America's Favorite Saltwater Fishing

BOOKS BY NICHOLAS KARAS

The Complete Book of the Striped Bass

Score Better at Skeet (with Fred Missildine)

Score Better at Trap (with Fred Missildine)

The Crow Hunter's Handbook

America's Favorite Saltwater Fishing

America's Favorite

Drawings by Vlad Evanoff

Saltwater Fishing

Nicholas Karas

A Sunrise Book

E. P. DUTTON & CO., INC. | NEW YORK

First Edition

10 9 8 7 6 5 4 3 2 1

Library of Congress Cataloging in Publication Data
Karas, Nicholas.
    America's favorite saltwater fishing.

    Includes index.
    1. Saltwater fishing. 2. Marine fishes.
I. Title.
SH457.K33 1976   799.1'2   76–12101

ISBN: 0–87690–205–0

Published simultaneously in Canada by Clarke, Irwin & Company Limited, Toronto and Vancouver
Designed by The Etheredges

This book is dedicated to my wife, Shirley,
who would spend much more time fishing if she
didn't spend so much time typing.

Contents

Preface

One of the most recognizable features of an affluent society is its leisure time. People completely caught up in the work of existence have little time to enjoy what they are doing or to sit back and absorb the world around them. But in America's society today we have found innumerable ways to consume our leisure time. Ironically, many of us turn to fishing. It was one of the few pleasures found in early civilizations, or even in medieval and colonial times.

There must be something special in the pursuit of fish that has drawn man to it, down through the ages, when he wanted temporarily to shrug off his woes and responsibilities. It has not always been the fish themselves that have most attracted people to angling, but often the sheer pleasure of catching them. Some say they fish to augment their larders; others claim they fish because of more primitive drives compelling them to gather and store, even though they are no longer dependent upon gleaning a life from the wilds. Still others—probably most of the others—will admit that they fish because it is fun. It is fun to be out in the elements; it is fun to become involved with one's tackle and equipment. It is fun to fight an adversary you cannot always overpower. And it is equally fun to consume the catch.

Today's America is still a coastal nation, much as it was in colonial days. More than half the people of this country live within fifty miles of salt water. And with the network of modern, easy-to-travel highways and expressways, it is easy to get to the salt quickly and often. But there are other reasons for fishing salt water. Growing populations in the interior of the country, loss of fish habitats through development and pollution, increased fishing pressure on freshwater stocks, all contribute to making saltwater angling appear a better diversion.

Saltwater fish are larger, they are more numerous, the waters are seldom crowded, there is always more space farther out, and the variety of fish is far greater in salt water than in fresh. Most saltwater fish resources have hardly been tapped. With all this going for the sport, it was only natural that the number of saltwater anglers should have grown rapidly over the last decade. Today, three out of five persons fish in salt water, where as short a time as ten years ago only one in five ever got to the briny.

Encouraging this seaward expansion in our leisure pursuits has been a remarkable advance in equipment, especially in good boats and outboard engines. These have approached a level where the average workingman can afford an outfit, and regardless of your income there is a boat and equipment built to fit it. Getting out onto the water is no longer limited to a very few wealthy anglers; it is within everyone's grasp.

Fishing equipment, too, has improved. Today's spinning reels and rods make it easy and quick to learn the fundamentals of casting. Modern lines, coupled with this gear, make fishing an instant sport.

Because of the great variety of species that swim the oceans, anglers have a vast range from which to choose. However, those fish within easy traveling from ports and marinas, or along a beach, and those fishing activities that require a minimum amount of investment in time, equipment, and money are pursued most frequently and have become America's favorite types of saltwater fishing. It is the purpose of this book to introduce anglers to the fishing that is near at hand and to those species that have proven most popular with anglers. The selection of what are the most popular species could have been much larger, but the line had to be drawn somewhere.

America's Favorite Saltwater Fishing is divided into two sections. The first sixteen chapters deal with different species of fish, their characteristics—ranges, seasons, descriptions—features that make them different from other fishes. The second part of the book is concerned with how to get fish out of the water and into your frying pan and covers rods, reels, and all the other equipment necessary to practice the sport successfully. The last chapter helps you deal with the fish on the way to the table and makes everything else that precedes it worthwhile.

NICHOLAS KARAS

St. James
Long Island, New York
April 1976

Part One

America's
Favorite Saltwater
Fishes

1. Striped Bass

I doubt that there is another gamefish that captures the imagination of the inshore saltwater fisherman more strongly than the striped bass. Striped bass, rockfish, linesider, squidhound, or whatever you choose to call it, is the optimal fish for many anglers. It swims close to shore; runs in numerous bays, estuaries, and rivers; delights in "holing up" along rips and cross-currents; and is fond of cruising the countless miles of seemingly monotonous beaches. The fish is everywhere within reach of the salty fisherman.

Many anglers with years of experience after other species try from time to time to take striped bass. Unfortunately, the number of unsuccessful striper fishermen is large. Much of the failure of this can be attributed not to a superintelligence on the part of *Morone saxatilis*, but to a lack of knowledge on the part of the fishermen. Striped bass demand some degree of attention if you are to master the art of taking them. You must know where they swim, why they are there, what they like to eat, how and when they like to eat it, and a host of other variables before you can take striped bass consistently and call yourself a striper fisherman.

Even though they are not taken with the ease and regularity of bluefish or weakfish, striped bass are still an extremely popular fish and have a legion of followers. This can be attributed mostly to the wide variety of techniques with which striped bass can be fished. Anglers can choose among a dozen ways to approach them. Stripers can be taken by trolling, spinning, or still-fishing; in big water or along the beach. They can be caught in a pounding surf or in a placid back bay. They can be found in slowly meandering tidal rivers or at the violent rips that meet in the open ocean between two strong currents. They can be taken off the bottom in water 80 and 90 feet deep, and they are caught on the surface with popper lures, spoons, and dainty flies. They can be taken by spinning, trolling, flycasting, drifting live-bait, or waiting on a sandy strand at the end of a line baited with cut-bunker.

DESCRIPTION

Striped bass are a fusiform fish; that is, they are sleek in their body shape, patterned somewhat after a cigar or torpedo. This is a characteristic of a fish capable of swimming rapidly when the need arises and a fish that likes to chase its food . . . an aggressive feeder.

Dual fins on the back are composed of, first, an anterior dorsal fin that is supported by sharp spines, is roughly triangular in shape, and is convexed on its trailing edge. The second, soft-rayed fin rises on the back after just a short space separating it from the anterior dorsal fin. It is triangular in shape and ends well forward on a stout caudal peduncle. The ventral, caudal fin reflects the top, soft, dorsal fin in shape and construction, though it is slightly smaller and begins a bit farther back on the body. The pelvic fins are located close to the middle line on the underside, in an area just under the pectoral fins and come equipped with sharp spines on their leading edges. The pectoral fins are medium to small in comparison to the same fins on other fish; they rise well below the middle of the side and below the apex of the gill cover.

The tail fin on a striped bass is large, almost square across the back, with only a slight concavity to it. It adorns a stout caudal peduncle that is the source of the fish's great speed and maneuverability. Such a tail is typical of fish capable of short, powerful bursts of speed, the kind needed to catch prey and then return to their lair.

In proportion to its body length, a striped bass sports a large head. It forms the front quarter of the fish. To match the large head is a large mouth with an underslung jaw filled with numerous small teeth. The head slopes to a pointed snout and the lower jaw rises to meet it, giving the striper an overall pointed or sharp-nosed appearance. A pair of large eyes are set high on the head and are capable of some binocular vision. The gill covers on the head are well scaled and the remainder of the body is covered with large scales that respond easily to scraping with a sharp knife.

On a striped bass, the lateral line starts near the top of the gill cover and as it passes aft remains in the top half of the body and then

The author displays one of several striped bass after successfully working a bucktail jig and porkrind combination in water 60 feet deep.

drops down, ending midway on the side of the peduncle. The longest stripe on the side of the bass follows this lateral line. The base or background color of a striper is silvery or white. Over this is laid a series of dark, horizontal lines. Normally, there are three to four above the longest line that overlaps the course of the lateral line and three to four below the lateral line. Those on the underside are not as long, ending short of the posterior portion of the fish, and are somewhat lighter in color. The back displays an overall black tone, ranging from blue-black to greenish-black in various individual fish, a coloration developed from a broadening of the lines or stripes.

The head varies in color from overall gray to green across the top and down to the snout, becoming lighter and turning to silver on the sides. The underside of a striper is pure white. The fins take on a gray to reddish-blue tint, but are always dark in tone or cast, and often reflect a brassy to gold iridescence.

Striped bass vary widely in size, from 1 pound in 1- to 2-year-old fish to 50 pounds for 15- to 20-year-old fish. Old records tell us that numerous striped bass at one time were caught commercially that weighed over 100 pounds, many as much as 125 pounds. Today, these catches are never equaled. The record rod-and-reel striper is a 73-pounder taken off Cuttyhunk, Massachusetts, and several fish between 68 and 73 pounds have been taken during the last fifty years. One or two larger stripers have been netted by commercial fishermen.

On the average, the bulk of the striped bass population is made up of 2- to 6-year-old fish, and these range in size from 2 to 10 pounds. As striped bass mature, more and more are lost to predation and other factors which reduce the overall population of stripers. There are still plenty of fish taken, however, in the 20- to 30-pound weights, and every year a few dozen fish over 50 pounds are recorded along with a handful of bass over 60 pounds.

Striped bass, like many saltwater species, are schooling fish, occurring in large numbers at one time. And, like most schooling fish, striped bass segregate themselves according to size. Thus a school of 3-pound fish are likely to contain only 3-pounders and a few smaller and a few larger fish, but all usually of the same age class. As stripers grow older and attain weights of 20 pounds and up, the schools become progressively smaller and there is a tendency for the different size and age groups to mix somewhat. Really large striped bass, those of 50 pounds and above, tend to become solitary fish and school only occasionally, while migrating or during a part of migration.

RANGE AND DISTRIBUTION

In colonial America, the striped bass was established in almost every river along our East Coast that offered it a chance in the spring to enter fresh water and spawn. Its range extended in the north from the St. Lawrence River, and many streams and estuaries in New Brunswick and Nova Scotia, south to Maine, all along the New England coast and as far south as northern Florida. The lower part of Florida, because of its warmer water, is devoid of striped bass. But from the Florida panhandle west to Louisiana, the striper again appears.

In waters at the extreme ends of its range, from Quebec to Maine, and from South Carolina to Louisiana, the striped bass is basically a freshwater fish that comes down to saline estuaries to feed during the summer months. In some of the more southerly rivers, especially those along the Gulf states, this migration downriver is sporadic or does not occur.

As dams were built across the rivers and streams in New England, striped bass were stopped from entering freshwater portions and eventually local populations in these streams dwindled and disappeared because the fish could not spawn. Today, those stripers that do appear in New England rivers are migratory fish from the Chesapeake Bay region, supported somewhat by stripers from the Hudson River and somewhat less by fish from North Carolina stock.

Striped bass are not native to the West Coast of the United States. However, numerous rivers in California, Oregon, and Washington were stocked in the late nineteenth century with stripers brought from the Hudson River. Stockings over the years were vast, but the environmental requirements for striped bass are so explicit that they didn't become established in all the rivers in which they were planted. However, they did establish themselves well in the San Joaquin, Sacramento, Feather, and Middle rivers flowing into San Francisco Bay. In Oregon, they concentrate in rivers emptying into Coos Bay and in the Coquille and Umpqua rivers farther along the coast. Striped bass were also stocked in the Columbia River, which

forms a natural boundary between the states of Oregon and Washington. Although on the Columbia they have never developed such
concentrations as are found in San Francisco Bay, Coos Bay, and the
Umpqua River, they are still found there from time to time. Striped
bass on the West Coast exhibit the primary or nonmigratory nature
of stripers in the Hudson River. They will migrate out of fresh water
and summer in salt water, and will even trek a short distance up and
down the coast, but they do not embark on the long coastal migrations characteristic of striped bass spawned in some of the Chesapeake Bay rivers.

On the Atlantic Coast, there are stocks of migratory striped bass
that originate in the sounds and bays of North Carolina, and in the
waters of Chesapeake Bay in Virginia and Maryland, and a limited
number from Delaware Bay, as well as a rather large stock from the
Hudson River. For the most part, these fish migrate in the spring,
after spawning, out of fresh water to the bays and estuaries at the
lower ends of the river systems. Most of these stripers summer along
the outer beaches and in large estuaries along the coast. They winter
either inshore or in a pocket off the coast of North Carolina, in the
Cape Hatteras area. Hudson River fish move into northern New
Jersey waters in the early summer and east into parts of Long Island
Sound and along the South Shore of Long Island as far as Fire Island
Inlet and Great South Bay. The great migrants of the species, however, are fish produced in several rivers flowing into Chesapeake Bay,
especially the Potomac. These fish will migrate out of Chesapeake Bay
in Virginia, or out of Delaware Bay via the Chesapeake and Delaware
Canal, moving along the coasts of New Jersey, New York, and New
England, as far north as the waters of southern Maine. The bulk of
the Chesapeake Bay stripers, however, summer in a smaller area from
eastern Long Island to Cape Cod, with concentrations in Buzzards
Bay and around the islands off the coast of Massachusetts.

These fish begin moving north in April and May and are well
established in their summer range by early June. They will remain
there until September, when the first waves of stripers begin moving
south again. The bulk of these fish migrate in October and November,
and by the end of the year they are wintering in the warmer waters
off North Carolina.

Striped bass on the West Coast winter in fresh water or water so

A Cuttyhunk, Massachusetts, skipper shows how to correctly gaff a striped bass alongside his boat.

brackish it is considered fresh. In March, they begin dropping down-river to the spawning areas and after spawning move farther into the saltwater bays and estuaries to feed. They remain there throughout the summer, some fish moving even outside the bays in short, coast-wise migrations. In September and October, they are again in the upper bays and by midwinter they are in freshwater environments.

WHERE TO FIND FISH

Striped bass are a true littoral species of fish; that is, they prefer to spend most of their lives close to shore and in shallow water. During their migrations north along the Atlantic Coast in the spring, seldom do they venture more than a dozen miles from land, and only when they are crossing from one beach or island to another. For the most part, they are found within the first few hundred yards from the beach. When they again trek south in the fall, their migration paths are even closer to the beaches and this is the time of year when surfcasting comes into its own.

Striped bass are lazy fish that like to let the water work for them, bringing food their way, instead of expending energy in searching for something to eat. Their favorite haunts are where two opposing currents come together, or where a fast tide moves over shallow water and boulders, creating boils and turbulence in the water. Along a length of beach, they are found between the beach and the first bar that forms parallel to the land, or on the outside of the first bar in water separating it from the second, paralleling bar. They can be right in the wash where waves break and tumble, or they may set up a watch where breaks in the bars occur, or cuts, through which food and water can stream past.

Striped bass are fond of following a flooding tide as it crosses a bay or estuary and enters tidal rivers and small streams. They like to feed on other small fish—killifish and spearing are favorites—that prefer the upriver portions of an estuary. They feed on small shrimp in the flooded grasses and then search out sandworms, mussels, and crabs along the bottom. Striped bass will eat almost anything that swims.

During the day, they may hold in deep water, not far from a shoal area or beach where they can go to find food when hunger overtakes them. In deeper water they will prey on passing schools of squid or dense concentrations of small and even large menhaden. Striped bass feed both day and night, but they do their heaviest feeding from sunset to near midnight, then slow up for a few hours, only to feed heavily again just before daybreak. Once the sun is up, the feeding slows considerably and though fish may strike throughout the day, they don't do it with the consistency they exhibit at night.

At night, stripers are more fearless and venture into the shallows and along the beaches. Two of their favorite foods are lobsters and crabs. You'll find these around rocky sections of a beach and it wasn't by chance that the striped bass acquired his Southern name, "rockfish."

Gulls and terns are great squealers on the whereabouts of striped bass. When these fish feed or blitz on a school of baitfish, the birds gather overhead screaming and diving for leftover bits of food.

TACKLE AND TECHNIQUES

Striped bass are taken by almost every technique known to fishing and on almost every kind of tackle except the really large stuff used for big-game fishing. This great variety of tackle is also reflected in the wide range of sizes of striper outfits. These can vary from a willowy, 4-ounce fly rod used to take school stripers in a saltwater marsh, to heavy trolling rods and reels with the 40- to 60-pound-test wire line needed to pull them out of heavy rips and tides in 50 feet of water.

The traditional technique for taking striped bass is with your two feet firmly planted in the sand, and casting plugs or spoons into a wildly pounding surf. This is *the* classic approach to striped bass fishing and probably the oldest. Stripers were first taken by swinging handlines into the surf from the beach, tossing squid with a hook buried in the bait and then retrieving it rapidly hand-over-hand. Today's surfcasters are far more sophisticated in their tackle, but the technique hasn't changed much. Surfcasters are divided between the advocates of the conventional reel, who learned to fish before spinning equipment came along, and those sold on the easy-to-learn art of spin-casting. It is difficult to say which is the better type of outfit, but spinning can be learned and mastered in a far shorter time than

Striped bass are fond of swimming in estuaries and tidal marshes during the summer months. Here the author lands a striper taken while rowing and trolling large sandworms.

thumbing a spool, and as a result the greater number of anglers in the surf today use spinning equipment.

The size of a spinning outfit should be determined first by the size of the man using it and then by the bait and lures he plans to use and the distance he must cast to reach the fish. There are about five sizes of saltwater spinning outfits. The smallest is the ultralight equipment that doesn't adapt too readily to use in the surf. At the other extreme are the big, man-killing rods, 12 to 14 feet in length, and big, "coffee-grinder"-type reels capable of holding 400 yards of 40-pound-test line. Between these two extremes are two categories that might be termed medium and heavy saltwater spinning outfits, and it is from these that most anglers in the surf will take their pick. The medium outfit might be too light for a large man, but an 8- to 9-foot spinning rod, with double cork handles and a medium-sized reel capable of holding 300 yards of 10- to 15-pound-test monofilament will do in most striped bass. For the rough days when the fish are on the second bar, or when you want to toss larger plugs, baits, and sinkers, the heavy spinning outfit is more in order. It may range from 9 to 11 feet in length, possessing a tip that is considerably stiffer than a medium outfit, and may swing a reel that can easily hold 300 yards of 20-pound-test line. It takes a lot more effort to toss a rig like this, hour after hour, and isn't necessary unless you are watching other fishermen pull out 30- to 50-pound stripers in close or taking fish at greater distances.

If there aren't any rocks in the surf and bluefish are not around, you can fish without a wire or heavier leader. But if barnacle-encrusted boulders are out there and the sea is filled with choppers, then you'll need a leader. Best bet is a 2- to 3-foot length of braided wire leader, covered with a plastic coating. At times, stripers are shy of dark leaders and you may have to substitute a 60- or 80-pound test monofilament leader in its place. It doesn't perform as well as wire, but it doesn't spook the bass.

Plugs and spoons are the lure that most surfcasters prefer to toss into the surf at stripers. Surface plugs are especially popular because bass will rise to the top to take such a lure. The thrill of witnessing the strike puts more kick into the punch. If the water is fairly deep, and the bass won't rise to a surface plug, a swimming plug or hammered metal spoon is used to take the hooks down to the fish.

In lieu of plugs, fresh cut-bait can also be used, and many anglers prefer it when fishing blind; that is, when you cannot see the stripers surfacing or working on baitfish. Some fishermen use whole or cut pieces of menhaden or mackerel when they are available, or a blob of sandworms or bloodworms anchored to the bottom by a pyramid sinker on a fish-finder rig.

Hook sizes will vary greatly, depending upon the size of the fish you are after; they begin with hooks as small as a No. 4 for schoolies to 10/0 hooks for cow bass, the big females of the population.

The next most popular technique for fishing striped bass, and one closely akin to surfcasting, is used by the angler equipped with a small boat, one between 12 and 20 feet in length. He takes off to follow a school of wandering stripers where the surfcaster cannot go. Most of this type of fishing is done by casting plugs and spoons from a drifting boat, just outside the pounding surf, or following the schools of stripers as they move away from the beach chasing and feeding upon schools of baitfish.

Long casts and heavy equipment aren't needed in this method of striped bass fishing, because the fisherman is not anchored to the beach but can chase after a really large fish as it pulls him away. Spinning rods ranging from heavy freshwater to medium and heavy saltwater outfits are used in this type of angling. Rods vary in length from 7 to 10 feet, but all have in common a rather stiff tip action for throwing lures from one-half to 3 ounces in size. Reels need hold only 200 to 250 yards of line that tests from 8 to 12 or 15 pounds.

When the fish cannot be located by casting or following the birds, the boat-equipped angler can elect to troll. Trolling is the dragging through the water of two or more lines equipped with lures. It is a great method for locating feeding striped bass because it covers a lot of territory with a minimum of effort. Engines make the boat capable of one long retrieve.

Trolling or boat variety rods are 5 to 6 feet in length, in 20- to 30-pound classes, or sometimes lighter, depending upon what you are trolling and the size of the fish you anticipate. When trolling in shallow water or when you want to keep the lures high, as in the case when the fish are on or near the top, Dacron and monofilament lines are excellent. They should be wound on a 2/0 to 4/0 reel capable of holding 200 to 300 yards laid on a stronger backing line.

But when you must troll in deeper water or when fish refuse to rise to the top, you are forced to add weight, in the form of drails or diving planes, to your terminal tackle. This is often cumbersome and takes a lot of fight out of the fish. Instead, many anglers switch to lead-core or wire lines to reach the stripers. Tungsten steel guides are needed on wire-line rods but aside from that they don't differ too much from other trolling rods.

Trolling baits vary greatly, but are usually artificial or rigged baits except when sandworms are trolled very slowly in shallow water. The most popular artificial bait is a 2- to 4-ounce bucktailed jig adorned on the hook with a yellow or white porkrind and worked as it is trolled. A great favorite in recent years is the umbrella rig, a collection of tubes on a four-way spreader that resembles a small school of swimming bait. Swimming spoons, plugs, and feathers are also used. Rigged eels are by far the favorite natural bait for stripers and are rivaled only by live-bunker (menhaden) fished on a very slow troll or at a drift.

For the inshore fisherman, the angler who haunts the tidal streams, marshes, and bays of an estuary, there are few thrills to match a striped bass taken on a fly rod. Stripers readily strike at a number of simple fly patterns, most with a single hook at the head of the fly, mounted on a short shank. Striped bass typically take all food, live-bait, plugs, or flies, by the head. When rigging live-baits this is an important point to keep in mind. A long eel need only be hooked in the lips to take a striped bass effectively. Most fish that swallow their prey whole take it head-first. Fish like bluefish, with a good set of cutlery, chop pieces out of a fish wherever they want and baits for fish of this type need tail hooks.

Another, and one of the deadliest, methods for taking striped bass is live-lining. The bait is usually a live bunker or mackerel; even blackfish are used at times. One technique for live-lining is to anchor the boat in an area where striped bass are located and feed one or two bunker into the current. The bunker are usually hooked through the nostrils and will stay alive for long periods of time. A slight variation on this method is, again, to fish two live bunker, one off each corner of the boat, but in this method, instead of anchoring, the captain stems the tide. Stemming the tide is using only enough power on the engine to equal the force or speed of the bottom: the boat is running but not going anywhere in relation to the current. The captain then has critical control over the location of the bait and can swing back and forth across the current or move up and down in it, placing the baitfish over more than one spot and increasing his chances of catching a striped bass. This technique works well along many of the islands off Massachusetts where the currents move well in close to land. It is an equally popular way of fishing on eastern Long Island, off Orient and Montauk points.

A somewhat different way of fishing with live- or dead-bunker, usually whole if it is dead, is to move the boat close to the beach—as close as the skipper dares—and then lower the baitfish over the side. A small drail or weight is used to keep the fish swimming irregularly. Then the boat is put into gear and slowly moves away from the beach. The angler on the rod puts the reel into free spool and the line pours off the spool, with the help of a thumb so that it doesn't overrun the reel. The baitfish stays almost in one spot. The boat is run out 200 or more yards, or almost as much as there is line on the spool. Then the engine is cut off to insure silence and the bait is slowly retrieved across the bottom. If it is live menhaden, the fish supplies all the action necessary. If it is dead-bait, then an angler jigs and stops it from time to time to imitate a swimming fish.

This type of live-lining or bunker dunkin' is done along the South Shore of Long Island and along the New Jersey shore areas where there are relatively flat beaches and little or no immediate current. For either technique, a 2/0 to 4/0 reel is used on a 20-pound-test boat or trolling rod, or one of similar type. Some anglers use a single 7/0 to 9/0 hook in the fish's nostril, while others prefer a treble hook of the same size. They claim there are fewer misses with the treble hook.

Bunker or mackerel used for bait weigh anywhere from 1 to 3 pounds and this big bait means that the likelihood of catching a large fish is extremely good. It also means that it will discourage a lot of smaller bass, but if you want big fish, as the saying goes, you must use big bait.

As mentioned earlier, striped bass didn't develop the nickname "rockfish" for no reason, and one of the rockiest places along most beaches, especially flat, sand stretches, is where groins or jetties have been built to protect the sands from eroding away. Jetties are constructed of a vast assortment of materials and all create natural havens for fish. Among the best are the boulder or rip-rap jetties, with plenty of large holes and crevices inside to encourage a growth of grass, barnacles, and mussels and to provide havens where small fish can escape predation by larger fish. Such an area is a great hunting ground for striped bass searching for food—lobsters or anything that moves.

In turn, the fisherman comes as a jetty-jockey, searching for striped bass. An entire art has been developed around fishing jetties and some anglers become real masters at it. Almost anyone can plug or cast about a jetty, but on such a pile of rocks, the live-bait fisherman really seems to score more often. One of his best baits is a live eel, and when this bait swims around the jetty in the dark, the chances of collecting striped bass are excellent.

Jetty rods are usually similar to surf rods, but a bit on the shorter side because the distances the angler needs to cast are not so great. Shorter spinning outfits, 8 to 9 feet long and on the stiff side to pull a bass out of the rocks, and a medium reel loaded with 250 yards of 20-pound-test line, are adequate. Leaders are standard equipment on a jetty stick because of the ever-present rocks.

Jetties are fished at an angle, not straight out. This is because most of the fish are near the jetty and along its bottom where it meets the sand. The angler begins at the base of the groin, or rock jetty, and casts his live eel or plug obliquely away from the rocks. The last third of the retrieve is then close enough to the boulders for any lazy striper to see and swim out to take it. The jetty is usually worked from downtide to uptide in direction. That is, the side downstream of the direction in which the tide crosses the end of the jetty is worked first and the angler works from the base of the jetty toward the end. In this way, the eel is always being fished back to the angler where he has control of the line and lure with no large bows in it. With the eel drifting downcurrent its presentation to a waiting striper appears more natural.

One of the deadliest methods for taking striped bass is by chumming. Stripers can be chummed from a boat, off a bridge, or from a point of land. The requirements are, first, that you have some reason for picking the spot; you know striped bass have been taken from there, or at least it looks like a natural site for stripers to collect in. The next necessary condition is that the spot have a moderate current during two to four hours of the tide. Too swift a current will require too much chum to create an effective chumline and one that is too slow will not broadcast your intentions far enough to attract the attention of enough stripers.

Chumming is done with clams—bits, pieces, and juice—or ground menhaden. The fishing equipment is usually a good conventional reel with a star drag and a 7- to 10-foot rod or a comparable spinning outfit. Equally effective is a light to medium boat rod with a 2/0 to 4/0 reel capable of handling lead-core line. Many chummers prefer lead-core line to others because it doesn't require a weight on the terminal end to take the bait down. A weight might scare a striper away or discourage it from striking. Also, the lead-core line is color-coded, the length being marked at intervals with a change of color. If the angler gets a strike, he can record the distance, so that when he boats the fish and then rebaits the hook, he can return it in the chumline to the exact spot where the first fish struck.

Striped bass can also be taken with regularity from deep water by jigging diamond jigs or bucktails through their lairs. Bass will often take up residence in deep water, in places like Plum Gut between Orient Point on Long Island and nearby Plum Island. Here, the water varies in depth from 20 to nearly 200 feet, and at times the

Two striped bass that fell for an imitation minnow plug.

stripers are lying on the bottom in 80 and 90 feet of water. Here they rest during migrations or wait for squid and schools of other fish to pass through the narrows. About the only way to get down that deep is to run your boat to the head of the current and drop a heavy lure and jig vertically through the area. Once clear of the spot, the angler cranks up his lure and runs again to the head of the current to start it anew.

Such an operation needs a 6- to 7-foot boat rod, one with a soft tip, but not so soft as to lose the sensation of the bottom through it. The reel is usually a narrow-spooled affair but with a large diameter so that it retrieves line rapidly. The retrieve ratio on the reel should also be large, 1:3 or better. To add further to the retrieve ratio, many anglers even add a longer handle.

The lure, usually a plain diamond jig, or a jig with a piece of cut-bait added to it, is dropped in free spool until it hits bottom. The fisherman then immediately throws the reel into gear and retrieves 6 to 10 feet of line, only to let it fall free again to bounce off the bottom. The striped bass usually hit the lure as it is jerked off the bottom. A slight variation of this technique is to fish a terminal rig composed of a large sinker, ranging from 8 to 12 ounces depending upon the force of the current, tied to a three-way swivel. On the other eye, a 2- to 4-foot heavy monofilament leader is added and then a 4/0 to 7/0 hook and a small baitfish—butterfish, bluefish, or mackerel. This affair is dropped over the side and bounced along the bottom in a fashion similar to the diamond jig. At times when the fish are not taking the diamond jig, this rig with bait on it can mean the difference between fishing and just a day on the water.

2. Bluefish

It is difficult to say which fish along our coasts is the most popular because fishermen and fish never agree with each other. I do know, however, that the voracious bluefish must be among the top three or four fish in popularity, if not *the* fish. One reason is the bluefish's willingness to strike at almost anything that is offered it. It can be taken by almost every fishing technique or method in the book. And, bluefish are "in season," to be angled for during a great part of the year. Last, its distribution is one of the greatest of any saltwater gamefish. With all these factors going for it, bluefish have got to be one of our most popular fish.

As if all this wasn't enough, the bluefish, pound for pound, is probably the gamest fish to take on a rod. Some fish grow larger, others jump higher or more often, some make greater runs when hooked, but none equals the bluefish for tenacity and just plain cussedness when it comes to fighting. And, they don't stop fighting even when they have been brought into a boat or are laid on the beach. Many are the unwary anglers who got their fingers too close to a "spent" blue.

DESCRIPTION

Bluefish, *Pomatomus saltatrix*, is a heavy-bodied but streamlined fish designed for a fast life in an open ocean. It is the only species in its family and has no close relatives to claim kinship. Its eyes seem inordinately large for the rest of the body and make a bluefish one of the few fishes that are capable of seeing well out of the water. The eyes are placed well forward, near a somewhat blunt snout. The mouth, near the bottom of the head, has an underslung lower jaw that obliquely extends to just under the eye. Both jaws are well equipped with rows of sharp, canine teeth.

From the shoulders back, the body is rather uniform in shape but quickly narrows near the tail peduncle and then finishes with a large, forked tail. Two large fins on the posterior half of the body, on both top and bottom sides of the fish, mirror each other in shape and when combined with the tail create a large area that gives a bluefish its great speed in the water.

A shorter, spiny fin extends ahead of the dorsal fin but ends far short of the head. A pair of pectoral fins extend back along the sides of the body beginning just behind the gill covers, and the paired pelvic fins are located directly under the pectoral fins.

The lateral line begins high on the body of a bluefish, near the top edge of the gill cover, and sweeps down and aft to end at the middle of the caudal peduncle, at the base of the tail fins. Scales in a bluefish are quite large and uniform in size across the entire body.

Bluefish exhibit a coloration pattern typical of pelagic or deepwater species of fish: dark on the top, blending into a lighter shade on the sides, and then turning white along the bottom or belly. The top is often colored a dark blue or dark blue-green that turns a lighter shade below the middle of the sides, where it begins mixing with shades of silver. The belly is a pure, flat white. The base of the pectoral fin is often marked with a black or dark coloration and stands out in a side view of the fish.

Two youngsters, fresh out of the surf, hold a bluefish that came in close to the beach at Cape Hatteras, North Carolina.

Bluefish vary considerably in weight over their range. They appear early in the summer in many bays and inlets as 3- to 5-inch fish called snappers. By the end of the summer and early fall they often attain a length of 10 to 14 inches and are then called snapper blues. Bluefish most often range in weight from 3 to 12 pounds. Fish above 12 pounds, however, are also common and numerous schools of 18- to 20-pound fish are found in deeper, offshore waters.

For years, the world record bluefish was a 24-pounder taken off the Azores. But the record has been broken several times since 1968 with a sudden surge of large fish along the Atlantic Coast of the United States. Today, the all-tackle record bluefish is a 31-pound 12-ounce monster taken at Cape Hatteras Inlet, North Carolina, in January 1972 by James Hussey. Still larger fish have been recorded and even a 40-pound bluefish is reported to have been taken some years ago in a commercial net.

Bluefish tend to segregate themselves into age or weight classes. An important reason for this behavior is the cannibalistic nature of the species: small snappers would be just another taste on the menu for a school of maurauding choppers. As the size and weight of bluefish increase, the numbers in a school tend to decrease.

RANGE AND DISTRIBUTION

Of all gamefish, bluefish are among the most widely distributed around the world. For years, very little was known about the distribution and life of this popular fish. And today, a great number of questions still remain unanswered, though the distribution of the species has been more clearly defined. In the United States, bluefish range, at times, from the Gulf of Maine southward along the entire coast to Florida and in the Gulf of Mexico from the Keys to Texas. In a wider area, they are also present in the Caribbean and are found as far south along the Atlantic Coast of South America as Brazil.

On the eastern side of the Atlantic, bluefish appear everywhere along the coast of Africa and as far north as the coast of Spain. They are also present in large numbers in the Mediterranean Sea and are found quite often in the Black Sea. Bluefish also frequent the east coast of Africa and occur across the Indian Ocean to southern Malaysia, Australia, and New Zealand.

The range of bluefish is related quite strongly to the fish's sensitivity to water temperature. Bluefish have a penchant for warm water, and in the summer months they will migrate northward—or, south of the equator, southward—as far as the warm currents retain a temperature of at least 45 or even 40 degrees Fahrenheit. During certain years when the warm waters from the Gulf of Mexico in the Gulf Stream sweep close to the eastern parts of North America, bluefish are taken as far north as Nova Scotia. The normal northern limit of their range usually finds them only as far north along the coast as Cape Cod or the southern coast of Maine.

This sensitivity to cold water is what keeps bluefish from the Pacific states and northern Europe. Cold water from the Alaskan Current washes the West Coast and proves too cold for bluefish to be anything but rare visitors at best.

Some recent studies of bluefish migrations indicate that the populations we see on our East Coast are comprised of not one, but three separate groups that at times intermingle. One group is a southerly collection that migrates as far north in the summer as Cape Hatteras. These fish are generally smaller in size, seldom weighing more than 5 or 6 pounds. A second group winters in the Cape Hatteras area and then migrates north in the spring and summers in the waters from New Jersey to Cape Cod. This group of bluefish often averages larger in size, between 6 and 12 pounds and occasionally larger. The third group are the behemoths of the species. Bluefish in this group range from 12 to 18 pounds and are truly pelagic or ocean-wandering fish. They migrate transoceanically and their appearance anywhere has not been marked with regularity. They can spend several years on the southeastern coast, wintering off Cape Hatteras and summering in the New York Bight. The fish can stay in an area for two or three years and then fail to show for several, suddenly appearing unexpectedly and to the delight of many fishermen.

SEASONS

Seasons for bluefish vary greatly within each area and often with the group itself. When bluefish appear, they do so first in the offshore waters. Their migrations are usually not as coastwise oriented as those of such littoral fish as the striped bass. After moving north and appearing in offshore waters, the fish gradually begin a shoreward migration in the Atlantic and a northward or coastwise movement in the Gulf of Mexico.

It is believed that bluefish spawn at this time, prior to moving inshore to feed. They spawn in the open ocean and the larvae drift toward shore. As they develop into free-swimming forms the small bluefish head for the estuaries, protected bays, and tidal rivers to feed, grow, and mature as the summer progresses.

Bluefish in varying numbers are along the coast of Florida and in the Gulf of Mexico at all times of the year. But the bulk of this southern population seems to arrive onshore late in March and in early April. On the Atlantic side, there is a definite movement of bluefish north along the Florida coast by March; in April the fish are along the coast from Georgia to South Carolina, and are at Cape Hatteras by June.

Cape Hatteras has bluefish throughout the year, fish from either the northern or southern groups. But the large bluefish, those that are taken by fishermen from November throughout the winter, begin to disappear after April. This group heads north along the Virginia Capes and is off Delaware in April, along southern New Jersey by May; by the middle of June the first fish are moving inshore along the entire coast from Long Island to Cape Cod.

During the fall, bluefish will stay in the waters of Massachusetts and Long Island into September, and even October and November, during years with a late, warm fall. But the first cold snap that chills the water can suddenly send them out of the shallows and into deeper water. And then suddenly, they are gone.

July, August, and September are the best months in the waters of the northern Gulf of Mexico for taking large numbers of bluefish. However, the larger fish seem to be taken later, in the fall and early winter of the year.

TACKLE AND TECHNIQUES

Bluefish can be taken on almost every type of fishing gear that finds its way onto salt water. This may be some of the basis for the great popularity of this fish. The most thrilling way to take them is with a medium saltwater spinning outfit, by casting to the fish when they are on a blitz. A bluefish blitz is a feeding frenzy when a school of blues is herding a school of baitfish. Blues will slash at any type of lure that moves in the water, but if it imitates what they are feeding upon, it can't be dragged any distance without being struck.

A medium spinning outfit consists of a fairly stiff rod, about 8 to 9 feet long, with a stout tip and with double grips to help you fight the fish. Standard line can range between 10- and 20-pound-test, with something in the 15- to 17-pound class a good compromise. Because bluefish can easily chop through all but the heaviest monofilament lines, the end of the line should be attached to a foot or so of braided wire leader. A snap and swivel of from No. 8 to No. 10 size will do, but it must be black in finish. Bluefish will strike at brass or steel swivels and cut them, if you attach your monofilament to one.

Lures vary over a wide range. Blues will hit surface poppers as well as medium- and deep-running plugs. Hammered metal spoons have long been a favorite, and they account for great numbers of blues taken from the surf. They are popular for several reasons: they cast well and far, come in a variety of shapes and weights, but most of all, bluefish like them. What better reason can there be?

Fishing a bluefish blitz requires a boat. But when the blues are not on the surface, that doesn't mean they aren't around or can't be caught. Trolling is another effective method, and when searching for schools of bluefish it is one of the best techniques to use. Blues are usually trolled with lead-core or wire lines because they can locate themselves in the water anywhere from bottom to top. The lead and wire lines have the ability to sink deeper and thus present the bait where the bluefish might be. A plethora of trolling lures are available. Tube lures from surgical tubing, artificial eels, and jigged bucktail/porkrind combinations are among the more popular forms of terminal tackle.

The outstanding bluefish "killer" during the past several years has been the umbrella rig. This is a multiple lure consisting of two strands of heavy wire crossed at their centers and attached to a piece of lead molded at their junction. At the ends of the arms, four spinning tube lures are attached, using short pieces of leader material, and from the center usually a larger lure is attached on a leader a few inches longer than the rest. In the water, the umbrella rig simulates a small group of swimming baitfish and it is not unusual for more than one blue to hit such a contraption simultaneously.

Also from a boat, and often in deep water, bluefish can be brought to your hook by chumming. The chum fish, often menhaden, are ground up and mixed with seawater into a gruel that attracts bluefish. The small bits of oily fish are broadcast in the water as the boat drifts, or, with the boat at anchor, are carried away by the tide or current. Into the chumline a baited hook is drifted, where blues will take it in preference to the soupy mixture that has attracted them to your boat. The bait can consist of larger pieces of bunker or other baitfish, or of clams or seaworms.

For trolling and chumming, a rod heavier than a spinning rod is used, often one equipped with a level-wind reel. The reel is equipped with a star drag that is adjustable and allows you to fight a blue. Reel sizes vary from 2/0 to 4/0 and should be loaded with 20- or 30-pound-test Dacron or monofilament line.

Bluefish do not enter the surf as readily as striped bass. But there are exceptions to this rule, usually at prominent points of land where a tide-rip is found, or where two currents come together. The two best-known examples of points offering such conditions are Cape Hatteras in North Carolina and Montauk Point, on Long Island. There are scores of lesser-known areas that are often just as good. And from time to time bluefish will come in on a stretch of sandy beach. In such a case, they are following baitfish that have been driven ashore, and the actual location is a matter of chance.

To fight a blue from a fixed position in the sand is one of the real highlights of surfcasting and bluefishing. The tackle needed for this is a bit on the heavier side as compared to fishing from a boat. One of the standard outfits for surfcasting for bluefish is a rod about 10 feet in length, again fairly stiff all the way to the tip, and with double grips for really working the rod, and a heavy bait-casting, level-wind, or conventional reel. The reel is loaded with 15-pound-test monofilament line, the terminal end of which is finished off in a wire leader.

As an alternative method, this same type of rod may be equipped with a heavy spinning reel. The line test required is about the same. If you need distance in your casts, then you can drop down to a lighter line, but you'll be sacrificing strength. If a really large bluefish comes along, it is somewhat doubtful that you will be able to handle it on a lighter line.

A standard item in the bluefisherman's bag of equipment is a billy club. This is a self-defense instrument for the angler. Bluefish, as previously mentioned, have been known to bite when well out of the water, and the only way to get a bluefish to release its grip on a lure or hook is neatly to place a hard blow to the head of the fish between the eyes. Then, the fish will relax its grip and open its mouth. But even then, don't trust it, and if you use a de-hooking device, do so with one hand firmly on the head so the fish cannot move in any direction.

WHERE TO FISH

Bluefish are by nature pelagic creatures, preferring to lead a life in deep water, but not in water so deep that it is devoid of baitfish or other food. In reality, bluefish swim wherever their main supply of food decides to go. At any time of the year, this can be any species of food-fish, for bluefish will attack and eat anything that swims, even, as we have seen, their own kind. During years when the schools of menhaden, spearing, weakfish, and seatrout are close to the beaches, bluefish are taken there. At other times, when their food-fishes are after plankton and the cooler water is offshore, bluefish will follow them there.

Large bluefish, as I have mentioned, have a greater tendency to prefer deeper water and will not frequent the bays and tidal streams as often as smaller blues. Snapper are almost always found inshore, where they stay until they are large enough to fend for themselves in the open ocean.

Bluefish are voracious, constant feeders. Unlike other fish that might feed only to fill their stomachs, bluefish are chopping machines that know no satiation. They seem to kill for the sheer joy of killing. Bluefish will feed on a school of baitfish and then regurgitate all they have eaten just so they can continue to slaughter the school. They will drive schools of menhaden out of the water and literally up onto the beach as they try to escape.

This continual feeding, so characteristic of bluefish, is based on

A quintet of bluefish that fell for a Scotty Rig lure and diamond jig, bounced along the bottom of Long Island Sound off Connecticut's offshore islands.

their physiology and hyperactive style of life. Their digestive system reflects this life-style. About the only time blues are not in a feeding mood is when they first arrive offshore. Then their instincts are bent on spawning. However, once that is over, they will make up for the interruption in their food intake.

As mentioned earlier, bluefish are likely to be found in two distinct areas. Large bluefish prefer deeper water and seldom venture into protected bays, coves, and shallows. They seek out water moving over sandbars, rips between islands, or holes in which bait will congregate.

In the shallows, smaller fish also have a liking for moving water: the rips along a river's mouth, along bulkheads and pilings, and almost any location where two currents come together are features sure to attract bluefish.

An easier way to find bluefish than by trolling is to watch the birds. Terns and gulls will follow schools of bluefish for hours, feeding on what is left over or floats to the surface after the blues have attacked a school of smaller fish. Gulls are often the better indicators of blues because they are not as excitable as terns. You may see a flock of terns, on the other hand, milling about madly, diving and screaming. As you race to where they are working they will suddenly disappear and you may find nothing more than a lone anchovy, one too large for the terns to pick up, on the surface.

Offshore fishing for blues can be the easiest of all methods, at times, for often the large charterboats will congregate in an area where bluefish have been feeding. And then all you need do is follow the fleet out and imitate what they are doing!

3. *Seatrout and Weakfishes*

Seatrout are the bread-and-butter fish of southern waters and are available to anglers throughout most of the year. Their northern counterpart, the weakfish, or squeteague, occupies the same niche for fishermen north of Cape Hatteras. To them, the weakfish is a spring-to-fall fish, and though the season is shorter the fish are well pursued. Of the scores of names for this fish "seatrout" is probably the most descriptive, though the species is really not related to trout or salmonids. Nor is the weakfish actually weak, in general; this deceptive name was given to it by heavy-handed anglers who lost too many fish because of their paper-thin mouth parts. The mouth of a weakfish is delicate and won't take much horsing before it lets a hook tear loose.

RANGE AND DISTRIBUTION

There are more than one kind of weakfish; in fact, there are eight species, all of which generally resemble one another in body form and even in environmental requirements. The great range of these fish has probably been one of the factors contributing to the species differentiation that took place over eons of time. The weakfish with the greatest range is the seatrout, also known as the spotted seatrout, spotted weakfish, or *Cynoscion nebulosus*. During the summer months, the range of the spotted seatrout extends as far north as New Jersey, and it is even taken on occasion in the waters off southern Long Island. However, its greater concentrations occur from Virginia south to Florida, where it inhabits every bay, inlet, and river indenting the coast. It also occurs in all the waters of the Gulf states, from Florida to Texas, and in parts of northern Mexico.

Strictly an Atlantic fish is the common weakfish, gray trout, or squeteague, the Indian name by which it is known in New England. Its scientific name is *Cynoscion regalis*. This weakfish is most abundant during summer months from the Carolina Capes to southern New England. It occurs occasionally in the Gulf waters off Florida and during some years its range extends as far north as the Bay of Fundy.

The silver weakfish, or silver seatrout, *Cynoscion nothus*, has a more southerly range similar to that of the spotted seatrout. It is found as far north as Chesapeake Bay and as far west in the Gulf of Mexico as Texas. Larger concentrations of this species inhabit the warmer waters of the Gulf; it occurs in smaller numbers elsewhere in its range. Because of its smaller size, up to 1 pound on an average, it is not sought after as a gamefish with as much interest as is seatrout or weakfish.

The sand seatrout, *Cynoscion arenarius*, another small weakfish that will grow as large as 4 pounds but averages around 1 pound, is restricted almost entirely to those states fronting on the Gulf of Mexico.

Two species of weakfish are sought after as gamefish and food on the Pacific side of the United States. The larger is the California white sea bass, *Cynoscion nobilis*. This weakfish is distributed along the entire Pacific Coast but is not too common north of San Francisco. It

Tom Sing illustrates how he catches seatrout in the waters of Murrels Inlet, South Carolina.

attains weights of up to 70 pounds, with fish between 6 and 30 pounds more common. Individuals over 50 pounds are considered somewhat rare.

The second, the so-called California bluefish, is not a true bluefish but another member of the weakfish group. It inhabits the Pacific Coast from the Santa Barbara Islands south to Guaymas and Mazatlán in Mexico. A good food and game fish, *Cynoscion parvipinnis* is colored a steel blue, without spots, and sports yellowish lower fins.

The last two species of weakfish are restricted almost entirely to waters south of California on the Pacific Coast. The corvina, *Cynoscion reticulatus,* is found from Mazatlán to Panama. It is a large fish that often grows to lengths of 3 feet or more. The largest of the weakfish, however, is the tortuva, *Cynoscion macdonaldi,* and it is known only in the Gulf of California, often called the Sea of Cortez.

It is most abundant along the east side of the Gulf and often congregates in large numbers at the mouth of the Colorado River, even entering it. It grows to enormous size, some examples having reached 170 pounds. The tortuva thus becomes the largest of the weakfish group.

DESCRIPTION

The spotted seatrout, or speckled trout, as it is often called along the Carolina and Georgia coasts, is the most colorful of all the weakfish. This is especially true of the male, whose colors are brighter than those of the female at all times and take on added tints during spawning seasons. The body is colored a gray-blue on the back, but this quickly turns into a light blue on the sides and is then mixed with silver on the flanks and belly. The body above the lateral line is marked by various-sized black spots, some circular and others oval, which are surrounded by a lighter blue halo. These spots continue on the posterior dorsal fin and over the tail fin.

Eyes are set well forward on a seatrout, in a narrow pointed head that finishes in a protruding lower jaw. The jaw angle is sharply oblique but ends in front of the eye. The dorsal fins consist of a spiny fin that is separate from a soft-rayed fin behind it. The pectoral fins are attached to the sides of the body just behind the gill covers, and the ventral fins are located almost below the pectoral fins. The anal fin is tipped in black, while all the other fins are finished off in a pale yellow coloration.

The rather large mouth of the speckled trout is guarded by several rows of teeth, with two large canines protruding from the top jaw. The mouth is constructed of fragile cartilage and light bone that tears easily, thus giving the fish its other common name.

Common weakfish (gray trout) are very similar to speckled trout in overall appearance. The body shape is slightly fuller in the area behind the head and shoulders, but the fish still gives the same general appearance of slimness. The length of the body is approximately four times its width.

Coloration is the greatest difference between these two major species of weakfish. Weakfish are finished off in burnished sheens of blue, green, purple, and lavender, with a copper or gold tinge to the scales as the light plays on their surface. Weakfish are covered above a distinct lateral line with a fine series of evenly distributed small black spots, unlike the few, large, well-defined spots that appear on the speckled trout. In some weakfish, these spots appear in the form of parallel rows, running down and forward from the top of the weakfish's back. The lower sides and belly are finished in white and silver and are often without the darker, spot pattern.

The tail fin has a slight concave finish to it in the weakfish, whereas the speckled trout's tail is almost square. Like the speckled trout, fins of weakfish are colored light pale yellow.

SEASONS

Spotted seatrout are found throughout their range during the entire year. They spawn from March through November in all the bays, creeks, and tidal areas they inhabit. Fishing is usually best from November to March in the Gulf states and from September or October to April and May along the Atlantic states. Migrations are often from onshore to inshore and then reversed. Any sudden cold spell during the winter months can send seatrout scurrying from the shallows to the protection of deep water either offshore or in the deeper inlets and bays inshore.

Northern weakfish spawn in numerous bays and tidal estuaries along the coast from North Carolina to Long Island, New York. However, the two concentrations of the weakfish population seem to occur at these two extremes. Weakfish in North Carolina enter the bays in early April to spawn. Adults, soon after spawning, begin a northward migration along the coast. By June, these fish have spread from the mouth of Chesapeake Bay north to Buzzards Bay in Massachusetts.

Another part of the population enters Great South Bay and Peconic Bay in late April but does not indulge in spawning until middle or late May. These fish move very little after they have spawned. The greatest concentration of weakfish during the summer months thus occurs in the waters off eastern Long Island and inside its two great flukes, in the sausage-shaped Peconic Bays.

With the first hint of cool weather, in mid-September or at times earlier, weakfish will begin schooling, and then locating them can be difficult. Once you have found a schooled group, however, the fishing is often fantastic. As the weather continues to cool, weakfish will begin a westerly, then southerly migration along the coast of Long Island and then down New Jersey, Maryland, and Virginia. Weakfish winter offshore on the Carolina Banks, especially in the Cape Hatteras area, where commercial fishermen take them in great numbers. The fish will stay here until spring, when they again move inshore, to the sounds and bays behind the Outer Banks and begin again the spawning ritual.

Two anglers, working a chumline of grass shrimp, take a weakfish from the waters of Peconic Bay, Long Island, New York.

Spotted Seatrout

Tackle for seatrout is best chosen from a selection of light saltwater or even freshwater rods. Spinning tackle is ideal but spin-casting rods and reels, as well as bait-casting, level-wind reels and 5- or 6-foot rods, work equally well. Almost any rod used for seatrout should have a fairly soft tip, one that will take the force out of a strike and play the fish lightly because of the fragile nature of the fish's mouth.

I prefer a 6- or 7-foot, one-handed freshwater spinning rod and a medium or even ultralight spinning reel. Line test can vary from 6 to 10 pounds, depending upon the technique. Although the mouth of a seatrout is equipped with teeth, they present little threat to your line, so leaders are not normally used. Baits, hooks, and lures can be attached directly to the line.

Seatrout are aggressive, sight-feeding fish that chase mullet, menhaden, or any other small fishes. This makes them vulnerable to small plugs and spoons, and even surface plugs, which they hit with ready greed. Trout also feed on the entire list of seaworms, mollusks, and crabs on the bottom, but of all the foods, they seem to prefer shrimp.

Tommy Sing, a fine offshore headboat skipper out of Murrel's Inlet, South Carolina, likes to take a day or two off in November or December and go fun-fishing for seatrout. He has developed a rig that is rather standard along the Carolinas for inlet fishing. It involves chumming with shrimp from an anchored boat. Tom uses a pair of spinning rods as he angles, each equipped with small, level-wind reels. They are loaded with 12-pound-test monofilament. In rigging the outfit, he first slips a large red bead over the terminal end of the line, then fishes the line through a large spindle float, one about 6 inches long and painted half-red and half-white. Next, he ties the end of the line to a half-ounce beaded trolling drail. To the other end of the drail he ties another length of monofilament, usually 20- or 30-pound-test line, to act as a leader in case bluefish are in the creek he fishes. To this 3-foot leader he ties a No. 5 or No. 6 treble hook.

The entire affair would slip through the hole of the float except that Tom ties a stopper with a rubber band so that the shrimp, baited on the hook through its collar or back, is about 6 feet away, depending upon the depth to be fished, from the float.

Such a rig is fished about 100 feet astern of the boat. It is cast out and then the reel is put on free spool and the rig is floated out to the required distance. Then the clicker is put on, while still in free spool. When a weakfish or seatrout strikes, it can run with the bait.

Most seatrout are lost at the strike. A trout should be allowed to run. Its initial run is its greatest, and a 2- to 4-pound fish can peel out 100 feet or more of line. Slowing the fish down should be done gradually or the hook will be pulled out of the mouth. This feat is easily accomplished on a level-wind reel simply by thumbing the spool, gently at first and then adding more pressure as the fish nears the end of its run. With a spinning reel it can also be done effectively. With a lightly set drag, the fish pulls freely until its run wanes and then by applying pressure on the side of the spool, the fish can be stopped.

The trout's second run is never as strong as the first and the fish will often come placidly to the boat. Sight of the boat, however, may make it run or jump again, so let it go. Don't lift a trout out of the water with the rod or line, but net it. Otherwise, you'll be out a fish.

Weakfish

Techniques for catching weakfish of the North, or squeteague, are very similar to those used on seatrout of the lower Atlantic Coast. This, too, is an aggressive gamefish, and it will readily take plugs, spoons, and even feathered flies and poppers, as well as live-bait. Chumming is equally popular, and a light saltwater or medium freshwater spinning outfit is ideal for such a situation.

Grass shrimp are the preferred chum; from an anchored boat these small shrimp are doled at regular intervals into the water. Periodically, some of the shrimp are pinched so that they fall to the bottom in the chumline while the free-swimmers may move off to one side or the other behind the boat. Usually two or three grass shrimp are festooned onto a No. 6 hook and this is allowed to drift back into the chumline. The amount of tide or current will determine how much weight must be added to the line. Usually from one to three, or four, split shot will do. In deeper water, however, coupled with a faster current, a large sinker, often as heavy as an ounce, possibly heavier, must be used. In this case, the terminal end of the monofilament is tied to a three-way swivel. Off one eye, the sinker is attached by a foot or two of leader material, while to the other eye, two to four feet of leader is attached before tying on the baited hook.

Weakfish can be trolled as well as chummed, and with the return of large numbers of very large weakfish, trolling has proven a valuable way to locate and collect these tide-runners. Favorite places for trolling are off points of land where the tide currents are forced to run a bit faster, and between islands or even shoal areas where dead or slow water is next to moving water. Trolling can be done with spoons, plugs, or even umbrella rigs, but many fishermen prefer to drag large Willow Leaf or Cape Cod spinners with two or three large sandworms trailing off the hook.

Rods for trolling can be heavy spinning outfits, where the rate of speed is rather slow, or light trolling rods with level-wind reels, where more resistance is likely to be encountered in the water. Dacron trolling lines can be used but will ride rather high in the water. If you desire to go deeper, a lead drail must be used. Also employed are lead-core lines and light-test wire lines that troll rather deeply without the use of lead weights.

One really enjoyable way to take weakfish is from a drifting boat. This might be termed a very slow way of trolling. It is one of the preferred methods in the Peconic Bays of Long Island and usually proves quite productive. Here, a boat or spinning rod is used, often with the terminal end attached to a three-way swivel. More than one hook can and should be used. The extra hooks are separated by two or three feet from each other along the length of the line, and will quickly reveal at which depth the weakfish are located.

This technique is usually practiced over an area that has produced weakfish in the past. A fisherman runs his craft ahead of the area, either upwind or uptide, and then cuts the motor, allowing the boat to drift over the spot. Two or three lines can be employed in rod holders, if there aren't enough free hands onboard. The hooks can be baited with shrimp, sandworms, clams or mussels (without their shells, of course), or strips of belly meat cut from small bluefish or bunker, live killifish, or soft-shelled crabs.

As the boat drifts, the rig should be picked periodically off the bottom and bounced along to make sure the last hook is close to the bay floor. The boat is likely to drift faster than will permit you to keep the sinker on the bottom, so you compromise by paying out line from time to time, until the lines are 100 or so feet astern of the boat. Too much line is likely to put a bow in it and when a weakfish strikes you won't be able to record the hit immediately and may possibly miss the fish.

With cut- or dead-bait, weakfish usually nibble or mouth a bait and often you'll feel nothing but a gentle tug on the line. Don't strike the fish prematurely. Eventually, you'll feel a steady, sustained pull as the fish travels away with the bait. More than likely, it hasn't yet swallowed the bait, and if you strike before the fish stops and re-mouths the bait, you'll pull it from its teeth. On the second run, which may at times be no more than a tug after the fish stops, set the hook, but not too strongly.

Weakfish are equally fond of searching in the surf for food, and at times will be found with striped bass of equal size. If there are large striped bass around, the smaller weaks won't be, because bass love to feed on them. In the surf, weakfish make excellent fighters and will strike small, silver lures and spoons as well as small plugs. They can also be fished on bait, but the addicts of the suds prefer to wade after their fish and take them on artificial lures.

When a seatrout reaches 3 to 4 pounds in weight, it is considered a mature fish and capable of spawning. But trout up to 8 and 10 pounds are not uncommon. The largest recorded weighed a bit over 15 pounds and came from Florida waters. Weakfish, on the average, grow larger than seatrout. During the past few years, there has been a great explosion in the population of this northern fish, and large tide-runners, fish of about 10 pounds, are not only frequent but again almost common. In their prime years about thirty years ago, 15-pound weakfish from the Peconic Bays were almost a rule of thumb. The world record weakfish is a 19½-pounder taken way off its course in Trinidad, while the current record from U.S. waters is a 13-pound

2-ounce fish taken from Great South Bay, Long Island. The latter is being challenged by two larger fish still to be officially recognized. Larger weakfish have been taken from nets and even by hook and line but do not qualify for International Game Fish Association (IGFA) records.

White Sea Bass

This giant of the weakfish family roams the Pacific from Alaska to Chile but is found only occasionally north of the Golden Gate. In appearance it is similar to the other weakfish, but has a solid bluish-black back, silver sides, and white belly. The two fins on its back are touching at their base, unlike the separate fins found on East Coast weakfish. The two large canine teeth are also missing on the white sea bass, and the bar striations above the lateral line are found only in very young fish.

White sea bass spawn in late spring or early summer and then move inshore to the kelp beds, where they provide some great fishing

A mixed bag composed of spotted seatrout and weakfish.

between May and September. Sea bass have a penchant for squid but will actively feed on small fish as well as crustaceans, and most of the fishing for them is done with live-bait. However, like other weakfish, they are aggressive feeders and will readily chase food-fish. This makes them vulnerable to lures, spoons, and plugs, and they are often taken by trolling or casting from drifting boats. Though they are not as fast as their East Coast counterparts, trolling speeds and retrieval speeds on the slow side are the most effective, and lures should be worked close to the bottom for best results.

Many night cruises by headboats and charterboats from California ports produce excellent catches. White sea bass are active night feeders and often this is the best time to be out fishing for them.

4. Drums, Red and Black

It's difficult to imagine a greater adversary in the surf of the Outer Banks than a red drum. Red drum, alias channel bass, pescado colorado, or redfish, is a fish popular with anglers dedicated to wading in the surf and whipping the suds. A close counterpart, though not as great a gamefish, but still one that must be considered because of the great size it attains, is the black drum.

Black drum and red drum are both members of the croaker family of fishes and are somewhat similar in appearance. On the table, the two differ greatly. Small channel bass, called puppy drum, are great as a food-fish. Larger drum become a little coarse and flavorless. Black drum, on the other hand, are even less palatable and usually find their way into fish chowders, where their flavor can be disguised or supported by plenty of spices.

RED DRUM

Of all the names used for this species of fish, scientifically known as *Sciaenops ocellatus*, probably the most appropriate one is "redfish," which is in use over the greater part of its range. From a sporting standpoint, the redfish or channel bass makes up in sheer size and stamina what it may lack in acrobatics and it thus captures the imagination and will of fishermen dedicated to angling in the surf.

DESCRIPTION

The red drum is a heavy-bodied fish that searches for its food primarily along the bottom. Its body shape reflects this specialization with a belly or ventral surface that is rather flat or straight, from the snout back to the anal fins. The back is broad and somewhat humped. Two dorsal fins on the back touch at their base with the anterior fin, supported by spiny rays. The posterior fin is supported by softer, cartilaginous rays. A drum's tail is large, rising from a stout caudal peduncle, and squared on the trailing edge. The ventral and anal fins have a free, spiny ray at their lead and the paired pectoral fins are located low on the sides of the body.

The well-defined lateral line in the side of a red drum begins above the gill cover, arches toward the back, and then sweeps low along the side of the body. It crosses the middle of the caudal peduncle and is even evident on the rays of the tail fin.

The head of a drum slopes rapidly toward a blunt nose. The nose extends slightly beyond the upper jaw. Large eyes are set high on the head and the posterior edge of the mouth ends just behind a line below the eye. Scales on a drum are large and even cover the cheeks as well as the gill covers.

Even though, as we have seen, it is often called "redfish," the color of a drum may range from an orange or a brassy red to yellow, depending upon the most recent environment in which the fish has spent time. The red coloration extends over the back and sides of the fish and abruptly ends in poorly defined lines along each side of the belly. The underside of the fish is all white while the pectoral fins are almost opaque. Their trailing edge is adorned with a bright orange or brassy yellow color. Top and bottom of the tail fin have a bright streak of color through them while the center portion is a bluish-gray. Many smaller red drum in Florida and the Gulf of Mexico do not attain the reddish or orange coloration, but show a gray to blue color over most of their bodies, with silvery sides and white bottoms.

A characteristic large, black spot is located above the lateral line at the base of the caudal peduncle or tail of a red drum or channel bass. In very large specimens the single spot is often broken up into a series of black spots, but all restricted to the same general area. This large spot and a lack of barbels or whiskers on its chin readily distinguish a red drum from a black drum.

RANGE AND DISTRIBUTION

Red drum are distributed from Massachusetts south to the tip of Florida and then west in the Gulf of Mexico to the Rio Grande River. Though they occur north of Virginia, their appearance in these waters is rather rare. For some unexplained reason, redfish are not a common species in the waters around Key West, though just to the north, on both coasts, they are quite common. Along the coast of Texas, where they are usually spoken of as "redfish," they are frequently the most abundant food-fish found by anglers and commercial fishermen.

Red drum are not migratory, nor do they move over great distances. There may be a slight onshore-offshore movement with the season, but the fish are quite sedentary in relation to estuarine systems or bays. Redfish in the Gulf and those found along the Atlantic coast of Florida seldom attain a large size in comparison to the channel bass of Virginia and the Carolinas. In fact, many fishermen do not realize that they are the same species of fish. Florida and Gulf of Mexico redfish average between 2 and 4 pounds in weight, with few fish exceeding 20 pounds. Those in the upper weight range are redfish from the northern Atlantic coast of Florida and Georgia.

Behemoths of this species are fish that spend most of their lives in the waters off North Carolina, Chesapeake Bay, and the islands on

Virginia's Atlantic coast. While redfish of the southern waters are not especially migratory, channel bass in the mid-Atlantic states are. It is believed that the greater majority of these fish winter in the sounds and bays of North Carolina, with a lesser number in the rivers and bays of South Carolina.

About March of each year, these fish abandon their winter hangouts and move through the numerous inlets to gather around Cape Hatteras. After feeding for several weeks, they eventually begin a northward migration. This starts along about April, and the fish then work their way north along the coast for the next two months. Some fish move into Chesapeake Bay while others choose to summer along the Virginia islands. Some move as far north as Delaware Bay and the lower bays of New Jersey, but that occurs only during especially warm years.

In the fall, they reverse this migration route and again offer fishermen a chance at them during October and sometimes November. Eventually the red drum return to their deeper abodes to wait out the winter and start the cycle all over again.

SEASONS

There is some fishing conducted throughout the year in the back bays and sounds for channel bass in the Carolinas, but it doesn't compare to the activity and excitement when the first big "bass," as they are often called, begin to appear in the Ocracoke, Hatteras, and Oregon inlets. From the inlets the fish move along the outer beaches and spend some time gathering around Cape Hatteras in May. By June they begin to thin out at the Cape and give surfcasters from Virginia Beach north to Rehoboth Beach in Delaware a chance. Fishing there and in Chesapeake Bay gradually wanes as summer wears on and slowly the drum seem to disappear.

In late September, the first fish are suddenly again passing the numerous fishing piers off Virginia Beach, Kitty Hawk, and Nags Head. Once again Oregon Inlet comes alive with red drum in October and this is the better place to be, as opposed to Cape Hatteras or inlets farther to the south.

Just as the fishing in the northern part of the fish's range begins to slow, it begins to pick up on the north Florida coast and the waters of the Gulf. The best time for redfish in Gulf waters is from November to April and May, and at that time, large numbers are taken from Florida, Alabama, Louisiana, and Texas beaches, inlets, and channels.

TACKLE AND TECHNIQUES

Channel bass are primarily bottom-feeders, looking for food in the surf, over nearby bays, and across the sounds. The classic technique used in catching these fish is to stand in a pounding surf after a good northeast blow, and wield a long surf rod. The excitement and thrill of battling a really large fish while engulfed in the pounding surf are difficult to describe, but are well known to hordes of surfcasters along the middle-Atlantic seaboard.

Drum move in the surf between the wash and the first combers. They are searching for clams and other mollusks, which they can easily crush between two large grinder plates located in their mouths. Drum are equally fond of crustaceans, and if you were to open the stomach of every drum taken along the coast it would more than likely include blue crabs, one of their favorite foods.

When fishing the surf for migrating drum, live-bait seems to be the preferred enticement. It is best handled on a medium to heavy surf rod, either spinning or level-wind. Many anglers choose rods up to 12 feet in length to give them the added leverage needed for reaching the outside of the first bar. However, most rods for drum range from 9 to 11 feet in length, with 10-foot rods in the majority. They all have in common a stiff action, a solid play from butt to tip. An angry channel bass is a formidable fish and it requires a sturdy rod to impose your will upon it.

Lines do not vary greatly in strength when live-bait is used. Seventeen to 25-pound-test monofilament is standard, but some anglers elect even heavier lines. A heavy line reduces the distance you can cast but because the baits are heavy, and often equipped with lead weights, they can be tossed great distances into the surf. The terminal end of the line is finished off with a leader 4 or 5 feet in length composed of either braided wire line with a plastic coating or plain monofilament line but of a 60- to 80-pound test.

On the terminal end of the leader a fish-finder rig is attached. This amounts to a large snap that is clipped to a pyramid sinker by a

Ken Lauer, noted surf guide from Cape Hatteras, takes a breather after landing a 50-pound-plus channel bass.

leather thong or a large ring that cannot slip past the leader. A large hook, anywhere from 5/0 to 8/0 in size, is attached to the distal end of the leader.

The best type of sinker to use in the surf to keep your line from washing in or out is a pyramid sinker. This lead weight is attached to the fish-finder by an eye imbedded in its base. Weights will vary from 1 to 3, 4, or 5 ounces, depending upon the surf and the current. When a channel bass picks up the bait on such a rig, it can move away, pulling the line through the eye on the fish-finder without dragging the lead weight. The reel is usually set on free spool, in such a case, with only the resistance of the clicker to keep the line from coming off too freely. The fish never feels the resistance on the bait and the fisherman is given a chance to grab the rod, set the drag, and then set the hook.

Fishing with this type of equipment is usually done with the use of a sand spike, or rod holder. By the very nature of the fish, they demand large rods and reels. After a short time, this equipment wears upon the arms of even the strongest surfcaster. That is why sand spikes, or rod holders, are used. Sand spikes are driven into the sand near the edge of the surf and the butts of the heavy rods are placed in them, in an upright position. They not only free the fisherman's hands but allow him to increase his chances of catching a drum by letting him set out two, three, or more rods—as many as he can effectively handle.

Bait used for channel bass in the surf is usually in the form of cut-fish. The bass actively feed on dead or live fish they come across in the surf, and mullet are a favorite. Chunks of cut-mullet, skewered on a large hook and tossed into the surf, account for most of the channel bass caught by sportfishermen. Next in line are globs of cracked mussels or clams, secured with light string or twine. Equally good but often difficult to obtain are blue crabs, that prime food for channel bass. When in the soft or shedder stage, they are especially deadly. In this stage they are held on a hook with rubber bands.

When channel bass begin their northward migration, they seem to feed more readily and while live, cut, and natural baits are still good, the fish will begin striking at lures. At this time, the smart drumfisherman changes his tackle slightly. It would be all but impossible to wield a large bait-casting surf rod for hours. To do this with lures, the sizes of rod and reel must come down to match a man's ability. Rods of 8 to 9 feet in length, still rather stiff in the tips, are used, and line sizes drop to between 12- and 20-pound-test to accommodate lighter lures. Many anglers still prefer to use a level-wind reel in the surf, when the possibility looms of playing such large fish. The prime reason is that it gives them immediate control over the line and is more sensitive to the changes in fighting tactics of a drum. However, spinning reels are easier to operate, and with an especially effective drag they find greater use than the level-wind type. But instead of the large spinning reels used on a bait-rig, medium-sized reels are now in order for casting plugs and spoons.

Silver hammered spoons; lead-headed, feathered jigs; and large plugs that will run close to the bottom are used for drum. The fish are still scrounging close to the sand and any lure used on them should be working in this zone. Otherwise, the lure may pass unnoticed over the head of the fish.

The surf is not the only place where drum can be caught while they are gathering to migrate or while they are on the move. They are quite effectively fished both outside the surf in deep water paralleling the beach, and in the deeper holes and sloughs in bays, channels, and inlets on the inside. A boat, however, is of course a necessity for this fishing. The standard approach here is to troll lures until a fish is located. Channel bass usually run in pods or schools during the spring and early summer months. Once they are located they can be fished with cut or whole live-bait or cast to with spoons and plugs.

In the bays and sounds behind the barrier beaches of North Carolina, the optimal technique is to cruise in a boat looking for schools of fish. Drum often swim in shallow water searching for oysters and clams, many times with their backs exposed in the air. Once they are located, the boat quietly approaches the school and anglers begin casting to the fish. During the late spring and summer months, when the drum begin to take up an extended residence in the waters of Chesapeake Bay, and on the outside among the sea islands of Virginia and Maryland, the fish select deep spots in channels or backwater bays. Here the best technique is to drift cut-bait or crabs into the holes.

The redfish of southern Atlantic and Gulf states are fished quite differently than the big channel bass of the Carolinas and Virginia.

While they occur in these areas in the surf as well as back bays, the redfish can be found almost everywhere, from mangrove swamps to the pilings around bulkheads, channel markers, and especially around the footings at bridges. Standard or medium-weight spinning equipment can be used on these fish because they seldom weigh more than 4 or 5 pounds.

These smaller fish are more aggressive and active feeders than their northern counterparts. They often chase schools of mullet and other small baitfish to the surface. At such times they are suckers for popper plugs. At other times, they can be enticed out of the mangrove roots and pilings with small spoons and plugs. A highly effective lure, fished with a spinning outfit, is a bucktail jig, one-half to 1 ounce in size. The feathered or bucktailed affair is retrieved with a jerking motion and redfish pick it up as it comes off the bottom.

Live-bait also works effectively on redfish, and if it is still kicking, so much the better. Large shrimp are good bets, and when lightly hooked through the collar on their backs they will kick around for a long time, attracting the attention of any passing redfish.

As is always the case, you should match the size and weight of your equipment to the size of fish you are after. Overtackling your fish takes a lot of the fun out of the game. Redfish can be easily taken on light tackle, often medium freshwater gear. Hooks will vary, depending upon the bait you use, but should range between Nos. 4 and 1.

BLACK DRUM

The larger black drum gets along with almost as many names as a red drum—"drumfish," "barbed drum," "big drum," "sea drum," "gray drum," and "striped drum." In scientific circles it is known as *Pogonias cromis.* The black drum is a close relative of the red drum, its fellow member of the vast and varied croaker family. The ability to produce the drumming sounds characteristic of these fishes is the result of a special muscle that works by rapidly contracting the swimbladder. It is best developed in the male black drum and only slightly developed in females. It is believed to be involved with mating, for which it acts as a "call."

DESCRIPTION

A black drum is fairly similar in overall appearance to a red drum. It has the same characteristically flat, ventral body shape, one designed to meet better the demands of a life of foraging along the bottom. The back, however, is more highly arched in a black drum than in a red drum. The head has a greater slant as it meets a snout with the mouth located at the very end. The angle of the lower jaw is parallel to the bottom of the body and ends on a line directly below the middle of the eye. The lower jaw is equipped with a series of dangling barbels that help the fish find its favorite foods: oysters, clams, and mussels.

The anal fin is characterized by a very short first spine and then

Bob Hutchinson of Virginia Beach gaffs a monstrous 70-pound black drum for Roney Leitner in the waters off Cape Charles, Virginia.

an exaggerated second spine, followed by soft rays that hold the shape of the fin.

Black drum are colored a silvery gray that in live fish has a brassy luster to it. In a dead fish, the silver disappears, leaving an overall gray or black appearance. In young fish under 20 pounds in weight, also called puppy drum like the reds, the sides of the body are marked with 3 to 5 wide, dark bands alternating with the silvery gray base color.

Black drum are on the average a larger fish than redfish. The largest on record is a 146-pounder taken at St. Augustine, Florida. The fish often reach 50 to 80 pounds in weight, but specimens over that weight are rare nowadays.

RANGE AND DISTRIBUTION

Throughout most of their distribution, the ranges of black and red drum overlap. Black drum, however, extend a bit farther north along the Atlantic Coast than do the red drum, and are more numerous in the northern part of their range than red drum. For practical fishing purposes, black drum extend along the coast to Cape Cod, but are also found as far north as the Gulf of Maine. Here they are considered somewhat rare. Their distribution extends as far south in the United States as Florida and west into the Gulf of Mexico. Their extreme southerly range carries them all the way to Argentina.

But as far as fishermen are concerned, black drum concentrations in fishable populations occur in Delaware and Chesapeake bays, the waters around Cape Charles, and among the islands on the Atlantic side of Virginia, Maryland, and Delaware.

SEASON

Fishing black drum along the beaches begins in late March along the lower Atlantic states and becomes better in April and May in the Carolinas and Virginia. After the fish spawn, in late April and May, the fishing begins to pick up again and large hordes of black drum begin to move north of Cape Hatteras. Angling continues good through early summer, but as the heat arrives in August, the doldrums have their effect on the black drum. At this time of the year they become as difficult to find as hen's teeth. After the lull, the fishing again picks up in the fall, and late September and October are excellent times. The duration and intensity of these black drum seasons, however, do not equal the spring run.

In the Gulf states, the fishing seasons seem reversed. The better fishing begins in late December and lasts into late March. Although black drum are around at all times of the year in the Gulf, the fishing activity is best during winter months.

TACKLE AND TECHNIQUES

Black drum migrate and feed in the surf, and large numbers are caught there, but they are taken primarily from rowboats, runabouts, and headboats. Boat rods are in order, sticks 5 to 6 feet long, not too stiff, but with double handles for playing a large fish. A bay or trolling reel is the best bet, one loaded with 250 to 300 yards of 20-pound-test or better line. Monofilament or Dacron lines work equally well. Reel sizes range between 1/0 and 2/0 for puppy drum to 2/0 and even 4/0 when big fish are around.

The typical fish-finder rig of the surf works well on black drum. Drum do not strike especially hard and often will pick up a bait, mouthing it before slowly moving on to find another piece of food. If the drum feels a drag or weight on the bait while it is still sampling the food, it is likely to drop it. But the fish-finder lets a drum run without knowing there is a hook in the bait or that the line is weighted with lead.

Because of the tough, bulldog nature of the black drum and its relatively large mouth, the hook chosen is often in the range between 6/0 and 9/0. The O'Shaughnessy style is one of the more popular but others work almost as well. Hooked drum will immediately drive for deeper water and rocks or clam beds. You'll need a heavy wire leader, preferably flexible or multistrand, to keep the sharp rocks from chaffing the line. More often than not, battling a large black drum becomes a true tug-of-war. The fish possesses real power and will head for deep water. If you can keep its head up, you can guide it along. But if it should "head down" you're in for a longer battle.

Black drum do not feed as much on fish as do their cousins. The majority of baits should be their natural foods: oysters, clams, crabs, and the like, globbed onto a hook. From time to time they will take cut-bait, but given a choice, two or three shedder crabs sewn together will be a treat most black drum can't pass by.

5. Flounders

There is no more popular species of fish on the Atlantic Coast than the lowly flounders. If we had to rate fish in an order of popularity, I'm sure that the flounders would come out on top as America's favorite saltwater fish. It's difficult to say which might be the more important reason for its popularity, the fishing or the eating. As far as being a gamefish is concerned, flounders rate rather low on the scale. But they are everywhere available, can be taken on almost any tackle you might find in the closet, are cooperative feeders once they are found, and few fish provide better eating than butter-fried flounder fillets.

There are nearly 500 species of flounders to choose from but only three are of major interest to American anglers from a sporting and eating standpoint. They include the summer flounder, or fluke, as it is known along the more northerly part of its range; its near cousin the southern flounder, which is quite similar in appearance and habit; and the smaller winter flounder, or just plain flounder, which provides the bulk of the flounder fishing in the northeastern states.

SUMMER FLOUNDER

Fluke, or summer flounder, are the largest fish of this trio, with numerous examples on the records that weighed 20 pounds or better. The range of summer flounder, *Paralichthys dentatus*, is also the greatest, extending from the cool waters of the Gulf of Maine south to South Carolina and occasionally Georgia. As with most flounders, there is very little or no coastal migration from season to season but a migration from the shallow waters of bays, inlets, and rivers offshore onto the Continental Shelf and into deeper water.

DESCRIPTION

The summer flounder's body form is typical of most flatfish; it has been compressed dorsal-ventrally during the course of evolution. The eyes have migrated to the left side along with the mouth. The dark side, or that with coloration, is the left side and the fish lies on its right side in the sand and mud. In coloration, summer flounder offer the greatest variety, ranging widely in tints from a pale white on top through hues of gray, blue, green, brown, orange, and almost black, depending upon the bottom over which the fish rests. The underside is usually white but in some fish it, too, can be colored.

The flounder is covered with a series of dark spots, approximately ten on the body and four or five more on the tail fin. The lateral line forms a large arch as it passes aft from the gill, around the pectoral fin, and then divides the body equally. The jaw is turned back on a sharp, oblique angle and filled with numerous, sharp teeth. The presence of teeth readily distinguishes the summer flounder from the almost toothless winter flounder. Its elliptical body is surrounded by continuous anal and ventral fins that edge the entire body almost completely. The base of the tail, or caudal penduncle, is scaled. In relation of width to length, the summer flounder is one of the narrowest of the flounders, with a body twice as long as it is wide.

Summer flounders grow to a maximum of about 15 pounds and many fish weighing between 10 and 13 pounds are regularly caught over their range. On the average, however, most of these fish are smaller, weighing somewhere between 2 and 4 pounds.

SEASON

Summer flounder spawn while offshore, in late fall, winter, and early spring. During late March and early April and May, depending upon their location along the coast, they begin a shoreward migration, entering the surf and many of the bays, sounds, and estuaries inside the barrier islands. Large fluke, or doormats, as they are sometimes called, tend to stay in deeper water even after the migration is completed. One of the best big fluke areas in their range is in the waters between Montauk Point, Long Island, and Block Island.

Fluke are within easy reach of fishermen throughout the summer, but as the waters cool in the fall they begin a return migration to deeper water on the Continental Shelf. After September, their numbers begin to thin, especially toward the northern end of their distribution. They are, however, quite active in the surf off Cape Hatteras as late as January and February.

TACKLE AND TECHNIQUES

Fluke can be taken by surfcasting, trolling, jigging, drifting, or at anchor; from the beach, in partyboats, or in the bays from small rowboats. In other words, the fluke is a versatile gamefish and offers anglers a variety of ways to catch it. The most efficient and preferred method is drifting in a bay or channel. Because of the great range in the possible size and weight of fluke, rods and reels will vary to match the possibilities. The standard fluke rig, however, is a 4- to 6-foot boat rod, not too stiff in nature unless there have been some doormats around, and equipped with a 1/0 to 2/0 reel having a star drag and filled with a minimum of 100 yards of 20-pound-test line.

Fluke can be taken on lighter outfits but this one will nicely handle a 2- or 3-ounce sinker, one or more hooks, and the accompanying bait that must adorn the hooks. Better, it will take care of any large fluke that happen to come along unexpectedly.

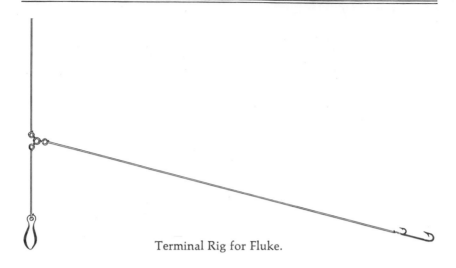

Terminal Rig for Fluke.

There are several basic rigs to put on the end of your line that will catch summer flounder. Initially, they all start with a three-way swivel attached to the end of the line. On one of the eyes of the swivel, the sinker is attached, either directly or with a short, 6-inch leader. Fluke are bottom-feeding fish and that is where your hooks and bait should be located. To the remaining free eyelet tie a 2- to 3-foot length of monofilament heavier than the line you are using. Attach the hook to the free end of the leader. A slight variation to this rig is to add one or two Willow Leaf or June Bug spinners just before the hook. The flashing does attract the attention of fluke. Still another variation on this rig is to tie a loop in the leader line about one-third of the way from the three-way swivel. Another hook with about a 1-foot leader is slipped onto the loop and provides a high hook for fluke that may be on the move.

Hook sizes and shapes will vary with the size of the fish you expect to catch and your personal preference for hook style. Styles range from Carlisle, Sprout, and O'Shaughnessy to Eagle Claw and the short-shanked Kirby hooks. When it comes to sizes, you can put them in three classifications. Small fluke will easily find their way onto a 1/0 hook because of their well-developed mouths. Medium fluke, those 3 to 5 or even 7 pounds in weight, can best be baited on a 2/0 or 3/0 hook. Doormats, fluke of 8 pounds or better, will stay on a 5/0 or 6/0 hook.

In the surf, fluke can be taken on most conventional surf outfits, depending upon the size of the fish. I once ran into a school of fluke almost at my feet in the wash off Cape Hatteras. They averaged about 3 pounds in size. We had along several ultralight freshwater spinning outfits and the fish on light tackle provided us with great sport.

Bigger fluke in the surf are best handled on a medium surf outfit, a rod about 8 feet long and a medium-sized spinning reel capable of holding a few hundred yards of 15- to 20-pound-test line. If the fluke are running farther off the beach and you are tossing large chunks of lead to hold your position, you should switch to a larger outfit, but the fun lessens, in an inverse proportion, as the size of your equipment increases.

When fishing from a partyboat or headboat, where other anglers are around and must be considered, you will want to use a heavier boat rod, a rather stiff 5- to 6-foot pole and a 3/0 or even 4/0 reel with 25- or 30-pound-test line. Once a fluke is firmly hooked, you can dominate its direction and haul it aboard. Many partyboats chum for fluke with smashed mussels or clam bellies. When this is done outside the beaches, the chances of calling up a really large doormat are good. In this case, the heavier tackle justifies itself. A large fluke, because of its flat shape, can turn sideways to your efforts and provides more of a fight than most fusiform fish.

WHERE TO FISH

Big summer flounder are big-water fish, not necessarily offshore, but in the larger bays with depths of at least 30 to 40 feet, or on shoals with deeper water not too far away. Inside the barrier beaches, the first place to begin looking for fluke is near an inlet or where numerous channels come together before pouring out into the ocean. Fluke like a current because they can lie near the bottom over mud or sand, and watch the world of food and bait pass them by without having to expend any effort.

Fluke are aggressive, sight-feeding fish and will chase baitfish and other foods into shallow water. Areas with meandering guzzles draining a thatch bed or stands of marsh grass are good spots for killifish and thus good places to go hunting summer flounder. Long bulkheads on the edge of a passing tide or salt river produce good catches of summer flounder because they encourage weeds and grass to grow. Smaller fish in turn like to hang around for their protection. Then come the fluke and eventually you.

The confluence of two creeks, or even where two currents pass side by side in an open bay, are also good spots to try for fluke. Current seems to be the key factor in any environment that fluke like. Where you find a current in action, that is where you are likely to find fluke.

The outside beaches of a barrier island fronting on the open ocean are also likely spots to find summer flounder, both large and small. Because of their flat body shape, they can swim in rather shallow water and can approach the edge of the surf, where the combers do the most work on a standing beach. Here wave action erodes the sand, releasing marine worms and crustaceans into the water and its turmoil. Here, too, is where summer flounder come searching for food.

In the surf, most of these flatfish will be found between the first bar and the beach itself. Bars are built up by wave action and form in a line parallel to the beach. But they are not continuous. Open spaces or sloughs occur where running tides build up force and the waves escape back to open water. At such breaks, the current heads out to sea, and here is where fluke take up residence, waiting for food to pass by.

BAITS AND LURES

Summer flounder take their bait alive if possible, and dead if nothing else is around. One of the best live-baits for summer flounder are killifish. Some anglers add a killifish and spearing or sand eel to the same hook. Each fish is hooked through the lips and dangles in the current. The idea of the spearing is to add a flash of light or color to attract the attention of a fluke. Spearing are almost impossible to keep alive on a hook. Killifish, far more hardy than spearing, stay alive and add action to the color.

In place of spearing, many anglers substitute strips of fresh squid. Squid are cut into full lengths, 3 to 4 inches, depending upon the size of the squid, and in strips about three-quarters of an inch wide. The affair is often cut in a wedge-shaped pattern, with the thinner portion at the tail and often split in two for more action in the tide.

Seaworms, both sandworms and bloodworms, are also good fluke baits when killifish and spearing are not available. Seaworms are hooked through the head, allowing the tail to flow freely. Often two or more seaworms are attached to the same hook.

In lieu of squid, the underbelly or white skin and meat of almost any fish will do as a substitute. The white bait fluttering in the current attracts the attention of fluke. It can come from the underside of mackerel, menhaden, or even fluke themselves. Once when fishing the surf with a small, lead-headed jig, we first attached strips of squid. We were casting into a rough sea and the squid couldn't take more than three or four castings before tearing loose. One smart angler then cut strips of the tough skin of a fluke we had just caught. He used it as a substitute that proved superior in staying power.

Because summer flounder feed readily on small fish, they are then susceptible to plugs and lures. Small bucktailed jigs, up to an ounce or ounce and a half in weight, adorned with a porkrind tail on the hook and bounced in a jerking retrieve across the bottom, account for many fluke. Small plugs and spoons that will travel along the bottom when cast, or even trolled, are also good for fluke. Light-colored patterns are preferrred over dark colors in a lure. Those resembling actual fish also seem to have an advantage. Lures colored and patterned like small mackerel are murder on fluke.

SOUTHERN FLOUNDER

The southern flounder, *Paralichthys lethostigmus,* is in a way a geographical extension of the summer flounder into more southerly waters. It is a closely related species that looks and acts extremely similar to the summer flounder and is more closely related to it than the winter flounder. It differs in size, with most southern flounder, or southern fluke as they are sometimes called, averaging only between 1 and 2 pounds. A few examples of larger southern flounder have been taken, but they are rare; the largest such fish recorded was a 26-pounder, with very few fish ever approaching this maximum. But when compared with several other species of flounder that occur in the Gulf, the southern flounder is often the largest.

Southern flounder take over in range where summer flounder leave off, inhabiting the waters of the capes of North Carolina and mixing with summer flounder at this point. They then extend south along the coast of the Atlantic and are spread everywhere along the Gulf Coast states to Texas. The greatest concentration of southern flounder occurs in the Gulf, with the coast from Panama City west to the Mississippi Delta the best southern flounder grounds.

Southern flounder do not range as far offshore or into deeper water as do their cousins, seeming to prefer shallow water and the inner bays and harbors. Given a choice, they will even work their way into brackish water and many are caught in totally freshwater sections of rivers and estuaries.

DESCRIPTION

Southern flounder are left-handed fish, that is, their mouths are on the left side of their bodies, similar to fluke or summer flounder. They differ somewhat in color from summer flounder, with a white underside and a top side brown to olive drab in color. The similarity of appearance is easily broken down when the two species are compared side by side. Southern flounder usually lack the distinct black or darker spots over the body that characterize summer flounder. When the spots do occur on a fish, there are only three or four in number. The southern flounder is quite similar to the Gulf flounder, but is distinguished from it by its color and by the diffuse dark spots.

SEASON

Southern flounder are found inshore throughout the year in all the states along the Gulf. On the Atlantic Coast, they move offshore slightly with winter weather but return again in early spring or with warmer weather. These fish spawn in winter and make the shoreward migration after spawning.

Because of their penchant for shallow water, southern flounder are most often encountered in shallow bays and lagoons, or at the heads of estuaries. They seem to prefer a mud, or a mud and sand bottom, as a place to look for food. They are most numerous along the beaches at high tide, where they swim practically out of the water chasing food. This is more prevalent at night when they are in the wash of the surf.

This habit gives rise to a way of catching this species that is popular along the Gulf shores. A strong spotlight and a spear or gig are used to take the fish in shallow water. The light seems to daze them momentarily and gives the spear fisherman a chance to strike at the fish. But they camouflage so well with the bottom that spearing them is not as easy as it might appear. Only the fluttering movement of their fins gives them away.

TACKLE AND TECHNIQUES

Tackle for southern flounder is the same as that used for fluke and varies only in size. Along the coast, they are often taken with light saltwater or light freshwater outfits. When fishing in the bays and lagoons, or tidal rivers, a boat rod, 5 to 6 feet long and a bit on the limber side, and a 1/0 or 2/0 reel with 8- to 10-pound-test line, is adequate. Hook sizes are somewhat smaller, between No. 6 and No. 1, and may be in any of the styles used for fluke.

BAITS AND LURES

Though they are aggressive feeders, southern flounder are not taken as often on plugs and spoons as are northern fluke. Instead, live-bait is the preferred choice. The fish feed heavily on anchovies, mullet, and other small fishes, showing a pronounced liking for shrimp. Any of these baitfish will do. Hooking them under the dorsal

Fluke (summer flounder) run in the winter surf off the Carolinas and Chuck Roberts was there to catch them.

fin will keep them alive for a longer length of time and live-bait is decidedly better than cut- or dead-bait.

WINTER FLOUNDER

When someone north of Cape Hatteras calls a flatfish a flounder he is usually referring to the winter flounder, or *Pseudopleuronectes americanus*. This fish is one of the best-known flounders along our coast and ranks at the top of the popularity poll. It is a right-handed fish when compared to the fluke and southern flounder, with its eyes and mouth on the right side of the body. It is popular with fishermen, young and old alike, and is sought after for the table as well as for the sport it affords millions of Americans. Whether you call it flounder, blackback, blueback, flatfish, black flounder, or mud dab, you'll find it a double-barreled treat.

DESCRIPTION

The mouth of this flounder is located on the right side of the body, along with a pair of rather widely-set eyes. The mouth is small, with the edge of the jaw ending well ahead of a line below the eye, quite different from the fluke. Also, unlike the fluke, the winter flounder has small teeth on its upper jaw and few or none on the lower. The lateral line is almost straight, except for a very slight arch just behind the gill covers. The tail is rather stout when compared to other flounder and fluke, and the back is covered with small scales that extend over the head and up to the mouth. Eyelids are also exceptionally heavy on the winter flounder when compared to other fluke and flounder species. The underside of the flounder is white and often very smooth.

Coloration in winter flounder can vary, depending upon the bottom they are over, a characteristic of most flatfish. It is usually an overall brown to olive drab in appearance, evenly colored and without spots or markings on the dark side. As in other flounder, the dorsal and ventral fins encompass the outside of almost the entire body, and the tail fin has a uniform, convexed shape.

RANGE

Winter flounder are found from the Straits of Belle Isle, separating Labrador from Newfoundland, south as far as Georgia. They are equally abundant on some of the offshore grounds, and Georgia's banks produce the largest flounder found anywhere. The fish are distributed most evenly from Cape Cod south to Cape Hatteras, with the centers of concentration from southern Massachusetts waters to the New York Bight. Winter flounder inhabit Chesapeake Bay and at times are found as far north in the bay as the freshwater sections of the Susquehanna River.

SIZE

Winter flounder do not approach the northern fluke in size. The average fish taken from inland bays and estuaries range in weight from one-half to 2 pounds. Snowshoe flounder, large members of the species and probably older adults, range up to about 5 pounds, the maximum for this species. The snowshoe seldom moves into the more protected bays and harbors. Prime summering grounds for these large fish are the waters of Block Island Sound, off the eastern end of Long Island, and as far east as Buzzards Bay on the Massachusetts coast.

A tribe or strain of flounder from the Georges Banks off Maine and Nova Scotia does grow consistently larger, weighing from 5 to as much as 8 pounds, but specimens are taken only in deep waters on this fishing area by commercial draggers.

SEASON

Though active throughout the year, winter flounder are so called primarily because they seem to feed best from September to December and again from late February to April and May. Many anglers believe that winter flounder become dormant during the winter months and bury in the mud. This is not supported by some observations. Flounder have been seen by divers to be actively swimming about during January and February. Their inattentiveness to feeding during this period is owing mainly to spawning activity. The fish fast when they are concerned with the job of producing more flounder.

The doldrums of the flounder season do occur during the warm months of the summer when smaller flounder begin to move from the shallower bays and channels, seeking relief from the hot water there, into deeper holes and faster-moving water. Where this isn't available on the inside, the fish begin a migration toward the Continental Shelf. As soon as the shallow water cools, they again head back to it.

WHERE TO FISH

Winter flounder prefer water with a mud or mud-sand bottom. Their chief foods, small crustaceans and seaworms, are found in such habitats and attract flounder to these bottoms. Winter flounder are not as piscivorous as fluke, but they will feed on small sand eels, killifish, and menhaden. Flounder do not bury themselves in the mud but lie on the bottom, stir up the mud, and let it settle onto them. They lie in wait for worms and small fish to swim by and make a short but extremely rapid dart after the food.

Flounder are found outside the bays, harbors, and estuaries in March and are taken in somewhat deeper water, between 20 and 40 feet, at this time. As the waters inside warm, the fish move in to feed near the bottom. A winter flounder spends almost its entire life in the bottom 6 inches of the water, as opposed to fluke, which at times range off the bottom and will even chase bait to the surface.

Flounder will be taken in the channels during the early part of the season and on the flats as the waters warm even more. As the water becomes too warm, these fish tend to stay in the deeper channels and holes, moving onto the flats only early in the morning and returning to greater depths as the sun warms the shallow waters.

TACKLE AND TECHNIQUES

Tackle for winter flounder, because of their small maximum weight, can be on the light side and offers a good deal of sport. A great number of spinning or spin-casting outfits are used, from either a boat or bank, to catch these flounder. A light freshwater outfit, with a rod 6 to 7 feet in length loaded with 100 yards, or even less, of 10-pound-test monofilament, will do. Often an angler will fish one or more rods until the action gets hot. When it is, one rod is about all anyone can handle.

Some anglers prefer a conventional rod and reel, usually a light bait-casting reel on a light, 5- to 6-foot boat rod. In some cases such a rod is better because it can easily handle a multiple-hook rig. Flounder rigs on the terminal end are often two-hook affairs, attached to a three-way swivel. Little or no line is used to attach the weight to the terminal end, because the bait must be on the bottom. Instead of the spreader devices that are popular with some anglers, other terminal flounder rigs consist of one snelled hook attached in tandem to a second. Two-hook rigs are standard when fishing for flatties.

Chestertown hooks, with their sharp, almost reverse bend in the hook and long shank, have come to be the standard flounder hook. One reason is that flounder tend to gulp the bait and the long-shanked hooks are much easier to retrieve. Because of the small mouths on flounder, smaller hook sizes are in order. They can range from No. 7 or No. 6 for the smaller fish to a hook as large as 1/0 needed for snowshoes or sea-flounder taken in deep water early in the season. You should stock several sizes in your tackle box and then match them according to the size of the fish you begin catching.

Flounder can be taken by casting in the surf or from a dock, pier, or sod-bank alongside a channel. Usually it is a cast, set the pole down, and wait game. To be land-bound limits your potential for flounder catching, and thus most anglers wanting to fill a pail with flounder take to a rowboat or small powerboat. Drifting does produce some flounder, but more are caught when you can keep your bait on the bottom and wait for the flounder to come to you. As a result, flounder fishing is done most often from an anchored boat.

One trick many flounder fishermen employ before settling down to wait for the fish to come to them is to lower the anchor onto the mud but not pay out enough scope for it to take a bite. Then they drag the anchor around in small circles with the use of the outboard or row power. They then anchor at the head of the disturbed area. The stirring of the bottom acts to release a natural chum, letting go with smells, tastes, and foods that drift out with the tide or current and call the fish to your area.

Chumming is a standard part of the flounder fisherman's bag. It is an easy way to call flounder to where your hooks and bait are waiting and keep them there once they arrive. One of the best forms of chum is crushed bank or blue mussels. They are gathered together in a can, crushed, mixed with a bit of seawater and sand, and then periodically doled out into the current. If mussels aren't available, bunker chum or even a can of cat food can be used. In the case of bunker, it must be added to a chum pot and lowered over the side to put the flavor and feed on the bottom where the flounder will come swimming.

Bloodworms or clamworms are the best bait for winter flounder because they are easy to skewer on a hook; they can be cut into small pieces so that they cover the barb and force the flounder to bite where the point is located; and best of all, flounder like them. They are easily dug from the beaches or readily available at bait shops. Small pieces of sandworm, which cut and hold better than bloodworms, are all that are needed on a hook.

6. Codfish and Pollack

Codfish and póllack, two offshore species of fish, make annual journeys shoreward and come within easy reach of smallboat anglers and the party-boat fleet. Codfish are almost always a bit offshore, though in rocky areas like the coast of eastern Connecticut, Rhode Island and southern Massachusetts, they often come within easy casting distance of shore. Here, many dedicated codfishermen never set foot in a boat. Almost the same is true for pollack. These great tacklebusters make a spring pilgrimage to the beaches of the Northeast Atlantic coast and provide great fishing for those anglers willing to brave the waters of a cool spring. Though the two fish may swim near to each other, a world of differences separates their behavior. Codfish scavenge the bottom for what slow life exists there, but pollack are aggressive game fish that chase their food with gusto.

CODFISH

Each fall, when all other fishes of the Northeast Coast seek the warmth of deeper water or take a southward trek to avoid the cold, there is one fish that comes into its own and captures the attention of a host of fishermen—the lowly codfish. Within its realm, the cod provides activity for all those anglers who refuse to put their fishing rods in the closet come October or November. The cod provides angling in salt water when no other species does.

Almost anyone who has fished for cod is likely to agree that as far as being a gamefish is concerned, cod would not rate very high. But they are sought after by so many fishermen and pursued for so many months during the year that their popularity has been firmly established. Fortunes have been earned from the great hordes of codfish in the Atlantic. Today, they support a well-organized and profitable headboat sport fishery out of numerous ports in Massachusetts, Rhode Island, Connecticut, New York, and New Jersey. There must be something about a cod that everyone likes.

DESCRIPTION

It is difficult to mistake a codfish for any other kind of fish, even its near cousin the pollack. Most apparent are the three separate, soft dorsal fins found on the cod's back, mirrored on the underside by two more similar in shape to the two posterior fins. The tail fin is rather small compared to the rest of the body, with rounded corners and a slight concave edge. The ventral fins on the bottom are located ahead of the pectoral fins on the side and the anal vent is situated ahead of the two ventral fins.

Generally, the cod is a heavy-bodied fish. Most of the body is up front, the deepest part being located under the front dorsal fin. But at its widest a cod is never more than one-quarter as wide as it is long. The head takes up an equally large portion of the body, about one-quarter of its length. The posterior part of the body rapidly grows slimmer and ends in a narrow caudal peduncle.

A cod's nose is conical, and blunt at the tip, with the lower jaw ending behind the tip of the nose. It possesses a large, wide mouth capable of swallowing a great array of things found on the bottom, with a posterior edge that ends under the eye. The jaw is lined inside with numerous small teeth. A single barbel dangles from beneath the chin and aids in locating clams on the bottom.

Cod have a unique lateral line and this is one of their key distinguishing features. In almost all other kinds of fish the lateral line is dark or black but in the cod it is the reverse. The line starts high in the head, at the edge of the gill cover, rises in a smooth arch over the pectoral fin, and then slopes to the middle of the flank to end at the pointed posterior edge of the peduncle.

Color in codfish varies greatly, almost without limitation, but falls into two general phases, the gray-green and the red. Some anglers call the red cod a rock cod but there is no justification for regarding it as a separate species.

The Atlantic codfish, *Gadus morrhua*, grows to enormous sizes. The largest one ever taken off the New England coast was a 211½-pound monster that measured over 6 feet long. It was captured by an otter trawl off the northeast coast of Massachusetts in May 1895. There have been numerous examples of cod weighing between 100 and 175 pounds, but the average fish, the big fish of anglers, weighs only about 35 pounds when taken from the northeastern shores. Large cod approaching 70 and 75 pounds are taken with some degree of regularity each year. The hook-and-line record is a 98-pound 12-ounce fish caught in June of 1969 off the Isle of Shoals, by Alphonse Bielevich, and on only 20-pound-test line. Other record fish for differing classes weighed 81 pounds 12 ounces, 81 pounds, 80 pounds 9 ounces, and 71 pounds 8 ounces.

The Pacific codfish, *Gadus macrocephalus*, occasionally called the Alaska cod, is identical to the Atlantic cod in almost every respect. It is impossible to separate these species externally; the only difference between them is internal, the Pacific cod having a larger air bladder. The Pacific cod, however, doesn't grow as large as its Atlantic counterpart. It is distributed from Oregon and Washington north across Alaska. It is also found on the western side of the Pacific as far south as Japan, where it is commercially fished quite heavily.

The Atlantic cod has a wide range, from the sub-Arctic waters along the northern part of the coast to as far south as Georgia. On the eastern side of the Atlantic it is found in Novaya Zemlya off Russia, south into the Baltic Sea, and along the coast to Spain. In the

United States, the greatest concentrations appear from New Jersey north to the Gulf of Maine, with the coast of Massachusetts the nucleus. Cod are deep-water, offshore fish and have been found off the edge of the Continental Shelf in more than 1,000 fathoms of water. But seldom do they venture more than 250 fathoms in depth. For the most part, they inhabit the various banks or fishing grounds on the Continental Shelf of the Canadian Maritimes and the New England coast.

Cod prefer cold water varying from 32 to 50–55 degrees Fahrenheit and because of this they stay offshore during the warmer half of the year. As the waters from New Jersey to the Gulf of Maine begin to cool in September and October, cod begin a shoreward migration. When this has been completed, they remain within a short run from most ports, from November until April.

Three unique areas exist in the range of the cod that maintain a fishery through the year when the cod have abandoned all other inshore points. These are the banks east of Nantucket; a smaller area between Montauk Point and Block Island; and another area just southeast of Block Island, named Cox Ledge. For some reason— perhaps a steady supply of food or an unusual cool-water current, or maybe a combination of both—cod hold in these locations for anglers throughout the year.

SEASON

During late fall and early winter months, cod will move onto the offshore fishing banks or into the large bays and sounds along the northern Atlantic coast. At times they are in so close that they can even be taken by surfcasters or anglers fishing from docks, jetties, and piers. The fish will remain at these inshore grounds as long as the water stays cool enough for them. Smaller cod have a higher tolerance for water of from 50 to 60 degrees Fahrenheit and will move closer to shore at these temperatures than do the larger cod. In some years the season lasts into May and June, but on the average, cod begin a migration to deeper water and to the deeper banks during March and April. Spawning takes place during late winter months and it is found that fish filled with roe or milt, when taken in nets, have empty stomachs.

Codfishing is for everyone, and here a youngster proves it aboard a party-boat fishing Block Island's Southeast Ledge.

WHERE TO FIND THEM

Codfish prefer a bottom with some grit to it, in the form of either hard-packed sand or gravel, stones, or old shell beds. In certain areas off the coast of Massachusetts, they will be found over soft or muddy bottoms but this is the exception to the rule. If the bottom is hard, cod are likely to be feeding over the area. And because cod are strictly bottomfish, their entire life is spent within one fathom from the bottom. And the larger the cod the closer they stay to the bottom; that is where their foods lie. Bigger fish get big by keeping the smaller fish floating higher. If you want to catch big cod, keep your baited hooks on the bottom.

FOOD

Codfish have often been called the garbage cans of the sea. Everything has been found in their stomachs, from finger rings to tin cans, corn cobs, rubber dolls, clothing, scissors—in short almost anything. When given a choice, however, they prefer to eat mollusks. These shellfish make up the chief or primary foods of a cod. While cod are omnivorous, often eating crabs, lobsters, shrimp, small fish, and even Irish moss, they like to dine on cockles and sea mussels, swallowing the entire shell and worrying about digestion later. Cod have been caught with several sets of mussel shells in their stomachs, at different stages of being dissolved.

TACKLE AND TECHNIQUES

Most fishing for cod today is done from headboats or party-boats. One reason is that the best codfishing is during the winter months and a large boat, one with heat and capable of taking rough seas, is the smarter way to go codfishing. But on a headboat you are often fishing with scores of other anglers, and of necessity your tackle must be rather stout.

Another reason for a sturdy rod is the terminal gear needed to fish cod at great depths, 50 to 200 feet at times, and in currents that may often need a pound or more of lead to keep your bait on the bottom. And on the bottom is where it must be to catch cod. On the fishing grounds off New England and New York, the average cod run larger in size than those on the Grand Bank. Heavier tackle is regularly needed because there is always the chance that a 50- to 60-pound fish may be caught on a trip by some lucky angler.

Tackle for cod falls into two basic categories: medium and heavy boat rods. Spinning rods and reels have little or no place in codfishing because of the great depths and heavy lines and weights needed to take them. The standard conventional or level-wind reel, with a star drag, sometimes equipped with an extended handle for faster retrieving, is used by most experienced codfishermen. A medium outfit for cod weighing between 5 and 25 pounds consists of a 1/0 or 2/0 reel loaded with 200 to 300 yards of 20- to 30-pound-test line on a 20-pound-class rod. This is a medium-action boat or trolling-type rod, between 4 and 6 feet in length and capable of handling a sinker up to 8 ounces in weight. For those long offshore trips to some of the famous wrecks around which cod like to congregate and where the chances of catching really big cod are better, switch to a heavier outfit, either a 30- or 50-pound-class rod, a 3/0 to 5/0 reel, and load approximately 300 to 400 yards of 30- to 60-pound-test line.

There isn't much variation in the terminal rig for cod. As mentioned earlier, the bait must be on or close to the bottom to pay off. That means your sinker can't be too far up the line from the hook. If you are codfishing correctly you are likely to be hanging on the bottom quite often so it won't pay to put together an expensive terminal rig. Begin with a piece of 50-pound monofilament as a leader. A 6-foot length will do. Tie the sinker to the lower end. If you want to get fancy you can add a large sinker snap to the end in the event that you will be changing sinker weights often to match changes in the current. About a foot above the sinker, tie a drop loop and then slip in a snelled hook. You can vary this slightly by tying a second drop loop two or so feet above the first and adding a second snelled hook. This is likely to take smaller fish unable to get to the bottom.

Hook sizes are not that important for cod because even the small fish are endowed with large mouths. But you should try to match hooks to the size of the fish to develop an efficient rig. For a medium outfit, use 5/0 to 6/0 or 7/0 hooks with straight shanks. For larger cod on a heavier rig, use hooks between 5/0 and 9/0 in size. There is one hook pattern known simply as a cod hook, and it was designed for use with a set line. Other shapes that hold well in the tough mouth of a cod are the Sprout and O'Shaughnessy patterns.

POLLACK

The American pollack, *Pollachius virens*, is probably the most misunderstood and least appreciated gamefish that swims in our oceans. This is partly because of its close relationship to the Atlantic cod. Pollack are members of the cod family, and the two species look so much alike that some anglers can't tell them apart even when both are lying side by side in the bottom of a boat. The pollack is a great gamefish and is much underrated as far as sportfishing is concerned. Unlike the cod, the pollack is an aggressive, voracious fish that feeds more by sight than by taste or smell. It is not a bottomfish but ranges the entire spectrum of the ocean from top to bottom and everywhere in between.

Pollack are not mollusk feeders like cod, but live mainly by feeding upon other fish with appetites that are seldom filled, even when they are in a school of small bunker or mackerel. One of their favorite foods is the young codfish. They are the codfish's number one enemy and will charge into a pack, scattering the cod to cover. The fact that they are primarily piscivorous in their diet makes them great gamefish, suckers to be taken on plugs, spoons, and spinners. You haven't really fished until you tangle with a big pollack on a fly rod.

DESCRIPTION

The pollack is not unlike a cod in general body shape and in the plethora of fins on its top and bottom sides. In location, the fins resemble those in a cod, but they are shaped somewhat differently. The greatest physical difference between the two fish, however, is the forked tail of the pollack as opposed to the almost square tail of the cod. Next, the mouths are different. The pollack's lower jaw protrudes beyond the upper lip, which makes bottom-feeding nearly impossible for it. It has the same chin barbel as a cod, but this barbel disappears in older fish.

The two fish also differ in color. Whereas a cod has either a reddish or gray phase, the pollack is usually colored a beautiful olive green to greenish-blue. (Hence it is often called Boston bluefish, green salmon, coalfish, or green cod.) The sides fade to a smoky gray along the lateral line and to a silvery gray on the underside. The ventral fins are white with a tinge of red in them.

Pollack do not grow as large as cod; adults average in size

Two anglers weigh a large pollack taken from the surf in central Maine. The fish weighed 20 pounds.

between 3 and 15 pounds. Plenty of larger pollack up to 20 or 25 pounds are taken, but rarely do they exceed 35 pounds. The world record rod-and-reel fish was caught off Nantucket Island and weighed 43 pounds 12 ounces, while a 40-pounder was taken out of Brielle, New Jersey.

RANGE

The American pollack ranges on both sides of the Atlantic from Cape Hatteras north along New England, Maritime Canada, Greenland, and Iceland to Great Britain and then as far south as Spain. The greatest concentration of these fish on our side of the ocean is in the Gulf of Maine, with fishable populations extending as far south as eastern Long Island. The fish called the European Pollack is not the same species, but a separate one, *Gadus pollachius,* called green cod or saithe by British, Scotch, and Irish fishermen.

Pollack are cold-water fish and where the summer temperatures rise above 52 degrees Fahrenheit you won't find too many of this species. The fish begin a migration shoreward early in April on eastern Long Island and in late April and May farther north. The younger pollack, called "harbor pollack," move in closer to the beach and shoal water than do the larger fish. They are taken inside rivers, estuaries, protected harbors, and bays as long as the water there does not rise above 60 degrees. These smaller fish, weighing from 1 to 3 pounds, provide excellent angling for rowboaters and jetty-jockeys and occasionally for surfers.

One of the great areas for surfcasting for pollack is Montauk Point. For about a week, or two at the most, in April, the fish are abundant around the point. They provide fantastic fishing for anglers from the beach or in small craft. Unfortunately, this occurs but a short time each year, but when it does, large pollack, mixed with smaller fish, offer anglers a bonanza.

During most of the summer months, pollack are within reach of boat anglers from Cape Cod north along the coast of Maine and off New Brunswick and Nova Scotia. The smaller fish are in close while the larger pollack, not totally averse to shoal water, are generally found chasing schools of young cod, spearing, herring, or shrimp in the deeper waters on the outside.

Pollack are taken often while fishing for cod, when working about on the bottom and occasionally when the bait is being raised and lowered. They have also been taken inshore by anglers trolling deep for striped bass or while working the water with a bucktailed jig and porkrind. Under such conditions, a light or medium boat or trolling rod is the best stick, one classified as a 20-pound rod by IGFA standards, or even a popping rod. A 1/0 or 2/0 reel loaded with 15- to 20-pound-test line and capable of holding a few hundred yards of line is your best bet. Under such bottom-fishing conditions, clams make the best bait.

But to really do a pollack justice, it should be sought after with a medium saltwater spinning rod or a 7- to 8-foot conventional rod and reel that can handle a fair-sized plug. Pollack will rise to surface poppers and plugs, but lures that run under the surface will catch more fish until you locate a school. Even spinners, No. 3 to No. 5, with big brass blades are great for taking pollack. For the smaller harbor pollack, smaller spinners, light freshwater and saltwater rods, even ultralight outfits with 3- to 6-pound-test line, will put a lot of sport into the game.

Pollack are not finicky feeders. When you locate a school they will charge your bait and make a mad dash for it if they miss the first time. After you have one hooked the fish doesn't like being pulled and is more than likely to tear off with a hundred or more feet before you can turn it.

Dedicated pollack fishermen watch the birds. Pollack are almost as aggressive as bluefish and feed much in the same manner. They will slash at schools of small fish, letting the birds pick up what is left. If you chase the birds and find them over feeding schools of pollack, try a fly rod and streamers or bucktails. A really hot pollack fly, according to Bud Leavitt of Bangor, Maine, a dedicated pollack fly fisherman, is any of the Wolff salmon flies. A 20-pound pollack is likely to have you panting for a good hour before you can grab its tail.

Some of the best fishing for pollack is at night. Given a windless evening with a tide well on its way to flood, you'll be in for a treat. Pollack come closer inshore and even bigger fish come to the top, chasing schools of bait and foraging among the rocks and grass for shrimp. Some anglers claim that pollack feed only at night. This isn't quite true, but they do feed better then than at any time during the day.

WHERE TO FIND THEM

In the extreme southern part of their range, pollack are taken from time to time off Cape Hatteras, but only in fairly deep water. With more regularity, they are taken out of several New Jersey ports, Brielle being the most popular. On Long Island, Sheepshead Bay and Captree partyboats occasionally take pollack in the spring, while fishing off Great South Beach and Fire Island for cod. The run off Montauk is unique. Pollack are taken there in the spring and again in the fall, along the rip that forms between Montauk and the southeast point of Block Island. Buzzards Bay offers on-and-off-again catches.

Provincetown's Race Point on Cape Cod is a hotspot in mid-May similar to Montauk. Fortunately, the pollack hang around Race Point a big longer than they do off Long Island. Most of Cape Cod Bay offers pollack fishing in the late spring and early fall, but it isn't until you approach the coast of Maine that you can count on catching them with some degree of regularity. The islands and the waters off the mouth of the Penobscot River, especially near Rockport, are considered the heart of the pollack country in Maine. And the rips off Petit Manan Light offer some of the best fishing available during the summer.

7. Blackfish

Flounder may introduce the spring fishing each year, but it is the blackfish along the Atlantic Coast of the northern states that bring the fishermen out to stay. Blackfish, or tautog, as this heavy-bodied bottomfish is called in New England waters, is the mainstay of the rowboat fleet during spring and early summer months. It is a delicious eating fish, excellent in any fish salad, and no fish soup or chowder is complete without the sweet, white meat of the blackfish.

From New York and New Jersey south, the fish is known as blackfish, or sometimes chub, and along the lower part of its range it is an "oysterfish," so called because of its love for these shellfish and its ability easily to crack their shells with its huge, grinding teeth.

81

DESCRIPTION

There aren't many fish with which to confuse *Tautoga onitis;* built with a stout body that reminds one of a lineman on a football team, the blackfish is unique in design. The body is broad, somewhat compressed from side to side, with a steeply sloping head that ends in a snout that resembles that of a sheepshead. Its caudal peduncle is so thick that it is difficult to hold a large blackfish by its tail. The tail fin is almost straight on its trailing edge, but with rounded corners. The dorsal fin is of uniform length across the back, where it is supported in its spiny section and ends with a large, fan-shaped, soft-rayed fin on the back edge similar to those on a largemouth bass. The soft anal fin on the bottom is, in shape, a mirror image of the soft dorsal fin on top, but is guarded in the front by three large spines. The large pectoral fins on each side are made to match the specialized technique blackfish use to feed, straight up and down. This standing-on-their-head feeding position allows blackfish to get into small cracks and crannies, and the large pectoral fins help it navigate easily in an up-and-down direction.

A blackfish's blunt snout ends in large, thick lips. Inside the lips

Blackfish are so fond of rocks that they are seldom found outside them. To catch blackfish, an angler must work his boat among the boulders.

are two rows of stout teeth, conical in shape, with two or three in the front of the jaw that protrude far beyond the other teeth. Behind these are two rows of flat, rounded teeth in the rear of the mouth, designed to crush hard shells.

Most of the blackfish's body is covered with rather large scales that grow progressively smaller from the flanks to the underside. Gill covers are devoid of scales and feel velvety to the touch. A small patch of scales rings the area behind the eye.

Blackfish get their name from an overall black or gray appearance that blends into a mouse color, or even chocolate at times. The sides are covered in darker, irregular blotches. As a fish grows older the blotches tend to fuse together and present an overall dark appearance. The underside is usually a lighter gray color in relation to the rest of the body, but the lower jaw or chin in large blackfish is usually white.

The only close relative, an almost exact copy of the blackfish, is the cunner or bergall. But bergalls do not grow on the average as large as tautog. Tautog do grow large, up to 3 feet in length. The largest on record is a 22½-pounder caught off New York in 1876, which can be seen preserved in the U.S. National Museum in Washington, D.C. The current rod-and-reel record blackfish is a behemoth taken off Cape May, New Jersey, that weighed 21 pounds 6 ounces, followed closely by specimens of 21 pounds and 20 pounds 14 ounces taken off Rhode Island. Average-size blackfish range from 2 to 4 pounds, with numerous fish approaching 10 pounds, but any over 14 or 15 pounds are rare.

RANGE

Blackfish are distributed everywhere along the Atlantic Coast from Nova Scotia and New Brunswick south as far as South Carolina. However, the major concentrations appear between Cape Cod and Cape May, with the greatest density between Orient and Montauk points on Long Island, east including the waters of Block Island, southeastern Connecticut, all the waters off Rhode Island, and into Buzzards Bay and the Elizabeth Chain of Islands off Massachusetts.

Blackfish are strictly an inshore species of fish from the coast of Maine to eastern Long Island. Seldom do they venture more than a mile or two from the rocky shores, and more often they take up their residence within the first 200 or 300 yards from the beach. But from southern Long Island west, down the coast of New Jersey and Delaware, blackfish tend to stray a bit to sea. They are found off the Cholora Banks and 17 Fathom fishing grounds in the New York Bight, 8 to 10 miles from land. Along the Jersey shore they congregate offshore around any collection of rocks on the bottom that will encourage shellfish growth.

SEASON

Blackfish make little or no migration up and down the coast. Instead, their movement with the changing seasons is almost entirely from inshore to offshore. They begin appearing along the outer islands near the end of March and are caught inshore by the end of April. Fishing usually holds well until late June or July, and slacks off first on the inside waters, in bays, rivers, and estuaries. However, they can still be taken throughout the summer months in deeper water where it occurs close to land. Late in August and September, blackfish again begin feeding inshore. They remain here as long as the water stays above the 50-degree Fahrenheit mark. When the waters cool below 50 degrees, often in October or early November, the fish head for deeper water on the Continental Shelf. Here they become sluggish, almost hibernating. Blackfish spawn late in the spring or in early summer after having moved inshore.

WHERE TO FIND THEM

Blackfish love a rocky shoreline because that is where their food is found. They prefer the submerged ledges along a wave-washed cliff, the leeward side of large boulders, or wrecks and artificial reefs—places not far from shore, in deep holes in bays and estuaries with steep banks; around piers, docks, and bulkheads. It is in such places that shellfish grow. Tautog feed heavily on mollusks: mussels, clams, barnacles, oysters. Shellfish don't stand a chance against their picking teeth and grinders. They are also equally fond of crabs, hermit crabs, scallops, shrimp, lobster, sand dollars, and seaworms, when blackfish swim in more shallow water.

John Naimoli of Amityville, Long Island, New York, beams with pride as he hefts two 6-pound blackfish after a day's fishing.

TACKLE AND TECHNIQUES

The tackle used to subdue blackfish is necessarily somewhat on
the heavy side. The reasons for this are twofold. The first is that a 4-
to 6-pound blackfish is a tough customer to handle and puts up a
fierce struggle. There is always the possibility of catching a large fish
and in that case you won't stand a chance on a light boat rod or
spinning outfit. The second reason is that if you fish where blackfish
like to call home you are going to be hanging up with great regularity.
If you can't yank your hook out of the rocks you will leave a lot of
terminal gear on the bottom. Once a blackfish strikes it is likely to try
to escape :o the rocks, behind pilings, or lodge itself in a crevice. You
have got to put muscle to the rod so the fish doesn't get there—hence,
a stout rod.

A good blackfish stick is a 4- to 5-foot boat rod with a rather
stiff tip. The reel should be a 1/0 to 3/0 conventional model that can
easily hold a minimum of 100 yards of 30-pound-test line. A good
star drag is also essential in the event that you do tangle with a large
fish.

The terminal end of your line should be finished off in a 4- or 5-
foot length of braided wire leader, possibly with a plastic coating, and
end in a snap and swivel. Then add a three-way swivel to the snap.
To one eye add a 1- to 2-foot length of 8-pound-test monofilament
and then tie a loop at its end over which you can slip on a 1- to 5-
ounce sinker. The actual weight of the sinker will depend on the
current in which you fish. Add only enough to hold bottom. It may
have to be changed regularly as the force of the tide changes. The
weak leader material on the sinker is there so that if you do hang
your sinker, and you should from time to time if you are fishing
where the blackfish are, then it can be broken. All you lose is the lead
and not the entire rig.

To the other eye, add a 3-foot length of 60-pound-test monofilament as a leader. In it tie a loop to which you can add your hook.
Hook sizes will vary in accordance with the size of the fish you are
catching. Small tautog, fish weighing from 2 to 4 pounds, can be
handled on a No. 1 to 2/0 Sprout or Virginia-style hook. Fish above 4
pounds, those usually found farther from shore or on deep-water

wrecks and reefs, should be fished with hooks that range in size from 2/0 up to as large as an 8/0 for the monsters of the tribe.

BAITS AND LURES

Blackfish are taken almost exclusively on bait. One time, though, while I was trolling a large plug for striped bass along the edge of a collection of submerged boulders, an 8-pound blackfish liked what it saw and struck the 7-inch plug.

Generally, however, small green crabs are the standard blackfish bait, either whole or cut in halves or quarters. They are held on by skewering the bait onto the hook and then wrapping on a rubber band or two for insurance. One reason for green crabs being so good is that the pesty cousins of the blackfish, bergalls, will nibble away any other bait you offer if they are around. But crabs are usually too large or too hard for most bergalls to handle. As other choices you can use rock crabs, hermit crabs, or mussels. All are good baits, hooked through their siphon and then crushed slightly to let their juices out as an added incentive to call blackfish. If bergalls are absent, sandworms are also an effective blackfish bait.

Most blackfishing is a straight up-and-down proposition. I have been in a boat when the fish were hitting on one end of it and not on the other. Blackfish will lay claim to a very small area and are not prone to chase after a bait. It must be lowered directly to them, sometimes down into a hole or among the rocks. Blackfish will often rest in between feeding forays by lying in the rocks, sometimes on their sides and sometimes along with several other blackfish all in a bunch. At such times, they won't venture for your offerings unless you drop it on their doorstep.

Most first-time blackfishermen are frustrated by the biting or feeding technique of these fish. When they feel the first nibble anglers will automatically respond with a yank, pulling on nothing. Blackfish at first will nibble a bait with only their front teeth. If they like it, a few moments later they will pass the bait down to their grinders. Then come the most powerful tugs and this is the time to set the hook. Once you have mastered the ability not to strike on the first tug, you will easily fill the bucket with blackfish.

8. Porgies

The porgy is another bread-and-butter fish of the Atlantic Coast and provides anglers with untold hours of fishing, as well as some great eating. The porgy is *the* fish for the bottomfisherman, the angler content to fish close to shore in protected bays and harbors, at anchor or while drifting. It is the contemplative, unharried way of saltwater fishing. As a result, the porgy has developed a large following.

There are scores of names for this little fish. While the most widely used is "porgy," in New England waters it is known as the "scup" or "scuppaug," a corruption of the Narragansett Indians' name for this fish, *mishcuppanog*. In New York and New Jersey, its name is often spelled "paugy," while farther south along the coast it is labeled the "fair-maid." Some carpetbaggers must have established themselves in Charleston, because here the name "porgy" again comes into use.

RANGE AND SEASON

There are two species of this fish in the Atlantic, both identical in appearance and similar in habit. The northern scup or porgy is *Stenotomus chrysops,* or *versicolor,* according to more recent taxonomy. Its extreme range is from Nova Scotia to northern Florida, but it is rare at both these extremities. It seldom ventures north of the elbow on Cape Cod or much farther south than Cape Lookout in the Carolinas. The best concentrations in the summer occur from western Long Island or northern New Jersey east to Rhode Island and western Massachusetts waters.

The southern porgy, *Stenotomus aculeatus,* was supposed to have taken over the range where the northern version stopped, and to have spread from South Carolina around the tip of Florida and appeared in all the Gulf states to northern Mexico. More recent studies have found that this isn't quite true: the range of the northern fish extends to southern Florida, but not into the Gulf. The porgy or scup of the Gulf waters is now classified as *Stenotomus caprinus,* or *aculeatus.* It ranges from the Carolinas to Texas, with its greatest concentrations in the Gulf, especially in Texas waters.

NORTHERN PORGY

The northern porgy appears on the Atlantic coastal calendar shortly after mackerel make their sweep up the coast. They show in inshore waters around the mouth of Chesapeake Bay during early April and are along the shores of Buzzards Bay, Massachusetts, by early May. The fish are found in shallow waters, mostly within six miles of the beaches, or less, during most of the summer. In late September, October, and occasionally as late as December, the fish begin to move toward deeper water.

Large concentrations of these fish appear off the coast of Virginia and North Carolina from December to March, and have been taken in deep water by commercial draggers. It was thought that all

A doubleheader on porgies (scup) is not something rare. If the angler had had three hooks on his rig he probably would have caught a third fish from the school.

the porgies migrated south, but recent evidence of winter dragging off Rhode Island, Massachusetts, and the South Shore of Long Island, has revealed wintering populations of porgies in 45 to 70 fathoms of water, where the temperature usually doesn't fall below 45 degrees Fahrenheit. Porgies remain in the inshore waters during most of the summer; they prefer the warm waters in protected bays and sounds. About the middle of September in the northern part of their range, these fish become supersensitive to cold water. A sudden cold snap can send them scurrying offshore and then they are unlikely to return until the following spring.

DESCRIPTION

The porgy is a bottom-feeding fish, and its body shape reflects this favorite mode of eating. The body is oval in overall form, but flattened somewhat along the bottom, with the mouth located low on the head and rather small in size. The teeth are sharp and designed for tearing away at mollusks and crustaceans, a favorite food. The back is high and humped, with a sharp slant toward the mouth and a slight indentation in the incline in the area just above the eyes. The eyes are large and set close to the top of the head. A large, even dorsal fin covers most of the back and flares into a fan shape near the tail. The tail fin is long and heavily concaved, with sharp tips on each end. The ventral fin is shorter and not as long, and is guarded on its leading edge by three stout spines. The pelvic and pectoral fins are rather large, with long, sharp points.

Scales are large on porgies and light scales alternate with dark. This creates, over the surface of the fish, a series of twelve to fifteen somewhat indistinct, dark lines or stripes that parallel each other in a horizontal pattern. The light-colored lateral line starts at the top of the gill cover and parallels the shape of the back before ending along the side of the moderately thick caudal peduncle.

Porgies are not large-growing fish. It takes them four to five years to reach a pound in weight. But what they lack in size they make up in numbers. They are one of the most prolific fishes that swim along our shores. In weight, porgies range from one-half to 5 pounds with rare individuals going to 6, 7, or 8 pounds. As a rule, porgies come in two general sizes; bay or sand porgies that weigh from three-quarters to

1½ or 2 pounds, and ocean porgies that weigh between 2 and 4 pounds.

Porgies spend their lives on the bottom, looking for clams, mussels, crabs, and sandworms and even eating vegetation from time to time. To fish for them effectively you must fish on the bottom. As a rule, they are more likely to be found over hard, shell-covered bottoms or those with gravel or boulders to which mussels and grass can attach themselves. But they are also found over mud or mud-sand combination bottoms when rooting for sandworms and small crustaceans.

Sand or bay porgies swim in water much shallower than the adult or older fish. They can be anywhere along the beach in from 6 to 16 feet of water. Larger porgies prefer water from 2 to 10 fathoms in depth, but still on the bottom. Favorite haunts of these fish are points of land where a current or tide sweeps over shoal water, and spots where two currents come together, but almost always in well-protected areas. They can be found in open water between islands and on offshore wrecks and reefs, artificial or man-made.

One technique that often pays dividends when used to locate a school of porgies is to begin by drifting, bouncing baits along the bottom until the fish are located. Once you find them, throw over a marker and come back to the spot and anchor.

TACKLE AND TECHNIQUES

Even ocean porgies can be taken on light tackle, and almost any freshwater outfit or light saltwater rig will suffice. The only time heavier gear is needed is when you are after ocean porgies in deep water and need a lot of lead to hold to the ground. In such cases, a 1/0 to 2/0 reel and a 4- to 6-foot rod, loaded with 10- to 12-pound-test line, is the maximum. For most other situations, a small boat rod, or even a freshwater bait-casting outfit, is enough to handle the fish. Many anglers prefer a spin-casting or spinning outfit loaded with 6- to 8-pound-test line, and seldom do you need to go heavier.

The terminal end of the line can be equipped with a three-way swivel and the sinker can be attached directly to the swivel. To the other end, a single- or even a double-snelled hook, No. 9 or No. 10 Chestertowns, to match a porgy's small mouth, may be used. Some fishermen add a second swivel above the three-way, or simply slip a snelled hook over a loop about a foot above the first one, to catch the attention of any porgies that may be swimming a foot or so above the bottom. In the case of ocean porgies, the hook size is a little larger, a No. 6 or No. 7 Chestertown or Virginia pattern.

Monofilament leaders and terminal tackle should be used instead of wire. Porgies seldom cut the line, but they do become leader-shy with the metallics. The monofilament becomes transparent in the water and doesn't disturb the fish.

Multiple-hook terminal rigs are standard fare with porgies, because they are schooling fish. When or where you catch one, you are likely to catch another and another. The fish hit well, but with light taps or nibbles. Set the hook briskly and he's yours. But don't be in a hurry to pull him up. Jiggle him around for a while and you are apt to feel another tap or even three and are likely to haul up double- and triple-headers.

When you have located a school of porgies and they are biting, they can easily be kept around your boat with a little bunker chum. Get the chum on the bottom where your bait and hooks are located, and you'll fill a washtub. This can be accomplished by adding your chum to a brown paper bag along with a large stone. Tie a string around the bag and lower it over the side, to the bottom. After a few minutes, yank the line and the bag will break on the bottom, spilling the chum where you want it.

Baits for porgies vary only slightly. Top choices are pieces of shrimp or sandworm, not large, but enough to cover the barb on the hook and remain interesting. Clams and mollusks also make excellent baits and chunks of cut-fish are also good. Especially good are strips of cut-squid, and often you'll be surprised by the firm yank of a fluke.

Porgies are great fish to eat, one of the best from salt water, closely resembling a batch of panfried sunfish from fresh water. The sand or bay porgies are best scaled; then cut off the head on a diagonal. Larger porgies are best skinned and filleted.

SOUTHERN PORGY

Southern porgies are almost identical in habits to their northern cousins. On the average, they run a bit smaller and resemble the northern variety so closely in external shape and color that they are difficult to tell apart. Baits differ only slightly between those used on northern varieties and for the fish in the Gulf of Mexico. Live shrimp are by far the best bait and account for more porgies than any other baits.

These fish run between one-half and 2 pounds in size, and bay porgy tackle is more than adequate for any southern porgy.

9. Rockfishes

As in baseball, where you can't tell the players without a scorecard, so rockfishing can be confusing if you don't have a guide to the fishes of the Pacific Coast in one hand while you angle with a rod in the other. Rockfish come in all sizes, shapes, and colors but have one trancendent quality in common, their love of a rocky habitat.

Rockfish comprise a very large family of marine fishes, with more than 30 genera around, divided into 250 or so species. These fish inhabit all our seas and oceans, especially the temperate parts of the Pacific. The only important species on our Atlantic Coast is the rosefish, with its score of aliases. But on the Pacific side of the United States and Canada they become an important and prolific game and food fish, with more than 85 species to entice the imagination and ability of the angler.

DESCRIPTION

There's a rockfish for almost every color of the spectrum: black rockfish, black-and-yellow rockfish, blue rockfish, greenspotted rockfish, orange rockfish, and even vermillion rockfish. Other rockfish species are even more varied and include Bocaccio rockfish, chilipepper rockfish, China rockfish, flag rockfish, gopher rockfish, kelp rockfish, longjaw rockfish, quillback rockfish, strawberry rockfish, tambor rockfish, and even a rockfish called a treefish.

Even with this great variety in names that reflect a great diversity in rockfish size, shape, pattern, and color, rockfish still have a lot in common, more than just a penchant for life on the rocks. All rockfish are easily identified through anatomical features. The most salient feature is a single, long, dorsal fin which is very distinctly notched in its spinous anterior portion, with a softer, ray portion just behind it. In all rockfish, this foresection has thirteen or fourteen strong and well-defined spines. Spines are a way of life with rockfish, and even the anal fin, on the bottom of the fish, is equipped with three long, sharp spines.

Rockfish have large heads comprising nearly a third of the length of the body, which is somewhat laterally compressed. They are also endowed with one or two ridges that form under the eyes and run back across the cheeks. These ridges end in spines, adding to the spinous nature of these rock dwellers.

Rockfish differ from most fishes in the way they produce their young, which are born alive.

The different species of rockfish vary greatly in size, as well as in other characteristics, ranging from the tiny gopher rockfish, which grows to 10 inches, to the spectacular vermillion rockfish and tambor that can exceed a yard in length.

RANGE

Rockfish are distributed nicely along the West Coast of the United States and Canada so that fishermen everywhere on that coast have an equal opportunity at them. Anglers in southern California have a wealth of varieties to draw upon. These include the kelp rockfish, speckled rockfish, greenspotted rockfish, chilipepper, and

Bocaccio. Point Conception, north of Santa Barbara, seems to be a dividing point for southern and northern species of fish in California. North of it we find black-and-yellow rockfish, black rockfish, and flag rockfish. In Oregon we find that the black rockfish have spread this far north and have been joined by three big bruisers of the rockfish clan: the vermillion, tambor, and orange rockfish, which are all basically deeper-water dwellers.

With coastlines as rocky and rugged as those of Oregon and Washington, we have prime rockfish waters that are just loaded with these fish. They are abundant along the coast and in the numerous bays and sounds extending up into Canada. While there are many species in these waters, the most sought after are barred rockfish, China rockfish, and strawberry rockfish.

TACKLE AND TECHNIQUES

Rockfish range over a great variety of water depths, from 6 inches to 600 feet, and a diversity of fishing techniques and tackle must be employed to cope with these varied conditions. Rockfishing can be divided into three general categories: shallow water or shoreline fishing, with the angler restricted to the beach; reef and shoal fishing from a boat in water of moderate depth—up to 100 feet or so; and deep-sea fishing, with rigs that must reach the bottom in as much as 100 fathoms of water.

Needless to say, shore fishing is the most popular and attracts the greatest number of anglers, who can practice it with a minimum of financial outlay and effort. But even in shore or surf fishing, there is great variation because of the differing character of the way the land meets the Pacific Ocean. The most popular method is casting among the rocks and breakers with either a spinning or conventional, level-wind outfit. Rod, reel, and line will differ with the species you are after. Many anglers, however, have a tendency to select equipment on the heavier side because of the great variety and often the unexpected size of fish that haunt even shallow water.

In addition, your tackle will take a greater beating from the water and rocks than from the rockfish. Lines of between 15- and 25-pound test, with lengthy leaders, are a standard part of a surf fisherman's gear. Sinker weights are determined by the size of the surf and the strength of the running tide, but all should be shaped so that they don't hang unnecessarily on sharp rocks. And come prepared to lose a lot of terminal tackle. If you don't, you aren't rockfishing correctly.

Rockfish are omnivorous, eating almost anything that swims. They will readily take cut-fish, shrimp, squid, mussels, clams, seaworms, and whole baitfish, alive if possible but dead if live-bait is not available. Of these baits, probably cut-squid and shrimp are the most preferred.

Another type of fishing along the shore does involve deep water wherever the shoreline consists of cliffs. Cliffs have their opposite counterparts in the water, deep holes immediately adjacent to the land. Some holes drop a hundred or more feet within just a few feet of land. There are numerous cliffs and outcroppings along the California-Oregon-Washington shore where anglers after rockfish become cliffhangers. They cautiously work their way to the edges of these spots and then fish vertically in the deep holes.

It takes a fairly heavy chunk of lead to fish a 100-foot hole and maintain contact with the bottom and 8-, 10-, or 12-ounce sinkers are often employed. To save a lot of hauling up and letting down just for one fish, many anglers go to multiple rigs; that is, four to six hooks tied on short leaders off the main line with the sinker always on the terminal end of the outfit. Bait for such rigs is usually something that will stay on well while a lot of fussing is going on with the other hooks, and strips of cut-squid seem to be the best bait.

The rod, reel, and line are also on the heavier side with this "yo-yo" type of fishing, as some anglers call it. The main reason for this is that you never quite know what will be swimming along with the rockfish, and 60-pound rock cod or 100-pound halibut are just as likely to strike your baits as a 5-pound rockfish. So, a 25- to 30-pound-test, or heavier line is used; a 2/0 to 4/0 reel with a lot of line; and a good star drag that can be turned down quickly in case the tug is a lot harder than you anticipate. Another trick the up-and-down anglers use is to select hooks with their points turned in, or to turn in the points on their hooks themselves. They claim this saves a lot of rigs from fouling on the sides of rocks and ledges as they are repeatedly hauled up, especially with a fish on that may take the line under a ledge and foul the free hooks.

In shallow water, rockfish move close to shore with a flooding tide and then away from shore as the tide ebbs. Fishing action for the shore-bound angler is usually best when the tide is near its flood and falls as the tide moves away. This introduces the second category of rockfisherman, the boatman. Usually in a small craft, he fishes the rocky shore from the outside in. The technique here is to anchor your boat within reach of the shore at low tide. Thus, as the tide rises and falls, you'll always be in rockfish waters.

Many rocky points and coves occur with intermittent sandy bottoms, and a rockfisherman will find little to catch over such an area. The trick is to feel out the bottom with your sinker and bounce your bait along it. If it has a soft, mushy response, then you are over sand or mud. Pay out more anchor line and continue to bounce on the bottom to the hard stuff. This action is employed not only to determine what sort of bottom there is, but also to attract the rockfish if you are over one of their homing areas. The bait should be kept moving, and if the swells and waves don't lift you a half-dozen or so feet on each sweep, then you should be gradually lifting and lowering your rod tip to give the bait the same type of movement.

In a boat, with your greater mobility, you can switch to tackle a bit lighter, even though you may take on some heavier fish. Twelve- to 20-pound-test line, a medium-action 5- to 7-foot boat rod, and a 3/0 to 4/0 reel will do. You can even switch to a medium or heavy spinning outfit and come away with fish. The only drawback with spinning gear is that the lighter lines don't hold up as well on the rocks. But if you check them regularly, as you should with any outfit, and replace frayed line, you shouldn't run into too much trouble. Of course, you use wire leaders on either type of tackle.

The third type of rockfishing is deep-water stuff, and usually requires boats capable of handling this kind of water. For the most part, this form of rockfishing is pretty well organized by the commercial headboat or partyboat fleets. Finding rockfish in water up to 600 feet deep requires rather sophisticated electronic gear. You need it to locate the fish and to get you back onto the same spot after you have them pinpointed. Only commercial craft can make such an effort pay.

To fish the big holes for the deep-water rockfishes, the tambor, vermillion, and orange species, you'll need rather special gear if you don't rent it on the partyboat. The depths are greater, the water

This lucky West Coast angler hit the jackpot with a good pair of rockfish that came from deep water.

currents stronger, and the fish larger. To match these demands you need a reel capable of holding anywhere from 300 to 600 yards of 50- or 60-pound-test line. All this line is loaded on a 6/0 to 8/0 reel and that means your boat rod must have a lot of beef to it because you'll be playing with lead weights of from one-half to 3 or more pounds. If you're lucky, you'll encounter big rockfish, but you can also expect to catch almost anything else in the ocean. Hook sizes rise in accordance with the size of the fish being encountered, and the other equipment being used, and you should tote along a selection of 3/0 to 10/0 hooks in one or more styles: Siwash, O'Shaughnessy, or Eagle Claw.

Some anglers revert to wire line for fishing at such depths, and there is justification for it. There is little or no stretch in wire line and the bottom can be felt easily. Any light fish nibble is immediately relayed to the fisherman. Long Dacron and monofilament lines absorb all but the hardest jolts, and you must keep as much sag or belly out of these lines as possible. That means heavier weights. But this can be avoided to a degree with wire lines. The wire lines most often used test at 40 or 60 pounds, but a lot depends upon where you are fishing and the remainder of your tackle.

Most of your deep-water action, after you set the hook on a rockfish, will be on or near the bottom. Once you have fought the fish for an appreciable distance up the line, the fight may suddenly end. The fish is stopped by the rapid decrease in pressure, and the sudden change causes the air bladder or stomach to extrude from the mouth and immobilize the fish. It is no less good to eat.

10. California Yellowtail

No one who has ever fished for yellowtail takes them anyway but seriously. If there ever was a brute that roamed the oceans at its will, it must be the California yellowtail, the Pacific counterpart in style to the Atlantic bluefish. The yellowtail is a mean, nasty, aggressive, finicky fish that comes as close to pure muscle as can be imagined. It strikes with the momentum of a steam locomotive, runs with the speed of a thoroughbred racehorse, and battles with the tenacity of an English bulldog. In other words, it is sheer pleasure on the other end of a fishing rod.

I've met the yellowtail off San Diego, among the Coronado Islands near Tijuana, and deep up the Sea of Cortez in Mexico. And each time I was not disappointed. The fish's only drawback is its erratic nature, striking only when it is ready and with no regular pattern of action. Your real problems begin when you think you have the fish figured out. It will toss you a curve every time.

The yellowtail has earned for itself the reputation of being the most popular gamefish in southern California waters. One of the centers is San Diego, where an annual yellowtail derby is held to organize the fishing. It is one of the prime fish of the charterboat fleet in these waters. When the yellowtails don't appear or are in scant numbers, the area's economy feels the pinch.

DESCRIPTION

The California yellowtail has several other, popular names, such misnomers as amberjack and white salmon, and is sometimes also called the Pacific yellowtail. South of the border it is known as the juarel. While it resembles somewhat the amberjack of the Atlantic Coast, it is, instead, a member of the Crevalle Family, and thus a cousin, but not kissin' kin, of the amberjack. It is powerfully built fish with massive shoulders and a fusiform body designed for a fast life in the open seas. The body is laterally compressed, but only slightly, to add more thrust to its drive when swimming. The snout of the fish tapers to a blunt point, somewhat as in a bluefish. The aftersection, however, tapers rapidly, as in all pelagic species of fish designed for open ocean life. The body is tipped with a sharply forked tail, the dorsal and ventral halves being mirror images of each other.

The dorsal fin is in two sections, with a minute separation between the spinous, anterior portion and softer dorsal fin that begins about midway on the back and extends almost to the caudal peduncle. A pair of pectoral fins are located just aft of the gill covers and below the middle of the body, just slightly ahead of a pair of ventral or pelvic fins on the bottom of the fish.

The lateral line begins high on the shoulders, sweeps aft and downward to the last third of the fish, and then ends in the middle of the caudal peduncle. A freshly caught yellowtail sports bright metallic blue-to-green colors above the lateral line. Below the middle of the body this color gives way to a silver-white and white underside. A bright brassy or yellow sheen band begins near the eye and runs down the side of each fish to taper off in a thin sliver at the tail. The body fins are a dusky olive drab except for the fish's flag, a brightly colored yellow tail fin.

Pacific yellowtail vary greatly in size. On the maximum end, most of the big fish have come from the waters off New Zealand, and the current world record is such a fish, a monstrous 111-pound yellowtail that measured 5 feet 2 inches in length and was caught in June 1961. Prior to this, the world record fish had been a 105¾-pound yellowtail taken out of Topolabompo, Mexico, in the Gulf of California on April 30, 1955. Zane Grey, a devotee of the yellowtail, took a 111-pounder in the South Pacific while he was still fishing. However, it was never logged as a record.

The fish we are more likely to encounter, however, do not run anywhere near that large. At one time, 50-pounders were not uncommon, but today they are a rarity. Instead, we satisfy ourselves with fish ranging between 8 and 12 pounds, with a 20-pounder considered a very good fish.

RANGE

There is some confusion about the California or Pacific yellowtail, *Seriola dorsalis*. There are similar—indeed, nearly identical—fish that cruise along the coast of South America and as far west as New Zealand and Australia, and so all yellowtails are grouped together. The only major difference is one of size. The western fish are considerably and regularly larger than those found off California. There has been some suggestion that these yellowtails be classified as another species or subspecies of yellowtail, possibly *Seriola grandis*.

The yellowtail we are concerned with swims the Pacific Ocean from as far north as Oregon to as far south as Panama. For the most part, however, it is concentrated from La Paz on the tip of Baja California in Mexico to as far north as Los Angeles.

Yellowtails are migratory by nature and begin to appear in the waters off Tijuana and the Coronado Islands near the U.S.–Mexico border as early as April. By May they are in the waters around San Diego and spread north depending upon the water temperature. The fish have been observed spawning on the banks off southern Baja

California from July to September. They do not spawn all at once, so that the spawning season is stretched out over a few months.

The yellowtail is a deep-water fish but likes to concentrate where the bait swims. This is normally outside the kelp beds, or in deep channels separating islands and points of land, near drop-offs to far deeper water.

SEASON

Along the coast in the area of the Mexican border, fishing for yellowtail begins in April and improves to about early July, when the first run is said to be over. The run appears again in September and continues until October and November. But, as I said earlier, don't count on yellowtail being bound to a habit. Water temperature is a far better indicator of what the yellowtails will be doing, and where, than the calendar.

Yellowtails are warm-water fish and like the warm water with them when they travel. When the waters of the Pacific off California are cold, or cool, the fishing can be late, slow, or even almost nonexistent. But when warm waters are pushed farther north along the coast by heavy oceanic currents or strong winds, the yellowtail follow. During such years, there are two very definite seasons: one when the fish move north and a second when they pass south. When the warm waters reach only the San Diego and Los Angeles area, the season can be solid throughout the summer. Many dyed-in-the-wool yellowtail fishermen do, however, catch their favorite prey throughout the summer season. In some areas it is the fishermen that fall off and not the fish, as they switch to the taking of albacore and other sought-after species. In some exceptional years, yellowtail have lingered in the San Diego area as late as December and early January. But this is a rare happening.

TACKLE AND TECHNIQUES

There are two general methods of approaching yellowtail, and both involve a boat. If you are a first-time yellowtail fisherman, then you might be wiser to opt for a party headboat or openboat. These communal craft sail daily out of ports in southern California on half-day, whole-day, and multiple-day trips. On some craft, the tackle is supplied or rented, and this takes the guesswork out of what to use. Bait is usually included in the fare, which can range anywhere from $6 to $8 for a half-day or day, to $40 and $50 for multiple-day trips, including bunks and food.

Tackle aboard a headboat will naturally be heavier than otherwise used because of the great number of fishermen angling close to one another. It will probably consist of a 30-pound-class rod, between 4 and 6½ feet long, with a 3/0 to 6/0 level-wind, star-drag reel loaded with all the 40- or 50-pound test line needed to fill the reel. The terminal end of the line is finished off with a wire leader and tipped with a hook ranging in size from a No. 2 to a 2/0, depending upon the size of the fish the skipper hopes to encounter.

If you are running your own boat and fish with but a few anglers, and your craft possesses an inherent mobility greater than a headboat, you may then naturally switch to lighter tackle and put more sport and fun into it. A headboat skipper measures his success tomorrow by the number of fish he can have his sports throw onto the dock today. Heavier tackle makes sure that fewer fish break away

It was a good day of yellowtail fishing aboard this California partyboat.

by accident, especially for new or novice anglers. In your own craft, you can switch to 3/0 or 4/0 reels on a 20-pound-class rod and use monofilament line ranging from 18- to 30-pound-test for the bigger fish, and drop proportionately down the scale for smaller fish.

Or, you can put real fun into the game by switching to spinning tackle. The lighter tackle makes pinpoint casting a lot easier and you are in touch with the yellowtail all the time it is on your hook. However, you should match the tackle to the technique that is taking fish. Some anglers troll, while others drift and chum; still others prefer to jig. Any of these methods can pay off at the right time, so when the finicky yellowtail is not cooperating, switch techniques and tackle to sample its moods.

Yellowtails are schooling fish and move around with other fish of nearly the same age-class and size or weight group. When they begin feeding, it is usually as an entire school that is moving past you. Smart skippers, especially those who run charterboats or headboats, chum as a regular technique. The chum is usually ground up anchovies or sardines, with plenty of live fish tossed regularly into the chumline to make the yellowtails chase their food. The biting can stop almost as quickly as it begins, with the fish moving off after something more interesting, even though you are still doling chum and anchovies into the slick. That's the kind of fish they are.

If you are on a partyboat and use a level-wind reel and rod combination, there is no way you'll be able to cast with live anchovy on your hook. If you try to cast, you'll likely snap the bait off on every attempt. Instead, you'll peel off line, ease the bait into the water, and let the current move it. If, however, you switch to spinning tackle and use live-bait rather than "iron," you must pick a rod with a soft tip. The soft tip or "anchovy" tip is designed to take up some of the thrust of the cast and ease the live anchovy into the air without casting it off.

BAITS AND LURES

The diet of yellowtails changes with the waning of the seasons. Early in the year, during April and May, the fish come ashore following schools of squid onto the flats. The bait to use then is, of course, squid or any good imitation of it. Once the squid move offshore, yellowtail feed on schools of mackerel and then anchovies. Anchovies are probably the best standard bait when those baitfish are in season.

The yellowtail is a unique feeding fish. Almost invariably, it will dine only on the main fare in the water at that time. That is, if the fish are feeding on squid it will be almost a waste of time to toss sardines or anchovies at them. But when they are feeding on anchovies, the little fish can be used alive as the bait and others ground up in a chum. Or larger cut-fish can be used in the anchovy chum as bait on the hooks.

Yellowtails can also be trolled for, using feathered lures or strips of cut-fish that troll without fouling the lines. In addition to trolling, yellowtail can be jigged with diamond jigs or other, similar, metallic lures. This can be performed in three ways. The trolling jig works well for fish near the surface of the ocean. The boat moves along at a steady pace and with 100 to 200 feet of line astern, or more if you desire to fish at a greater depth. The rod is periodically jigged to make the lure dance on the opposite end. Or, from a drifting or anchored boat, you can cast a jig or metallic lure away from the boat, and after allowing the lure partially to sink, retrieve it with a jigging or jerking action of the rod and reel.

The last form of jigging is called vertical jigging or yo-yoing. The lure is allowed to drop to the bottom in free spool; the clutch is then set and the lure retrieved a dozen or so feet in a series of jigging movements and then dropped again to the bottom. Or, it can be jigged up a few feet off the bottom, bounced around, reeled up again for a few more feet, bounced around again, and this action continued until the jig is out of the water, after which the entire performance is repeated.

There are also those grand moments of angling for yellowtail when the fish have corraled a school of bait or squid near the surface of the water. They thrash about wildly, feeding and gorging themselves on the bait without regard to what's happening around them. At times like this, they can be taken on plugs, spoons, or almost anything that is tossed at them. However, times like these are few and far between, and you must resort to more conventional and less exciting approaches to catching yellowtails if you want to do it consistently. That's the real mark of a fisherman.

11. Mackerel

There is no more confusing group of fish to an angler trying to keep names in order than the mackerels. It is quite true that many of them look so much alike that you almost need to be a biologist to keep the various species clear in your mind. The interchanging of names from one locale to another along the coast compounds the confusions. Nor are the mackerels themselves of any help, because of their wide range of distribution and extensive migrations.

There are nearly 60 species of mackerels, ranging from the small tinker mackerel to the monstrous horse mackerel, alias the tuna. In addition to the giants, included in the family of mackerels are another half-dozen tunas, bonito, albacore, and wahoo, as well as all those with "mackerel" as first or last names. Luckily, only about 15 species swim in North American waters and of the mackerel-type fish we are accustomed to, only a half-dozen are common enough or sporting enough to be sought after on a regular basis by fishermen.

ATLANTIC MACKEREL

This great gamefish is also called the common mackerel, *Scomber scombrus,* by biologists, or Boston and spikes, a common mackerel of two sizes with market terms for identification. The common mackerel is a fish with a huge following because it ranges so widely along the Atlantic Coast. It comes into the bays, harbors, and sounds, as well as along the inshore waters of the open ocean, so that thousands of fishermen in headboats and private craft can take their turn at the vast schools.

DESCRIPTION

Mackerel hardly need description, so familiar are they to fishermen and nonfishermen alike. They are high-speed, oceanic fish that wander over waters of all depths. To meet the requirements of such a life they have developed an extremely streamlined body shape, one with very little drag or resistance, so that high swimming speeds can be attained without a lot of effort. The head or snout is sharply pointed, with the mouth fixed on the very end. The body is 4½ to 5½ times as long as it is deep, and somewhat cigar-shaped. It is oval in cross-section. The jaw is large and gaping, ending under the eye, and filled with numerous small but sharp teeth.

There are two large dorsal fins. The first is over the middle of the back, just behind the pectoral fins. The second is well separated from the first and begins at the lower third of the back. Five smaller, triangular-shaped dorsals graduate to the thin peduncle. A set of ventral fins on the bottom of the body mirror the rear dorsal fins in size, shape, and number. A sharply forked tail finishes the thin peduncle.

The lateral line of the Atlantic mackerel is dark, originating from the top of the gill cover and riding rather high along the back as it moves aft and comes to the middle of the side near the end of the first, large dorsal fin. It ends in the caudal fin.

When mackerel blitz you can't stop them from biting. On a partyboat, one angler takes on a tripleheader while others anticipate their turn.

Coloration in a mackerel ranges from a dark green to a dark blue, with almost a solid blue-black on the head. The top side of the body is barred, with vermiculations or wavy lines that run from the back down the side for about a third of the width of the fish. There are from twenty-three to thirty-three of these lines, also colored a blue-black and alternating with a brassy green or blue background. The lower sides of the fish are white, with silvery or brassy iridescence as the light changes.

Atlantic mackerel are not the big mackerel of the seas, nor are they the smallest. Adult fish vary from 14 to 18 inches in length, with some growing as large as 22 and 23 inches. Weight varies from 1 to 2 pounds in the spring, to 1¼ to 2½ pounds in the fall, after they have had a time to feed and fatten. One of the largest common mackerel on record was a 7½-pounder taken in 1927.

Commercial fishermen have contributed a lot to the confusion over mackerel names. They often classify their catch for the market according to size. Small mackerel are known as blinkers, spikes, or tinker mackerel. Spikes are the smallest, while tinkers are the largest in this category. Really large mackerel are referred to as Boston mackerel.

RANGE AND SEASON

Mackerel are strictly cold-water fish and are seldom found in the sea where temperatures reach 68 degrees Fahrenheit or higher. As a result, they are naturally confined to the more northern parts of the Atlantic in the summer. They are found on both sides of the ocean, from Spain north to Norway and on this side from Cape Lookout, North Carolina, to the Straits of Belle Isle, north of the Gulf of St. Lawrence.

It is believed that mackerel spend most of the winter months offshore, on the high seas. As the waters of the Atlantic begin to warm along the shore, they appear in late March and April, along Cape Hatteras. From here, they begin a definite migration along the coast, from a mile to 20 or 30 miles seaward. They arrive in the New York Bight by mid-May, in Long Island Sound almost at the same time, and in Buzzards Bay by the first of June. While the main body of fish migrates along the coast, smaller schools break away and enter the bays, sounds, and harbors all along the coast. These schools take up only a short-lived residence, from a week to four or five. Eventually they straggle back to the main body of fish and continue north as the waters warm. Mackerel summer in the waters from Cape Cod north, in the Gulf of Maine, and in Canadian Maritime waters.

The fish begin spawning as they approach shore, from Maryland in May to Massachusetts in June. Migrations southward in the fall are not as exact as the run north in the spring. With the coming of cold weather, mackerel begin schooling and make a southward-seaward run, oftentimes missing many of the points of land they lingered around in the spring. During some years they show up in the waters around Cape Hatteras in December and January, but in others they seem to have headed out to sea before running that far south.

TACKLE AND TECHNIQUES

Mackerel are not difficult fish to catch once you have located a school. The difficulty lies in locating them. Seldom do they travel in singles or small numbers. More often, they are a part of a school that can vary greatly in size but always encompasses large numbers. Schools can be spotted chasing small menhaden on top or by the activity of terns and gulls. The surest way to find a school of mackerel is to bring them to you. They answer readily to chum, and ground mossbunker (menhaden) is one of the best chums. Most chumming for mackerel is done at a drift because it covers more water, and because mackerel can often be in very deep water where anchoring requires a good deal of work. Sometimes the chum slick is used not to attract mackerel to the boat so much as to hold them in the area once they are located.

A variety of lures or baits can be worked in the chum once the fish appear. You can begin by casting small plugs and spoons, lures with a lot of flash to them. A light saltwater or light freshwater spinning or spin-casting rod and reel will do the trick. Most mackerel you'll run into won't weigh over 2 pounds and you're taking a lot of fun out of the game if you insist on heavy gear.

At times mackerel won't take artificials when chummed, so make certain you always have some bait along. It can consist of seaworms, strips of cut-squid, small baitfish, or even strips of belly meat from other mackerel. Seldom will they pass up live- or cut-bait.

An added bit of sport can be had by trying for mackerel with a fly rod in the chum. Streamer and bucktail flies do well, and one angler I know likes to dip his flies in sardine or bunker oil, to add flavor to the flash. He claims it makes every strike a sure thing.

Another technique for locating Atlantic mackerel is to drift and jig. Small diamond jigs, either plain or with a porkrind or a strip of squid on the hook, are used. One variation on the jig is a multiple-hook outfit. It consists of three or four hook-and-tube affairs tied in tandem and then finished off on the bottom with either a 2- or 3-ounce sinker or a larger diamond jig. This rig is jigged through a school of mackerel and oftentimes there are multiple strikes.

Mackerel can be trolled with a jigging outfit similar to the one just described, or by jerking a small lead-headed bucktailed jig. A porkrind on the tail is a good addition and adds action to the bounce of the lure.

Mackerel have large and tough mouths and sharp hooks are needed to plant them firmly. When using light tackle and bait for smaller fish, a hook anywhere from No. 7 to No. 3 is adequate, in either a Carlisle or O'Shaughnessy pattern. If you are offshore and consistently running into large Bostons, then a 1/0 or even 2/0 hook size may be more in order. Schools of mackerel usually contain fish of nearly equal size and weight. A consistent rule is that the smaller the size of the mackerel in a school, the larger will be the school.

WHERE TO FIND THEM

When mackerel are running offshore, they can be in almost any kind of water, ranging in depth from 5 to 50 fathoms. On the deeper end, they are not spooked too often by a boat. But once they enter the inside bays, harbors, channels, and sounds, they seem to become sensitive to boats and motors. Approach them cautiously and don't run over a school. Mackerel can be anywhere between the top and the bottom in a body of water. But because they prefer deeper water, they are seldom found in depths of 30 feet or less.

CHUB MACKEREL

There is another mackerel quite similar to the Atlantic mackerel in shape, appearance, and range that is called the chub or tinker mackerel. Its populations vary greatly from time to time and these fish are often taken with the common mackerel by anglers without knowing the difference. It is closely related to the common mackerel but *Scomber colias* (at one time known as *japonicus*) is consistently smaller in size. It is differentiated internally from the common mackerel because it has an air bladder. Externally, it has thirty or fewer lines on its back; these lines break up into spots below the lateral line.

PACIFIC MACKEREL

For a long time this fish, *Scomber japonicus*, was thought to be the same fish as the chub mackerel, but today it is regarded as a distinct but closely allied species. It is the Pacific counterpart of the Atlantic chub mackerel, but grows a lot larger, up to 6 pounds, though the average weight of the fish ranges only between 1 and 3 pounds. Its description is the same as that of the chub mackerel and its range covers the entire Pacific Coast of the United States. The best concentrations, however, are in the waters off southern California.

Because it, too, is a lightweight like the Atlantic mackerel, light tackle is the order of the day. Like other mackerel, it is taken by casting and fishing live-bait, or even trolling. Unlike their East Coast cousins, however, Pacific mackerel have a penchant for shallower water when they are in season and the best time to find them is during their fall migration southward.

SPANISH MACKEREL

What the Atlantic mackerel does for the coast of New England, the Spanish mackerel does for the states along the Gulf of Mexico. The Spanish mackerel, *Scomberomorus maculatus*, though not one of the true mackerels, fills the void in the southern distribution of mackerels. Once hooked, a Spanish mackerel loses its temper, hence the Latin name, and it is never a sure thing as to who will win in a battle. It is one of the best small sporting fishes available to anglers. It is a fantastic acrobat and doesn't tire easily. In the frying pan, it is equally as formidable.

DESCRIPTION

Spanish mackerel have the overall mackerel appearance and though not one of the genuine articles, they are so closely related that to the fisherman it doesn't really matter. They have the same cigar shape as the common mackerel, one designed for life on the high seas. The biggest difference, at first glance, is in the shape of a much larger tail. The dorsal fins that are separate in the common mackerel are attached in the Spanish and much differently shaped. The front dorsal fin is wedge-shaped, higher at the lead edge, and then grows smaller as it passes aft. Often attached to the front fin, or with just a small space between them, is the rear dorsal fin, triangular in shape but with a slightly concave rear edge. Approximately eight small, rudimentary dorsal fins line the top of the back from the large dorsal fin to the base of the narrow tail. On the sides of the caudal peduncle, the Spanish mackerel has two small, lateral stabilizer fins.

The anal fin on the underside is a mirror image of the rear dorsal fin, but begins just slightly farther back on the body, and small rudimentary fins, mirror images also, form a line all the way to the tail fin. The pectoral fin is located just behind the gill cover and on the middle of the flank. Unlike the cerro and kingfish, the Spanish mackerel lacks scales on the base of its pectoral fins. Also, to distinguish it from these two other near mackerels, the Spanish mackerel has large, oval orange or yellowish-orange spots on its sides, both above and below the wavy lateral lines. The cerro's stripes are missing along its sides and back.

The lower jaw of a Spanish mackerel protrudes slightly beyond the upper jaw and is well lined with sharp, conical teeth. In color, it is a dark green or bluish-green over the back and the upper sides, turning pale toward the underside and a silvery white on the belly.

In size these fish are considerably larger than common mackerel, with the maximum reaching 9 or 10 pounds, but with an average closer to 3 pounds. The largest ever recorded was a 25-pound monster taken in a pound trap off the mouth of Chesapeake Bay in October 1901. It measured 41 inches in length.

DISTRIBUTION AND SEASON

Spanish mackerel are distributed in the Atlantic from Brazil north to Cape Ann, north of Cape Cod. But for practical fishing purposes, they aren't too numerous north of Chesapeake Bay. For the most part, they are fished heavily from the Carolinas south to the Florida Keys and then west across the Gulf of Mexico to Texas and northern Mexico. The Spanish mackerel is one of the top inshore species along the Gulf states and second only to the grunt in numbers as a food-fish in southern Florida.

Spawning takes place on the Carolina coast during April and May. At one time they spawned in the waters of lower Chesapeake Bay during the first week or two in June. Nowadays, they are not as numerous inside the bay as in past years.

Spanish mackerel can usually be found anywhere along the coast where the water temperature is 60 degrees Fahrenheit or higher. As a result, they remain in the lower Florida waters and Gulf states throughout the year. However, the best fishing times—that is, when they are around in large numbers—are from about the first of February in southern Florida and the first of March in the Gulf. The fish then move north along western Florida and to Texas. Another group of Spanish mackerel moves north along the Atlantic Coast of Florida about the same time and kicks off the season in April, with the fishing getting better as the year progresses. Occasionally, some fish are taken as far north as the New York Bight in July and August, but not so often that one could say that he was going fishing for Spanish mackerel. Along about the end of September, or in early October, these mackerel have reversed their direction and are back in their more southerly waters.

WHERE TO FISH

Spanish mackerel are inshore fish, but in most of their range they often prefer the deeper inshore waters. One exception is along the coasts of the Gulf states, and they are frequent visitors to the fishing piers that jut from the Texas coast. Otherwise, they are taken over reefs and shoal areas in deeper water along the Florida coast north to South Carolina. From here north, they seem to be farther offshore and fishing for them can mean a run of from two to ten miles, depending upon where their food is swimming.

TACKLE AND TECHNIQUES

Spanish mackerel can be taken trolling, casting, or by drifting baits. Of the three, spinning or casting is probably the most enjoyable. When these fish are schooled and on the move, mob instinct prevails. At such times, they will strike at almost anything tossed at them, provided it is small enough for them to mouth. Once the schools break apart and pods become established in areas along the coast, taking them on spinning tackle or any other kind of equipment becomes challenging.

Most Spanish mackerel you encounter will range around 3 pounds in size, and you can tackle them with ultralite or light spinning gear. A standard freshwater rod, 6½ to 7½ feet long, with a moderate action and tip, and a reel loaded with 6-, 8-, or 10-pound-test monofilament will put a challenge in your fishing. Small plugs and spoons, lures that dip, dart, and dive, are what mackerel like. Even surface poppers that chug and dart make good mackerel lures when fished properly. Mackerel, being fast swimmers, like their food moving at a fast clip and thus to be effective, retrieving should be done at a rather rapid crank. Speed, movement, and direction are three aspects of a cast and retrieve which you can vary to obtain different effects on the fish.

Trolling also produces a lot of Spanish mackerel, especially when you cannot spot schools feeding on top. Spoons trolled at a fair speed are good lures, but if you've a mind to catch more fish, use a small bucktailed or feathered jig and jerk or jig it as you troll to impart added action to your lure. When a school of feeding mackerel does break to the top, troll along the edges and not through the middle of the action. Feathered jigs, plugs, and spoons, moving at a fair clip, will tempt the schooled fish.

As Spanish mackerel reach their goals in migration, they take up residence on or near the bottom, feeding on small shrimp, worms, or small fish in or above the grasses. At times like this, bottomfishing for mackerel is in order. They will take minnows, alive or recently alive, and live shrimp. Here, the bait is fished off a float or bobber, at varying levels to determine where the mackerel are striated. If they are on the bottom, you can angle without the float and even slip a split shot or two onto the line to get the bait down deep. Small baitfish and shrimp are best skewered on a 1/0 hook and this tied to a 2-foot length of light, braided wire leader. At times, Spanish mackerel become shy of lines and leaders and you may have to go to lighter, transparent monofilament lines and do completely without the leader. You may lose more hooks and fish, but you'll be catching mackerel instead of just drowning bait.

Spanish mackerel are also taken in the surf. Along the barrier beach islands of Texas, along parts of the islands off Louisiana, and on the Atlantic Coast from Florida to the Carolinas, these power-houses are prone to strike for the beach from time to time, tearing apart anything in their way. Fishermen don't normally go surfcasting specifically for Spanish mackerel because the appearance of these fish in the surf is so unpredictable. But when they do move within casting distance, they usually hit anything and everything, and while they are there, bedlam reigns.

KING MACKEREL

Anyone who has tied into a king mackerel will probably tell you that it is the greatest gamefish that swims in the ocean. It is a powerful fish, grows to heavy weights, is a master acrobat, and is filled with enough stamina often to wear away a hook and leader. It hits like a bolt of lightning and its runs are sustained and powerful. Whether you know it as kingfish, cero, cavalla, silver cero, Florida kingfish, or even black salmon, or by its Latin name, *Scomberomorus cavalla*, you must agree that it is one of the greatest prizes an angler can take within easy reach of most ports, harbors, or inlets.

DESCRIPTION

King mackerel are the biggest of the mackerels that swim the seas, some growing to as long as 5 feet and weighing over 100 pounds. The king mackerel is shaped much like all the other mackerel, cigar-shaped, with small, powerful fins and a body designed for a life on the high seas. Like all the other mackerel except *japonicus,* it is without an air bladder and would sink to the bottom if it didn't constantly swim. As a result, the king is a hyperactive fish, one that is always on the prowl.

The long, forward dorsal fin is short at the front and gradually grows smaller to end just before a small, high, second dorsal fin that rises out of the back. Unlike Spanish mackerel and the closely related cero mackerel (*Scomberomorus regalis*), the first dorsal fin is clear or transparent and uncolored, a distinguishing feature. The short anal fin rises in a line just aft of the second dorsal and is a mirror image of it. The king mackerel is often confused with the cero mackerel and the names are often used interchangeably. But when the two fish are compared side by side, several apparent differences are easily seen. The most obvious is the color. A king mackerel is a uniform iron-gray over the back and top sides, with the underside a silver gray and an all-white belly. In young fish, the sides are marked with weak gray or yellowish spots that disappear in the adult. In cero mackerel, a yellow to brownish narrow stripe runs the length of the body from gill cover to tail peduncle. Yellowish spots in rows above and below the lateral line also distinguish the cero from the king.

The lateral line is also a key distinguishing feature separating the two closely related species. The lateral line in the cero descends gradually from the back to the side under the rear dorsal fin, whereas in the king it descends sharply in the area, even to a location below the middle of the flanks.

DISTRIBUTION AND SEASONS

The king mackerel is a lover of warm water and plies the Atlantic Coast of this hemisphere from Brazil north to Cape Hatteras. At times, it is found as far north as Cape Cod, but it is only an incidental fish north of Chesapeake Bay. With a penchant for deep, as well as warm water, king mackerel follow the flow of the Gulf Stream from the Caribbean northward. On their migrations north, they often follow closely on the tails of the Spanish mackerel, out of which they don't hesitate to take a bite. There are some kings around the keys during most of the year, but about February and early March, large numbers migrating from farther south come close to land at the Florida Straits. The invasion then splits, sending kings north along the Gulf Coast, eventually to reach Texas, and east along the Atlantic Coast, to concentrate between the Savannah River and Cape Hatteras. The fish are well established at the Cape by May and produce excellent fishing throughout the summer. Along the Gulf states, they reach the panhandle of Florida then quickly spread westward in April. Concentrations become quite heavy at times in the waters from Ft. Meyers to Clearwater.

Fishing for kings in Florida falls off during the latter part of the summer months, but come September and October, the kings are suddenly back again, and in force. At this time they provide some furious fishing that doesn't wane until near the end of the year. It never really dies, because some kings take up a permanent residence off the southern end of the state.

WHERE TO FISH

King mackerel are not truly inshore species, though they frequently make sustained passes along capes and points of land in their migrations north from Florida. Ironically, however, the larger fish often stay in shallower water than the schoolies, fish from 2 to 5 or 6 pounds. The bigger fish prefer muddied or riled water where the Gulf Stream meets shore currents and bait is often plentiful. The smaller members of the tribe are clear-water addicts.

Because kings are school fish and because they are constantly on the prowl, they are difficult to locate except when feeding on top and attracting birds. They do have a penchant for the reefs located offshore, from the coast of Florida to Cape Hatteras. The Cape Hatteras area is more of a shoal than a reef but it serves the same function, that of attracting baitfish, and they in turn bring on the kings.

Anglers who know the locations of reefs start by fishing over such features where they exist. Headboats or partyboats out of many Florida ports specialize in chasing kingfish in season and are equipped with the sophisticated electronic gear needed to find them when concentrated over reefs. All you need do is follow such headboats and let them lead you to the fish.

TACKLE AND TECHNIQUES

Though king mackerel may weigh up to 100 pounds, fish above 50 pounds are quite exceptional. The current world record is a fish that weighed 76½ pounds and was taken off Bimini in the Bahamas. Other big fish have come from the Florida coast, with several record-breakers boated off Louisiana and a few in the Caribbean Islands. But big fish are not what an angler usually goes armed for, and the range of fish he is likely to catch varies usually from 5 to 15 or 20 pounds.

Matching your tackle to such a range isn't too difficult, and the preferred method of angling for kings is by trolling. Trolling is most productive because it allows an angler to keep up with a moving school of mackerel once they are located. A lot of kings are taken by accident, by fishermen trolling for marlin and sailfish, and as a result they are often overtackled and the fighting qualities of this great fish are not appreciated. Instead, if you troll exclusively for kings, an IGFA-class 20-pound trolling rod and accompanying Dacron or monofilament line are a good combination. You can, however, drop even lower, to a 2/0 or 3/0 reel and 15-pound-test line.

Regardless of the outfit you use, the terminal end should always be finished off with a 5- or 6-foot length of wire leader. Single-strand is often preferred because it works better with some of the lures and baits needed when traveling at a rather fast trolling speed.

On the terminal end of a trolling outfit, add a spoon, spoon-and-feather combination, Jap feathered jig, nylon-tailed jig, or even a sleek plug than can withstand a fast troll. Live-baits vary from balao to mullet, or strip baits, or a piece of cut-menhaden 5 or 6 inches long and 2 or so inches wide. Even the belly flesh of a mackerel is used and preferred by some anglers.

King mackerel will mix in many sizes in a school and at times 20-, 30-, and 40-pounders are numerous. To cope with fish of this range, you'll have to increase the size of your equipment, switching to a 4/0 or 6/0 reel, and a 30-pound-test trolling rod with 30- to 50-pound test line.

Most of the time, king mackerel swim on top or near the top of the water and Dacron and monofilament outfits work well on them. But at other times, kings will run deeper, refusing to come to the surface to strike a bait. You have to go to them. In this case, Monel or stainless steel lines are used to troll and at times weights, heavy drails weighing up to as much as 16 ounces, are added to get the bait where the fish are. It takes a little sport out of the game but does put fish in the cooler.

Kings are vicious, hard-hitting fish and nearly always hook themselves. It is customary, however, to strike back and set the hook deeper as soon as a fish strikes. It is usually a hit or clean miss proposition with kings, and striking immediately doesn't discourage them from coming back if you miss.

An alternate to trolling is drift-fishing for king mackerel, especially over some of the reefs over which they establish themselves when they stop wandering. The school is located by trolling or by electronic devices and the boat moves upstream or upwind of the reef. Anglers fish the drift in two ways. The first is to fish in the direction you are drifting. The bait must be cast ahead of the boat and allowed to sink to the bottom. As soon as it hits bottom, it is immediately retrieved with fast, jerking movements by snapping the rod tip. The kings come off the bottom and strike the bait with a vengeance. This type of fishing is best accomplished with a medium to heavy spinning outfit. It makes the cast easy and efficient. The bait is allowed to sink with the reel bail open. As soon as it is on the bottom the bail is closed.

Because the potential size of the mackerel can be great, a stout spinning rod, 8 to 10 feet long, is used, and a medium to large spinning reel capable of holding about 300 yards of 20- to 30-pound-test monofilament is standard. When the fish run under 10 pounds, lighter outfits can be used, with line between 10- and 15-pound-test. Leaders are mandatory here as well as when trolling. Cut-bait is usually in the form of strips of any fish found in the area. Artificials are generally bucktailed or nylon-finished jigs, 1 to 3 ounces in size. Colors are usually white or yellow, or combinations of the two. On the hook, a strip of porkrind, opposite in color to that of the jig, is used. Here, too, the retrieve is in a jerking or jigging motion.

The alternative drifting technique is to fish behind the drifting boat, as is the practice of the numerous headboats. Here, a piece of cut-bait or strip-bait is jigged or bounced along the bottom as the

boat drifts through the school of fish over the reef. In such a situation, fishing closely with other anglers, the tackle gets a bit on the
heavier side because an angler doesn't have room to play his fish. If
you fish out of a smaller craft or your own boat, you can go light and
use either a spinning outfit or light boat rod similar to the trolling rig
for schoolie kings.

12. Sharks

Ever since man discovered sharks in the oceans he has carried on a strange relationship with them. Most of it has been born out of fear and respect, with large doses of fascination mixed in. For eons the relationship has been rather standoffish, with only the sharks doing the approaching. But today, the iconoclastic fisherman has turned the tables on the primitive fish. Today, we've become shark hunters, a change that may compensate somewhat for the man-eating tendency of these wolves of the sea.

Maybe the fascination exerted by sharks arises from the fish's ability to take on man, from the unpredictability of its actions, or from the massiveness of the fish available to almost any angler. A lot of it doubtless results from the ability of the shark successfully to thwart a fisherman's attempts—and even after it has supposedly been subdued, a shark keeps fighting. The outcome of a hook-up is never sure until the shark is swinging by its tail from a gin pole.

All these factors contribute to the aura that surrounds fishing for sharks . . . the perfect adversary for man's intelligence. Man is also a sucker for self-punishment and the sheer muscle effort and tactical skill needed to take on a shark feed this masochism. A 400-pound fish dancing on the end of a gossamer line, with a real possibility of its joining you in the boat, will excite even the most lethargic angler.

There are more than 250 species of sharks that roam all the oceans of the world, some even entering freshwater rivers from time to time. The greater part of this massive fish population, however, prefers the temperate and tropical waters of the globe, where food is often more plentiful and where their cold-blooded nature is served more readily. Sharks have filled almost every environmental niche possible, and range in size from the tiny chain dogfish shark, that as an adult does not grow more than 17 inches long, to the behemoth of the family, the plankton-feeding whale shark that grows up to 45 feet in length, and is our largest living fish.

Sharks are easily distinguishable from all other types of fish because they have more than one gill opening on each side of the neck. Most sharks have 5 or more such openings. They also differ from other fishes in that while they have vertebrae they lack true bone. In its place sharks are held together with cartilaginous substitutes that may calcify slightly in the head. This cartilaginous skeleton is a feature of more primitive life forms and proves that the design of the shark must have been pretty good to survive in a world of intense competition down to the present time.

The skin of sharks is tough and leathery, totally unlike that of other fishes. It is covered with denticles that are not the same as scales in a true fish. These are formed in the embryological stages of the fish's development by both the dermis and epidermis.

Sharks' teeth are formed from the denticles or placoid scales. These modified placoid scales are thus embedded in the gums, a part of the skin around the mouth, rather than in the cartilage of the jaw. Last, the tail fins of a shark differ from those of other fishes, with the top half always larger than the bottom portion and with the spinal column continuing into the end of the top lobe.

Sharks are basically omnivorous feeders; that is, they will eat almost anything that swims, crawls, or floats. Only a few are strictly vegetarians, or plankton feeders, while a great number are scavengers, feeding on anything that is left over after other animals have had their chance at it. There is one group, however, that are aggressive feeders, basically chasing fish. These piscivorous sharks attract the sportsman because of their willingness to take a baited hook.

Of the scores upon scores of sharks, only a small group are of real interest to the fisherman: those that when hooked put up a sporting fight, or those that grow so large, even though they may be dullards on the hook, represent formidable opponents in themselves.

There are many sharks that can be baited, but the International Game Fish Association recognizes only a few for record keeping because they are a challenge to catch and when hooked offer the angler a real hustle for his money. These include the blue shark, *Prionace glauca;* shortfin mako shark, *Isurus oxyrinchus;* man-eater or white shark, *Caracharodon curcharias;* porbeagle shark, *Lamna nasus;* thresher shark, *Alopias vulpinus;* and the tiger shark, *Galeocerdo cuvier.* Of course, there are other sharks that do a creditable job on the end of a fishing line, for example, the hammerheads, lemon, bull, blacktip, and dusky sharks, but they aren't always as dependable in a fight.

Sharks do grow large and records, which are kept primarily of the gamefish species, include a blue shark of 341½ pounds, a mako shark of 1,061 pounds, a white shark of 2,664 pounds, a porbeagle shark of 294 pounds, a thresher shark of 600 pounds, and a tiger shark that went to 1,780 pounds.

Interest in sharks during the last year or so has been spurred by the book and movie *Jaws,* as well as a plethora of shark literature that followed them and some that has been around for years, extolling the virtues of sharkfishing. But an even greater impetus to a new interest in sharkfishing has come from the increased mobility of the smallboat fisherman, generally using extremely seaworthy craft between about 19 and 24 feet long, that can, at high speeds, run offshore for sport. With pressure increasing on billfish and other species, it is only natural that the big-game angler and the inshore sportfisherman should turn to a plentiful fish like sharks upon which to practice their skill and art.

Sharks are inshore as well as offshore fish and it isn't at all true that the farther you travel offshore the bigger become the sharks. Sharks are very accommodating in that respect; they enjoy swimming close to shore for the benefit of the fisherman if not the swimmer. Frank Mundus, the renowned skipper of *Cricket II*, who for the last forty years has pioneered sharkfishing, spends the better part of all his shark trips within 5 miles of Montauk Point, Long Island, and does quite well.

FISHING TECHNIQUES

Sharks can be trolled. When you spot one or more with their fins on the surface cruising an area, you can aggressively seek them out by putting one or more strip-cut baits or whole fish over the side and

Roy Sieber of Kings Park, Long Island, New York, brings a hammerhead shark alongside his boat while fishing out of Fire Island Inlet.

slowly trolling near to where they are feeding. But if you want to catch sharks with regularity you must do what most shark devotees do—chum.

There's almost no way to figure out where sharks are located in a flat, calm ocean. They may be at any level between top and bottom. About the only indication of where they could gather is over the type of bottom that would attract other fish upon which the sharks might feed. Other than that, you are at a loss to make an intelligent guess.

But the odds are not stacked totally against you. Sharks have a fantastically well-developed ability to smell and taste anything in the water. They can pick up the taste of food miles away in a moving tide or current. And through these keen senses you can undo a shark by chumming. For this, preferably highly oily fish like menhaden are ground up into a paste. The paste is then mixed into a gruel with seawater and this is ladled into the ocean astern of your boat.

Where to begin chumming is difficult to determine. But you must begin somewhere. A few skippers chum at anchor when the wind and tide are opposed to each other and might make the establishment of an effective chumline impossible, but for the most part a shark fisherman should drift and chum. This technique covers more water and is likely to expose your chumline to many more sharks. The rate of chumming is determined by the speed of the drift. One fact must be kept in mind whenever chumming; once you have started a chumline you must ladle the gruel into the water at a pace that keeps the line continuous. If there are too many breaks between blessings of the water a shark following the line of chum may lose interest and be unable to find the source of all the tempting taste and smells. It might swim off and you've lost it as well as wasted your chum.

From time to time the chum should be spiced with pieces, not very large, of menhaden or any other fish to give the approaching sharks something to whet their appetites and keep them coming. Since chum is usually of an oily nature, the oil will float to the top, revealing a slick in the direction it is traveling. Keep your eyes on the slick, because any surface-feeding sharks will be coming your way in it. But don't bet that that is the only way they'll come. Some may rise off the bottom to strike your bait and you'll never know it until it has happened. And it happens when you least expect a shark to be around; when the summer heat puts you and the crew into a stupor, then the activity suddenly explodes.

How long to feed an unproductive chumline before trying somewhere else is a difficult question to answer. In some cases, sharks will be behind the boat after the first few ladles of chum are spread. In others, it may even take an hour or more, and at times you just can't get a shark to play games with you. Experience and patience go hand in hand.

Bait on your hooks can be whole or cut fish, or even meat from a butcher shop. Sharks don't really mind what they eat, and if it is oily, or bloody, or both, so much the better. Sharks are real garbage cans when it comes to what to feed them.

TACKLE

Sharks vary greatly in size, as we have seen, ranging from 20- to 30-pound fish up to the monsters of over 1,000 pounds. Roughly, the fish and the tackle to match them can be divided into several categories. The lightest includes a 20-pound rod, which will take fish from zero up to 50 and 60 pounds without trouble when in the right hands. The next classification is composed of rods and line in the 30-pound class that will handle fish up to 60 or 70 pounds. This is followed by 50- and 60-pound-class equipment that begins to take on the big fish. At the end of the scale are 130-pound-class rods and lines and even special, large outfits for those fish too large to come aboard even the largest sportfisherman class of boat.

Rods and lines fall in the same classes; that is, a 20-pound rod will usually be fitted or matched with a 3/0 to 5/0 reel loaded fully with 20-pound-test line. There is a lot of monofilament used in shark fishing, but most shark lines are Dacron. The larger the rod, the larger the matching line and the corresponding reel, up to 14/0 reels that can take on the great white sharks.

Special attention must be paid to the terminal tackle used for sharks because of the large weight to which these fish can grow. The end of the Dacron line should be tied to a stout snap and swivel by a Bimini twist for maximum strength. The snap/swivel is used because you may be changing leaders and hook sizes frequently and the snap makes the job go faster and smoother. Because the rig isn't trolled, the swivel won't interfere with the action on the end of the line. Wire leader is a must in all forms of sharkfishing. The shark comes well equipped with teeth and only stainless steel or piano wire leaders will do. The latter is preferred even though it may rust out. After you use it once, the leader should be discarded but its superior strength and memory factor makes it more desirable than stainless steel. A minimum of 10 feet should be used but because some sharks like to roll on a line and leader, I'd suggest a 15-foot minimum.

Numerous hook shapes or patterns will work for sharks but they should be extra-strength hooks and welded ones are ideal. Hooks should always be razor sharp, so sharpen even new hooks. They'll range in size from 5/0 to 14/0, depending upon the size of the fish you are after and the remainder of your equipment. For live-bait, the hooks should be left swinging on the leader by looping it through the eye. Where dead-bait is used the leader can be passed through the eye and then wrapped around the shank for holding power, with the free end cut long. The free end can then be used to secure the bait to the hook and keep it from riding up the leader if it works free.

Experienced anglers with boats that are easy to maneuver and that can even chase a running fish will elect to fish with lighter equipment and thus get more sport into their fishing. They will also prefer to fight the shark standing up with a rod-butt holder mounted on a belt gimbal. Really big fish demand big tackle and it becomes impractical to stand up and fight the equipment as well as the fish, and in this case a good fighting chair becomes a must.

It's impossible, of course, to order up the size fish you want or to predict how large a shark you will catch. If the fish are running within a certain weight range, all you can hope to do is to try to match it. If a larger shark comes along and is too much to handle, you'll probably lose a lot of line as well as the terminal gear—that's the name of the game.

Sharks will feed in three general areas behind your boat, based on depth of the water rather than on proximity to the craft. Some fish prefer to feed along the surface, others will be somewhere between the top and bottom, and another group, often the larger fish, will have a tendency to hang near the bottom if you aren't in excessively deep water. To meet this variation, experienced skippers usually fish three or more rods, baiting them and then drifting the bait aft into the chum slick.

Getting the baited hook to the correct level isn't a problem. Anglers use a variety of floating devices, but I prefer small, toy balloons that can be picked up at a dime store. On the top or surface line, I'll attach the balloon via a weak piece of kite string to the leader, so that it drifts the bait about 15 feet under the surface. On another line, if I'm in 60 to 100 feet of water, I'll tie the balloon about 30 to 40 feet from the bait and pay it astern. When a shark hits and pulls the balloon under the water, pressure increases on the water-logged kite line and the balloon pops free. The bottom line may not need any weight to take it all the way down. However, if there is a slight current or tide running, a 3- or 4-ounce bank sinker, tied loosely with the weak kite string, will break free once a shark shakes the bait. The sinker is tied slightly ahead of the hook.

During long periods of sharkfishing the activity can become very slow. The only evident action is the duty fisherman manning the chum ladle. It would be a tiresome chore to hold the rods in the ready position so most skippers place them in the numerous rod holders around the gunwales and transom of the boat. Place the reel in free spool but with the clicker on and retire to bask in the sun or scoff a beer.

The strike of a shark can be slow or fast. In most instances the shark won't even know it's hooked and it may go on to take more than one bait. There is no hurry in setting the hook. In fact, it's a good idea to wait a few minutes so that the shark can work the bait down the throat and into its stomach. When you do decide to set the hook, two or three sharp yanks on the rod will do it. You have either a hook-up or a miss. Now the fun begins.

Almost always, the initial run of a shark is the strongest and longest. After that it is a seesaw battle, with you gaining a bit more line each time before the fish peels off the next run. The fish is pumped in; that is, the rod is lifted to pull the fish closer and as you drop the rod you crank madly to take up the slack. There should never be slack in the line because this allows the fish to rest. The rod should be arched during the entire battle or you aren't wearing down the shark.

The length of the battle is determined by the size of the shark, your ability, the size of the equipment, and how fast you want to put it into the boat. With all four of these variables at work at one time, it may take you anywhere from a few minutes to several hours before you see the wire leader. Boating a shark is a two-man job—at the least. The mate or assistant cautiously grabs the wire leader with gloved hands and pulls the fish alongside the boat. If it is a big shark either he or another assistant sinks a flying gaff into the fish behind its dorsal fin. The hook on the flying gaff is attached to a stout line that has been turned several times on a boat cleat. Then, with the aid of another gaff, at times, a traveling loop is worked around the tail of the shark and snubbed against the boat. It is lifted only when the shark is definitely known to be dead. *Never* bring a live shark into the cockpit of a boat, no matter how large your boat.

Sharks are difficult to kill and can often be kept out of the water for hours and still come back to life with enough energy to harm someone. One way to kill a shark is to tow it backward and drown it. This can take time. Another is to rap it a few times on the head with a pacificer or put a rifle round or two through its head. But if you have no use for the shark on the table, there is little or no reason to kill it. You can skillfully cut off the leader after you have tagged the fish with one of the plastic tags used to help study migration routes, and let it swim away to do battle another time.

Some sharks make especially good eating. While most sharks are edible, the steaks of the mako are almost, some fishermen claim, as good as swordfish steaks.

13. Groupers

The groupers, fish of America's warmer Atlantic waters, are represented by a vast array of species, with more than a dozen that regularly find their way into the angler's fish box. Because of their penchant for warm water the majority are found only in the waters that surround Florida and in the Gulf of Mexico west to Texas. One species, the black grouper, has been taken as far north as the coast of Massachusetts, but its practical northern range limit is off Virginia and the Carolinas.

As a body, groupers are not the gamest of fish in the oceans. But they are consistent good feeders and are sufficiently abundant in numbers to provide the skiff and rowboat fleet with countless hours of angling, not to mention the good eating.

Though nearly a dozen grouper species are found in our waters,

134

only three are considered really sporting, either because of their fighting ability or by virtue of their great size. These include the black, Nassau, and red groupers.

Groupers are often referred to as the bass of salt water and at a first glance they closely resemble the freshwater fish. But the appearance is only superficial and at closer scrutiny the similarities fade. Identification of groupers is also confusing because of the great similarity between different species. This is further compounded by numerous color phases within several species. Some vary in color from somber browns, blacks, and mottled casts to brassy reds and yellows.

Groupers are just that, fish that swim in groups rather than schools. I guess the difference between school and group is size. Groupers are more prone to swim in numbers of two, four, or six rather than in a real force of fish. Also, they are real homebodies. There is little or no migration of a group or school. Their wanderings are established by the food they eat, and this includes small fish, crabs, and other crustaceans fond of a sedentary life on a reef or coral shoal. Even on a reef, these fish seldom move great distances and may take up guard duty outside a crab hole or crevice in the rocks and wait for hours for the dweller to make a break.

BLACK GROUPER

The most widely distributed of the grouper family is *Mycteroperca bonaci*, alias the black grouper. Its range normally extends north to the Carolinas and Virginia but when exceptionally warm thrusts of water from the Gulf Stream push north, this grouper moves with it and has been recorded in such unexpected places as Montauk, Long Island, and Woods Hole, Massachusetts. Its greatest concentrations, however, are in Florida waters, with the Florida Keys the surest place to go if you want to catch a black grouper.

Like all groupers, this one has a single, continuous dorsal fin with at least ten spines and ten rays on the fin. The mouth is large, with a projecting lower jaw and a dandy set of canine teeth in the front. The head is large, about a third of the body length. In the genus *Mycteroperca* the space between the eyes is great and creates a fish with a rather broad head. In the *Epinephelus* genus the eyes are set closer together, giving the appearance of a fish with a somewhat narrow head.

Black grouper are not always black, but may vary in coloration from brown to dark orange, to almost any color in the spectrum. The base color is interrupted with shadings and bars of either dark gray or blue, and brown bars with green dots or a white phase with poorly defined dusky markings.

Black grouper can grow to monstrous sizes, which helps make up for their lack of game qualities. Fish above 50 pounds have been recorded, but the majority you are likely to encounter will range from 5 to 10 pounds.

This species is fond of feeding upon fish and crustaceans. Because of its less sedentary nature when compared to other groupers, it is found farther offshore, on coral reefs and rocky shoals where it is a bread-and-butter fish for the headboat fleets. Many such boats sail regularly out of Gulf ports for black grouper, and quite an industry as well as recreational effort has been built around them.

Fishing techniques for groupers vary but little. The basic approach is bottomfishing with live- or cut-bait. However, the black grouper is also partial to trolled lures. Feathered lures trolled by the sportfishing boats account for a lot of grouper. Usually these lures are weighted and adorned with porkrinds for more action, which must take place close to the bottom, in the realm of the black grouper, if the fisherman is to be successful.

Of all the groupers, the tenacity of the black is the greatest. It will lunge at the bait and then bore away for a spot to eat it unmolested. This is usually among the rocks and crannies on a rocky or coral reef, and here is where fish and fisherman often part. The only way that you are going to impose your will on that of a bullheaded black grouper is to out-tackle him, and this means rather stout equipment.

A rig for these grouper consists of a 5- to 6-foot boat rod, a bay reel, between 3/0 and as large as 5/0 if large grouper are on the reef, and line between 25- and 50-pound-test. If the fish are running smaller, lighter gear is then in order. The technique is to fight the fish with gusto, immediately after it is hooked. A grouper cannot be given its head. Once it goes into a determined dive it will be difficult to turn.

NASSAU GROUPER

As its name implies, the Nassau grouper, *Epinephelus striatus*, is common to the Bahama Islands and Nassau. It is equally as common, however, to the coast of Florida, and in Gulf waters as far north as Tarpon Springs. Of the three popular or fishable groupers, the Nassau is probably the best known as well as that most often taken by commercial fishermen. It is also the one that most northern anglers encounter during their midwinter trek to Florida to escape the seasonal cold of the north. If you take your vacation in Puerto Rico, you'll more than likely run into it there as well.

Nassau grouper are occasionally big fish, reaching a maximum of 50 pounds. But this is rare nowadays, and fish beyond 10 pounds are considered to be a good catch. The average fish is closer to 5 pounds and that's usually enough to make any angler smile.

The Nassau grouper is easy to distinguish from other groupers because of its color pattern. In coloration it resembles slightly the red grouper but the red grouper is considerably paler and lacks the black patch or saddle on the tail just ahead of the fin. Bars of darker color appear on both the head and body, with scattered black spots or dots around the eyes.

A Nassau grouper is the least groupy of the groupers, preferring to swim and feed alone whenever possible. About the only time you'll find it grouping is during the breeding season, from May to June. After that, it moves to the offshore or outside coral reefs and shoals to feed and forage on the bottom after fish and crustaceans.

It is found most often over shallow or only medium-depth reefs and thus is readily accessible to great numbers of fishermen. The depth of the water a grouper chooses corresponds somewhat to its size. Smaller fish are found closer to shore and in shallower water while the bigger Nassau grouper wander into deeper water, where they can cope more readily with their enemies in search for food.

On a rod, the Nassau grouper is often considered the best fighter in the family. It will always strike at live- or cut-bait and even falls easy prey to bucktailed or feathered jigs bounced around the bottom. Like all groupers, once it is hooked it will try for the bottom, hoping to cut your line on the sharp rocks or coral. Your task is to stop it from reaching there. And, because these fish don't grow as large as

Jerry Kenny of Flushing, New York, gaffed his own Nassau grouper while fishing off Walker Cay in the Bahamas.

the black grouper, you can accomplish the task with almost any good boat rod, a bay reel equipped with a star drag, and a line test between 12 and 25 pounds. Hook sizes will depend on the size of fish you are after or have been catching and will vary from No. 2 to a 2/0. Bait can consist of almost any fish, though cut-mullet seems to have an edge over other species.

The flesh of the Nassau grouper is as good on the table as on a rod and especially when cut into strips called grouper fingers and deep-fried, it is difficult to surpass. However, everyone recommends that the fish first be skinned. The skin is tough and does not add to the flavor of the meat.

RED GROUPER

When an angler refers to grouper without being specific he is usually talking about the red grouper. One reason for this is the greater range of this fish in tropical American waters; another is the great numbers of the fish available to the average angler. The red grouper is found as far north in the Atlantic as the coast of Virginia, but not in any real numbers north of Georgia. It is well spread along both coasts of Florida and captures the interest of numerous commercial fishermen out of Mississippi, Alabama, and Louisiana ports.

The red grouper is really a reddish brown in overall cast, somewhat mottled over the entire body. When its mouth is open it discloses a bright orange buccal cavity. The tail is stout and the trailing edge almost square. This fish is not spotted unless in the dark brown or white phase in which the fins are finished in light red blothces with white trim. Lack of a notch in the membrane between the spine on the dorsal fins distinguishes *Epinephelus morio* from other groupers.

Like other groupers, the red grouper is also basically a bottom-fish, fending for itself over rocky shoals, coral reefs, and old shell beds. Seldom is it found, other than as a transient, over sandy bottoms. If you are a first-time grouper fisherman or angling over unfamiliar waters, one of the best techniques is to drift and fish. Cut-bait, dragged along the bottom, is sure to turn up a grouper, grunt, or snapper. If either of the latter two species of fish is caught, grouper cannot be far away. Red grouper have a tendency to swim in larger groups or schools than other groupers. This may account for the large catches made annually along the Gulf states by commercial draggers.

Red grouper as large as 40 pounds have been recorded, but the chances of catching such heavyweights are extremely rare. Instead, you'll have to content yourself with fish between 3 and 5 pounds, because they are the most numerous and provide the best eating. Grouper in this size range are suckers for cut-bait; almost any kind of cut-bait or even shrimp will work nicely. If you've run into a school or know of a reef that harbors bigger red grouper, then your best bet for a bait is often a feathered lure or jig. This is administered via a moving boat and worked in a slow troll over the outer edges of the reef or shoal.

As with other groupers, you can easily be fooled by the initial strike or tug on the line. Even a big grouper bites with a rather dainty strike. The surprise comes after you have set the hook and think you have another runt on the end. The line begins slowly peeling off and if you don't immediately tighten down the drag and stop the run you are more than likely to wind up with a frayed and cut line for your efforts.

Smaller grouper are inshore fish and prefer shallow water, within easy reach of the small-boat fleet. Bigger grouper will tend to hang farther to sea and you'll need a better craft to seek them out.

While red grouper are good eating fish, I'd rate them a notch below the Nassau grouper. Like all groupers, the fish should be skinned to avoid a strong flavor. Larger fish should then be steaked and smaller ones filleted. Red grouper makes an excellent ingredient in fish chowder.

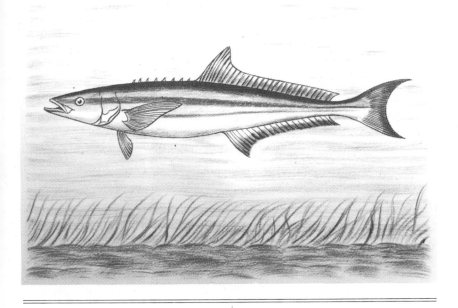

14. Cobia

The cobia is probably one of the most misunderstood and underfished species that swims close to our shores in salty water. This great gamefish, however, is undergoing a surge in popularity that finally is bringing it the recognition it deserves. Though cobia have been around our coasts as long as anglers have been here to fish for them, they were considered rare or not too abundant in most areas, with recognized concentrations occurring only here and there.

This sparsity on the part of cobia may have been due to low population numbers. Numerous species of saltwater fish are cyclical in nature, with alternating highs and lows in numbers. In some fish this cycle is short, lasting from three to five or six years. In other fish the cycles peak every thirty to forty years. In the case of cobia, the cycles could be even longer.

Another explanation for the small numbers of this fish in the angler's catch may not depend at all upon the abundance of the fish, or lack of it. Instead, it may result from anglers' ignorance about cobia, when and where they occur and what it takes to catch them. But the growing knowledge of anglers of how and where to fish for them has rapidly increased as pressures rise on other fish and their populations diminish. Whatever the causes, the cobia is rapidly gaining popularity and fast becoming a favorite.

One reason for this is certainly that cobia fishing offers an ever-present chance for shore-bound or inshore boat fishermen to catch numerous fish, often of a fairly large size. The average cobia seems to begin at around 15 pounds, and even a fish of this size is full of fight and power. Seldom is a cobia a sure thing . . . even after one is hooked, no one knows who will win.

DESCRIPTION

The cobia, *Rachycentron canadum*, at first glance looks like a successful cross between a large catfish and a shark. The body of a cobia is sleek and sharklike in appearance, with a high dorsal fin that looks somewhat like the top fin of a sailfish, but on a smaller scale. It rises sharply from a position about midway along the length of the body and then drops rapidly and follows parallel to the top contour of the fish. It abruptly stops at the caudal peduncle, the base of the tail. The tail fin is large, sharply pointed on both ends, and sharply concaved, a little longer on the dorsal half than the ventral half. The long ventral fin is a mirror image in shape when compared to the dorsal fin. It starts even farther back on the body than the dorsal fin. A pair of large pectoral fins are mounted below the middle of the sides and small pelvic fins are located just ahead of a line below the pectorals. Seven to nine small, short, triangular-shaped spines adorn the cobia's back in an area from the end of the head to the beginning of the large dorsal fin.

The head is flat on top, very similar to that of a catfish, with a wide, gaping mouth. The lower jaw extends well ahead of the upper jaw and when closed and viewed from the side gives the fish a sharply pointed head profile. But the view from the top is just the opposite. The head looks wide and blunt and very effectively designed for a fish that can feed off the bottom, shoveling up its food, or anywhere in between there and the top, taking floating crabs off the water's surface. A cobia's teeth are rather small and are located on both jaws, on the tongue, and on inside areas of the mouth. The head is depressed in relation to the rest of the body, extremely flat, and gives rise in many anglers to the notion that a cobia is related to the remora or sucking fish, which attaches itself to sharks and other pelagic fishes. This is just a resemblance and there is no family connection.

The lateral line on a cobia is continuous, wavy in appearance, and set high on the side of the body. Coloration in the fish does not vary greatly from one locale to another. It is dark brown or chocolate on the back, pales somewhat along the sides, and turns a creamy yellow to white on the underside. The side of the cobia is marked by several darker bands, with the widest one passing from the eye, expanding in the midsection of the fish, and then narrowing and extending onto the caudal peduncle and even tail fin. The fins are a very dark chocolate or black.

Dan Upton of Beaufort, South Carolina, shows what he does best . . . catching cobia, and tries to bring aboard a 30-pound fish.

Cobia can grow large and that is one of the fascinations of angling for this fish—never knowing what you'll get. In a school, they mix in size and you can get a 15-pound cobia on one strike and a 50-pounder on the next. The record for South Carolina, a place where large cobia hang out, was 78 pounds for several years and was just recently topped by an 82½-pound fish taken off the north end of Hilton Head Island in Broad River.

Ocean City, Maryland, produced a 90-pound fish in 1949, while Crystal River, Florida, boasts of a 91-pounder as its entry to the record book. The Pacific has cobia but few of them frequent our West Coast; they do, however, like Australia, and a 100-pound cobia was taken off Queensland in 1962. The world record, however, is an African cobia, a 110-pound fish (plus a few ounces) that came from Mombasa, Kenya, in 1964. Prior to the African record, the biggest fish taken in the cobia class came from Cape Charles, Virginia. The 5-foot 10-inch behemoth weighed 102 pounds and was caught in July 1938.

On the average, cobia range in size between 10 and 15 pounds, but fish up to 30 and 40 pounds are not rare. Plenty of cobia top the 30-pound mark in Chesapeake Bay in the summer, and when the fishing is really hot along the Gulf states, no one will pay much attention to your catch unless you have a 70-or-so-pounder in the batch.

DISTRIBUTION

Cobia enjoy worldwide distribution but are confined to warm, temperate, and tropical waters. In the Atlantic, they are found along the American coasts from New Jersey south to Argentina. A few fish make it north every year as far as Cape Cod, but these are rare. Cobia appear around Bermuda and on the east side of the Atlantic along most of the African coast. In the Pacific, they occur in the East Indies, Malaysia, and as far north as Japan. They are found on the eastern side of the Pacific, in its warmer waters, but in limited numbers. They are occasionally taken off southern California.

Cobia have a host of names, depending upon where they swim. In Australia they are known as "black kingfish," because of their somewhat mackerel-like profile. In the Gulf of Mexico and along the Gulf states, where they exist in high concentrations from western Florida to Louisiana and Texas, they are called lemonfish or ling. In eastern Florida and along the Carolinas, where they also appear in great numbers, they are called by their more universal name, cobia. A long-established cobia ground is Chesapeake Bay, where it is believed large numbers spawn each spring and summer. Here they are locally called "crab-eaters," "coal-fish," or "sergeant fish."

SEASON

Cobia are migratory fish and begin to appear along the beaches of the Gulf states as early as February and March. But they are fish that prefer warm water and warm weather and the angling for them doesn't become good until the weather is really hot. Cobia are first seen migrating along the Florida panhandle, heading west, in April, and the best months to fish for them in the Gulf are from May to August. On the East Coast, cobia begin showing at Cape Kennedy around April and almost simultaneously at the rivers and inlets of South Carolina. By May they are in the waters of North Carolina and by the end of the month in Chesapeake Bay. Good cobia fishing months in the Southeast are June and July.

At this time, the fish swim into all the bays, rivers, and sounds, and are within easy reach of boat-equipped anglers. The fish set up housekeeping in each river system and will extend their local range out to sea for ten to fifteen miles.

Biologists have not been able to establish firmly whether cobia migrate in a totally north and south direction along the Atlantic Coast and Florida, or in an offshore-onshore move. They feel that it may be a combination of both movements. In the Gulf of Mexico their migration patterns are somewhat different from those in the Atlantic. Cobia strike north in the Gulf, swimming in large schools, and make land near Panama City, Florida. A few fish head eastward into Florida, but the large bulk take a westward trek toward Texas.

On the Atlantic side, they appear almost simultaneously from Florida to North Carolina and then a little later off Virginia and Maryland. This has led biologists to believe that here the migration is

Cobia are inshore-offshore fish, and to angle the buoys in a channel safely, a seaworthy craft and plenty of fuel are needed.

first inshore and then northward. The fish are residents of inshore waters until the end of August and begin tapering off rapidly in September.

WHERE TO FISH

Angling for cobia is done inside, in rivers and bays, and outside the sea buoys, and can be done with almost any boat. Cobia have a penchant for hanging under buoys or any other structure but to fish these from inshore to the outside requires craft that can handle rough seas in the event they arise. The outside can be as far as twenty miles away, so this type of fishing demands a boat with a good engine and a gas capacity to run from forty to fifty miles a day.

Systems of buoys appear along all our rivers and channels and create good cobia fishing areas along the coast. Such hotspots include Chincoteague Inlet and a series of smaller passageways between islands on the Virginia Capes; the approaches to Chesapeake Bay; numerous rivers in lower parts of the Bay in both Virginia and Maryland; all the inlets punctuating the Outer Banks leading into North Carolina's vast and numerous sounds and bays, south to Cape

Lookout, New River Inlet, Cape Fear, and Little River Inlet, the latter shared by both the Carolinas. South of Port Royal Sound and St. Helena Sound, two great cobia grounds are the estuaries of the Savannah River in Georgia–South Carolina, and Ogeechee, Altamaha, and St. Andrew's sounds in Georgia. On the east coast of Florida there are similar estuarine situations in St. Marys River, St. Johns River (a vast fishery), Ponce de Leon Inlet near Daytona Beach, and St. Lucie Inlet near Stuart.

The possibilities for fishing cobia are almost unlimited on the west coast of Florida, but the better cobia fishing seems to be concentrated in the panhandle rivers of the state, from the Apalachicola west, but with Panama City the center. The fishing extends from Florida west to New Orleans, around the many delta channels of the Mississippi, and down the coast of Texas to northern Mexico.

TACKLE AND TECHNIQUES

Cobia aren't called crab-eaters for nothing, and that is one of their favorite foods. If you cut open every cobia you caught you'd find that only a few didn't have at least one crab in their stomachs. In addition to crabs, they'll eat almost any fish that comes along and can't swim faster than they do. In particular, cobia have a penchant for eels. Thus eels, crabs, and fish, alive better than dead, constitute the best baits.

A typical way of fishing live crabs is to anchor a boat above a known cobia hole, large buoy, or set of pilings that they inhabit and float a crab downstream to them. The crab can be handled without a float or weight if it is alive, or on the end of a bobber float if it is dead to keep it from sinking to the bottom. And because cobia inhabit all levels of water, a bait or two should also be weighted slightly and drifted along the bottom. Eels are fished in much the same way, drifted or floated to an area that cobia inhabit. Another technique is to cast the eel, usually the smaller ones—8 to 12 inches in length—to where the cobia hang out and then gradually retrieve the eel.

Another technique to use when you don't know exactly where cobia are hiding is to anchor a boat in a river or current and feed back several lines with cut-bait. One or two can be kept high with a float, but one or more should be on or near the bottom. Then the cut-bait is advertised with chum. Almost any kind of fish, ground and oily, will do for chum, and it should be used sparingly—only enough to attract the cobia. For cut-bait, mullet makes an excellent choice.

Cobia also are taken readily by casting plugs and spoons to them. In many areas of the Gulf, the cobia are spotted on or near the top of the water. They don't always spook when a boat approaches and will often come alongside an anchored boat to seek its shade. When the fish are cruising on top, one angler runs the boat, keeping it parallel to the cobia, while one or more begin casting to them.

Much the same technique is used around buoys where these fish like to congregate. The boat is slowed as the anglers approach the buoy and then begin casting plugs and spoons to the large floating device, whether they see fish or not. More than one fish will take up residence under a buoy, so if you get one, don't stop fishing until you have really worked over the area.

Cobia like large plugs, lures that swim on or near the surface, and favorites with anglers include Big-O, Redfins, Repalas, Rebels, Cisco-Kids, colored gray or a light shade of any other color. Lures should be retrieved evenly, but not too rapidly. When they strike a plug with its treble hooks cobia almost always hook themselves. A hooked cobia will often jump several times and then bore away for the bottom in a tug-of-war that can last an hour or more, depending upon the size of the fish and your equipment.

When taking live-bait, cobia don't fool around with it but pick up the food and run with it. Usually they take it down into the mouth far enough so that an angler can strike the hook almost any time. Out of habit, most anglers will let the fish run for a while and then set the hook. The mouth of a cobia is tough and if the hook is well set it won't pull out. The normal characteristic of the fish is to jump once or twice after the hook is set, and then it heads for the bottom or into rocks where it can sulk, cut the line, or just hold you off.

Tackle for cobia is naturally on the heavy side because of the mixture of sizes of fish you can encounter on a trip. If you do a lot of baitfishing and can handle a conventional reel, one with a star drag and no line guide, you'll probably do well on plugs. But most anglers never develop the educated thumb to handle a conventional reel and they elect a spinning outfit. It should be a tough outfit, and not unnecessarily long. A stout rod up to 8 or 9 feet is enough, but it should have a lot of power in the butt and only slightly less in the tip. You may be forced to pull a charging cobia away from a buoy chain or out of the rocks and you'll find it impossible to do so with a soft or weak tip. Nor can you easily cast the large and heavy lures needed to attract a cobia. Even a 10-pound fish can easily handle a 6- or 7-inch plug with its gaping mouth.

The spinning reel should match the rod and is often of the largest or next-to-the-largest size available. It should be capable of holding 300 yards of 30- to 40-pound-test monofilament. Cobia often make long, sustained runs and if it is a really large fish, and you are at anchor, you may be forced to chase it. More line on your reel will give your partner the time he needs to pull up the anchor and get the engine running.

Don't be alarmed if you see other shapes alongside your fish when you bring it to the boat. Instead, have your partner armed with another rod and lure or bait. Other cobia have a habit of following a hooked fish, trying to find out what it is chewing on. You can get a second fish if you keep your eyes open and a rod handy.

Cobia are powerful fish and if brought into the boat seem to come alive and can destroy everything inside. Dan Upton, a close friend of mine and one of the top cobia fishermen in the country, never brings a cobia into the boat on a gaff unless he has first had the chance to tap it on the head with a club or hammer. His technique is to gaff the fish, holding the club in one hand and the gaff in the other. As the fish comes up along the gunwale of the boat it is quickly tapped and then, in one sweeping movement, rushed into the over-sized fish box or cooler. The lid is quickly slammed shut. Even a well-tapped cobia will thrash around inside the fish box for a while. It's only common sense to use this self-defense tactic on cobia.

Cobia are excellent eating and, unlike some fish that become tougher or coarser as they get bigger, the larger fish taste as good as the smaller. The fish has flaky white meat and can be prepared in numerous ways. But smoked cobia is a gourmet's delight.

15. Black Sea Bass

One surefire way to tell whether a fish is popular is to count its aliases. And few fish outname the black sea bass of the Atlantic Coast. It is known by such various handles as blackfish, Black Will, Black Harry, black perch, rock fish, rock bass, humpback, and tally-wog—but the most common name of all is just plain sea bass. To the biologist, it is *Centropristes striatus*, a member of the large family of groupers and sea bass, and a member of three closely-knit species of sea bass, of which it is the most widespread and important.

To the charterboat fleets that sail out of southern Massachusetts, Rhode Island, eastern Connecticut, Long Island, New Jersey, and South Carolina, the sea bass is a fish that often saves fishing trips. When a skipper can't locate porgies, or weakfish have moved over-night, or fluke and flounder are seeking colder water, they turn to established sea bass grounds, secret concentrations that they call upon for help when all other fish abandon them.

RANGE AND DISTRIBUTION

At the turn of the century, one of the greatest concentrations of sea bass along the Atlantic existed annually in the New York Bight, and even in lower New York Bay. But during the past forty years, the populations of sea bass have steadily declined, becoming alarmingly low in the northern part of its distribution. But in the area from Cape Hatteras south to Georgia, it has remained rather stable. Fleets sailing out of Savannah, Charleston, Murrels Inlet, and Little River have always counted on and not been disappointed with sea bass. During the last three or so years, however, there has been a resurgence of this great game and food fish along the northern part of its realm and blackfish trips, sailings strictly for this fish, are again common in New Jersey and Long Island.

Marion Culp of Columbia, South Carolina, checks over his first black sea bass taken on fishing grounds out of Charleston.

In general range, the sea bass extends from Nova Scotia in the north to northern Florida in the south. Its fishable populations, however, are more restricted, from the Carolinas to eastern Massachusetts. Today, the prime sea bass grounds in the summer months are along the beaches of New Jersey and Long Island, or the New York Bight, and during late fall and early spring along the coast of South Carolina to northern Florida.

DESCRIPTION

At first glance, sea bass closely resemble many of the other sea bass: striped bass, cunner, wreck fish, and scup. But at a closer look, there is no mistaking this fish for any other. The most striking feature is its large fins, both dorsal and ventral, and on the tail, as well as its large pectorals, which extend halfway back on the sides. The caudal fin is unique among species in the northern part of its range, rounded and convex, but the top ray is extended past the rest and looks like an antenna. The fore-and-aft dorsal fins are attached with the front fin supported by 11 sharp spines, and the after dorsal fin is large, soft, and fan-shaped.

The body is rather stout, three times as long as it is wide, but with a bulge or hump near its shoulders. Males, approaching the spawning season, begin storing fat in the tissue under the skin in this area on the back and develop a decided hump; hence the name "humpback."

The snout is moderately pointed, with the mouth ending at the tip. The jaw is on an oblique angle, large but ending well before the eye. The eye is set high atop a head that slopes sharply from the back to the mouth. Gill covers are covered with scales and a large, aft-pointing spine exists on the apex of the last gill cover. Scales in the sea bass are rather large and well developed, even on the underside of the fish. The lateral line begins at the top edge of the gill cover and parallels the shape of the back to end in the middle of a heavy peduncle.

Sea bass, like most bottomfish, have developed the ability to change color, within limits, to match the bottom over which they are feeding or living. This is, however, a slow process and does not occur in a matter of hours, as in some tropical species. In general, sea bass range in color from a dusky gray to a muddled brown, black, or blue-black, or in mottled combinations of these dull colors. Regardless of the color, the belly is usually a somewhat lighter shade of the rest of the body. Much of the general appearance is that of striations or bars horizontally across the fish. This is created by each scale, whose base part is lighter than the edge and gives the illusion of a series of longitudinal lines.

A monstrous sea bass is any fish over 5 pounds; a few have even been recorded at 7½ pounds. The largest ever recorded was an 8-pounder taken off Nantucket Island. The average sea bass, however, is between three-quarters and 1½ pounds. A 1-pound fish will measure 1 foot in length, while a sea bass of 18 or 20 inches becomes stouter and weighs close to 3 pounds. Larger sea bass, those from 2 pounds and up, have a tendency to seek deeper water and stay farther offshore. Smaller sea bass, often referred to as pin bass, have no qualms about shallow water and filter into every channel, harbor, marina, boat basin, bridge, pier, and bulkhead available, looking for tidbits.

SEASONS

Sea bass are strictly bottomfish and range along the Continental Shelf from the beach to a maximum of 70 fathoms in the winter. The 70-fathom mark is usually where water temperatures seldom fall below 46 or 47 degrees Fahrenheit, the minimum sea bass will tolerate. Sea bass winter offshore where water reaches this temperature.

As the spring sun warms inshore waters, sea bass migrate inshore and many from southern offshore waters begin moving north. By the first or second week of May, they are on the fishing banks of New Jersey and Long Island. They will remain in this area longer than most bottomfish in the fall, holding their own until late October and November of most years.

At one time, sea bass were believed to move or migrate only from shallow to deeper (70-fathom) water in the late fall. But winter dragging off Long Island and Massachusetts reveals that while there are wintering sea bass at this location, the numbers are not what they should be. Instead, commercial boats winter dragging off Virginia and the Carolinas have seen their catches increase markedly at this time of year. While the sportfishing may dwindle in the Northeast, winter is often one of the better times for sea bass in the Little River and Charleston, South Carolina, areas. Here, they provide anglers with year-round fishing.

Spawning takes place in early May along the Carolina coast and by the middle of May and early June off New Jersey, Long Island, and southern New England.

WHERE TO FISH

The chief foods of sea bass are crabs, lobsters, shrimp, and an assortment of clams, mussels, and barnacles. Therefore, you must angle on the bottom for them. From time to time, sea bass even feed on small silversides, menhaden, lances, and killifish, and they will seldom pass up a tempting offer of sandworms or bloodworms. Most of these foods occur naturally over hard bottoms, among rocks where seaweeds and grasses grow to provide protection for small fish and a place for mussel shells to anchor. Pilings around wharves and docks are great for pin bass, while larger sea bass prefer offshore wrecks and reefs in water of 20 fathoms or less.

TACKLE AND TECHNIQUES

Most pin bass or smaller sea bass, those of up to 2 or 3 pounds, can be taken on the lightest of tackle. A 5- or 5½-foot boat rod with a 1/0 reel and 10-pound-test line is about all that is needed. A light freshwater spinning outfit will do, and for the youngsters a closed-face spin-casting rod and reel are ideal. When after larger fish and in deeper water, often accompanied with stronger currents, you could take fish on the same outfit, but handling the added depths, heavier weights, and larger hooks calls for a respectively heavier outfit. Switch to a medium freshwater or saltwater spinning outfit, 6 to 8 feet long, loaded with 200 yards of 12- to 15-pound-test monofilament or a 5- to 6-foot boat rod, one with a moderately stiff tip, a 2/0 reel, and a few hundred yards of line.

Hook sizes for the pin bass and smaller sea bass might range from No. 5 to No. 1, and hooks as large as 1/0 or 2/0 are adequate for the humpbacks or larger sea bass. Hook styles are not as important with sea bass as they are with some fish, say flounder or bluefish, and almost any pattern will do.

Most terminal outfits use two, sometimes three hooks for sea bass. One reason for this is that they school similarly to porgies and that if you catch one there are likely to be others around. A second reason is that sometimes the fish are just a bit off the bottom. If your first hook is in the grass then fish may not find it and a slightly higher hook gives top insurance. Also, porgies often mix with sea bass and you might find them at the bottom hook and sea bass on the second or third hook.

Such a rig is best tied to a three-way swivel, with the sinker attached directly to one eye. Sea bass can be leader-shy and you should use a slightly heavier size monofilament line to attach the hook to the swivel eye; a 1- or 2-foot length is enough. The second hook should be slipped onto a drop loop made above the three-way swivel a distance equal to or slightly longer than that of the snell or leader you use for the second hook. The principle is the same for a third hook if you choose to add one.

Baits for sea bass are cut larger than those for porgies because of the larger, tougher mouth of a sea bass. They include everything found on the bottom, from cracked mussels and soft-shelled clams, to skimmer clams, hard clams, shrimp, whole or cut; crabs, in either small, whole form, or cut in halves and quarters; seaworms, both blood and sand; and pieces of cut-fish ranging from killifish to menhaden, spearing, or eels.

One way to attract sea bass or keep them around once you locate them is to chum. Sea bass are bottomfish and the chum must be in that locale to be effective for you. A lead chum pot is the best way to get it there. Fill the pot with ground bunker (menhaden) or crushed blue mussels and lower it over the side of an anchored boat. The chum will dissipate quickly in a fast current so tend the pot regularly.

The more water you are fishing over the more difficult it is to locate schools of sea bass if your craft is not equipped with an elaborate fish locater. In deep water, while looking for big sea bass, drifting and jigging has proven a good technique. In such a situation, use a medium-action boat rod, 5 to 7 feet in length but with a tip of moderate action to give a jig added life. Reels on such an outfit may be 2/0 or even 3/0 in size. The lure to bounce is the diamond jig in 3-

or 4-ounce sizes or weights. Jigs come with single, treble, or fixed hooks. For this type of fishing a fixed hook is the better choice. The jig itself acts as the weight and the flash of metal is the lure, so bait is not needed on the hook.

The jig is lowered to the bottom from a drifting boat and then bounced 2 to 4 feet off the bottom as the boat moves. The angler releases line as it is needed in case the boat is drifting rapidly, so that the lure always comes off the bottom. Fish usually strike it on the way up. This is an effective technique for big sea bass, and can also be worked quite well on smaller ones where they occur in rather deep water near to land or in protected bays and harbors. Naturally, the size of the jig can be varied between 1- and 2-ounce sizes, and the line and rod can be lighter to match the lure and fish.

When sea bass strike at a diamond jig, or even a small bucktailed jig, there is no doubt that a fish is on. The mouth of a sea bass is large and tough, and once the hook is set there is little chance of a fish getting away. With live- or cut-baits, the fish bite somewhat differently. They tend to nibble and tease with a bait and this is registered to the fisherman as a series of taps. If you strike at this signal you are unlikely to have a fish on the hook. After teasing or mouthing the bait for a minute or so, sea bass then commit themselves and take it deeper. Then there is a definite tug on the line. Now is the time to set the hook with a short, but firm snap of the rod tip. Sharp hooks make the job surer and easier. To make sure that all these messages are telegraphed properly to you from fish to rod tip, you must maintain a taut line at all times. Any slack or bow in it will absorb the signals and you won't have any idea what is happening on the bottom.

A word of caution here may be helpful when handling sea bass. Those soft-looking and flowing fins are filled with sharp spines. A sharp spine also exists on the operculum, or side of the gill cover, and the sharp edges of the gill cover are also murder on fingers and hands. Be cautious when unhooking or handling sea bass, or it can be painful.

16. Pacific Salmon

As far as the sportsman is concerned, the salmon of the Pacific Coast are primarily saltwater fish. These fish differ vastly from the Atlantic salmon in habits and characteristics, even though they look like kissing cousins. Six species of salmon thrive in the Pacific; however, only five are indigenous to North America and all are members of the same family. Though they look very much like the Atlantic salmon, the latter fish is really more closely related to trout and chars than the Pacific species.

The single greatest difference, aside from body anatomy and habits, is that, unlike the Atlantic fish, salmon of the Pacific die after they have ascended their streams and spawned. There is no such thing as second spawning among these fish. Closely tied to this behavior is the fish's internal anatomy. It is designed to degenerate

Coho salmon spend more time out of the water after they are hooked, than in it. Here two anglers battle one of the great fish in Kilbella Bay, near Rivers Inlet, British Columbia.

once they enter fresh water, and though they occasionally strike lures and baits, for all practical purposes they have stopped feeding. This means that fishermen must seek these salmon while they are still in large bays and sounds, or at the mouths of estuaries, before they begin their upstream trek toward death. As a consequence, salmon angling on our West Coast is almost always on the salty side.

Of the five species of *Oncorhynchus* on our side of the Pacific Ocean, only two are of real interest to the sportsman, the Chinook and the coho salmon. Uniquely, these two species are the only piscivorous fish when compared to the other salmons, that is, they feed primarily on other fish, basically food-fish, in their adult stages of life. This makes them vulnerable to spoons, flies, plugs, and cut-bait and catchable by rod and reel, the only method used by sportfishermen.

CHINOOK SALMON

The Chinook is the heavyweight of the salmons, in fact, of all the salmonoid fishes, outweighing the heavy Atlantic salmon and even the largest of the northern lake trout. Size alone is often enough

5641

Ron Pedderson of Waukegan, Illinois, proudly displays a 12-pound, hook-jawed male coho salmon he took trolling a Grey Ghost fly.

to make a fish a worthwhile quarry but added to this, a Chinook fresh from the sea is a gamester with little parallel or equal on medium or even heavy fishing tackle.

Fascinating to the fisherman is the wealth of lore about the Chinook that has developed over the centuries and its reputation of making upstream migrations of nearly 2,000 miles. The Chinook angler finds himself pitted against a formidable fish. It's little wonder that on the West Coast, from California to Alaska, a special madness seems to develop when Chinooks begin returning from the sea. Derbies and fishing contests sprout in almost every bay, fishing village, or center along the coast. At these times, almost every craft available, from 40- and 50-foot cruisers to small fishing dories and skiffs, are out in search of this big fish.

The Chinook, *Oncorhynchus tschawytscha*, poses under a collection of pseudonyms. The name Chinook evolved from the first explorers who found Indians along the Columbia River with a culture closely allied to this salmon. They were the Chinook tribe and their fish became known as the Chinook's salmon. Along the coasts of Washington and Oregon this fish is known today as the Chinook salmon. In California waters and in Alaska—the name was probably taken there by miners—it is called the king salmon, while in British Columbia it passes under the name of spring salmon, from its habit of making an early or spring migration in that area. In the region around Puget Sound, however, it is called the tyee. In the Indian language a tyee is a chief and in many references a tyee salmon must be one of 30 pounds or more. Below 30 pounds it is referred to as a spring salmon.

DESCRIPTION

All salmon are handsome fish and the Chinook is no exception. A swath of dark bluish-green covers its back and gradually lightens toward the side and the lateral line. Color on the side blends into a silvery sheen and the reflection runs forward to the head. On the underside, the belly is more of a white than a silver. Fins across the top are grayish-blue or dusky while the lower fins are pale. The tail is stout, broad, and nearly square along its outer edge. Around the mouth, the gray or bluish tint covers the lips of a Chinook and even enters the buccal cavity to lend credence to still another name for this fish, blackmouth salmon. Many black spots cover the upper portion of the body and extend over the dorsal fins, the adipose fin, and on both halves of the tail fin.

Salmon fresh from the ocean and while still in the ocean have an overall silver appearance. After they enter the bays and tidal estuaries they immediately begin to darken, some exhibiting an even reddish tint to their skin. Once in fresh water they take on an even more somber appearance, dark and dusky, to help them blend with the bottom. As spawning time approaches, males develop a hooked jaw.

The flesh of a Chinook is a light pink to almost white and not as red as the coho salmon.

Chinooks are big fish, their maximum being well over 100 pounds. The largest Chinook verified by records was a 126½-pound behemoth taken in commercial nets at Petersburg, in southeast Alaska. A 95-pounder was taken 600 miles up the Yukon River near Tanana, Alaska. On rod and reel, the biggest Chinook was a 92-pound fish taken by Heinz Wichmann on the Skeena River, British Columbia, in July 1959.

Though Chinooks exceed 100 pounds they are rare above 70 pounds. In Alaskan waters, however, fish between 40 and 80 pounds are caught with more regularity than elsewhere. The average Chinooks are closer to 15 and 20 pounds. The waters of Rivers Inlet in British Columbia, however, produce fish whose average weight is around 30 pounds . . . that's quite an average.

RANGE

Chinook salmon are hatched in freshwater rivers, often at great distances from salt water. In rivers along the southern limit of their range, they may spend only a year in their natal stream before turning downstream. In Alaskan waters they may remain in the nursery stream for as many as three and even four years. Once in salt water, Chinooks grow rapidly and spend anywhere from one to eight years foraging in the ocean. Fish that spend only one year in the salt are called "jacks," and are usually precocious males that are mature almost at the time they head for salt water. Most Chinooks, however, spend six to seven years in the briny before returning to spawn in fresh water. This excessive time on the high seas is one reason Chinooks grow so large.

Chinooks are distributed from as far south along our Pacific Coast as Monterey Bay, California, to as far north as the Yukon River in Alaska. The Yukon itself houses a large fishery but salmon are rare immediately north of the river and beyond.

Somewhere in its range a spawning run is almost always in the works. The majority of Chinooks, however, are part of either a spring or fall run and appear at the mouths of river estuaries at these times. On the Columbia River there is an extra summer run. On the Sacramento River, spilling into San Francisco Bay, there is a late winter run. These latter fish, however, don't spawn until the following spring.

TACKLE AND TECHNIQUES

The standard technique used to catch Chinook salmon used to be trolling, using a stiff 6-foot rod and level-wind reel equipped with a star drag and Dacron or monofilament line anywhere from 30- to 50-pound-test. Almost exclusively, plugs, spoons, or wobblers were used to attract the eye of a Chinook. Favorite spoons were finished with brass on one side and chrome on the other. The favorite plug was one that resembled a wobbling or injured fish.

Bait, especially cut-herring, was also trolled. The herring was prepared in one of several ways, either with a single hook through the lip, but more often with two hooks, the second on a shorter piece of monofilament that forced the bait's body to curve. When pulled through the water, the curved bait went into a slow roll that resembled a wounded or dying fish. A favorite feeding technique of Chinooks that hunt and feed in a school is to rush a school of herring, tearing and biting as they go through it. Then they make a sharp turn and return to pick up what was stunned or injured on the first pass. And, because herring is a favorite salmon food and is most frequently found in their diet, it was the preferred bait-fish.

During the last decade a new technique has evolved and grown rapidly in popularity to the point where it now probably is practiced more than other forms of fishing for the Chinooks. It is called mooching. The essence of mooching is light equipment and hence it offers far more sport than any other technique. A mooching rod consists of a long fly rod, 9 to 10 feet in length, with a large reel loaded with monofilament line. Or, it can be a large spinning rod with a suitable reel loaded with tons of 8- to 12-pound-test line.

The lure again is cut-herring. The bait is either cast out and retrieved at a very slow pace, working the bait, or trolled at a snail's pace. The fish can be used with the entire body, or with the head cut off so that the angled blunt surface causes the body to roll and wobble; or just the flanks of the herring are sliced away and used with two-hooked affairs that make the fillet roll; or a special rig is used whereby the head of the fillet is placed into a cupped plastic device that imparts an action to the rest of the bait when it is moved through the water.

Mooching is done from boats equipped with small motors at a slow speed or, even better, against a running tide where the motor does little more than stem the force of the current. A mooched bait can also be drifted on a moving tide, and the bait fished at a depth between 10 and 20 feet and slowly raised and lowered as the boat drifts.

Fishing for Chinook is best from that period called daybreak to midmorning. The fish are often on or near the surface of the water and only a small kidney-shaped sinker on the line ahead of a flasher and bait needs to be used. As the day progresses, Chinooks have a tendency to drop deeper. Slightly larger weights are then needed.

Spoons are used with the standard trolling gear when the fish are down deep and refuse to rise to where they can be mooched. The spoon along with a flasher or several resembling a Christmas tree are trolled deep with the aid of weights needed in fast currents. At great depths, many Chinook fishermen resort to wire-line outfits and their size ranges anywhere from 20- to 60-pound-test.

COHO SALMON

What the coho lacks in size, when compared to the Chinook, it makes up in stamina and acrobatics on the end of a fishing line. A 10-pound coho hooked on a fly rod or spinning outfit is good for a minimum of a half-dozen jumps and 15 to 20 minutes in the water before you can even think of slipping a net under it.

The coho is the darling of the sportfisherman because it readily takes artificial lures. Even when it is on its spawning run up freshwater streams, it still has the occasional desire to strike a fly or spinner and accommodate fishermen.

DESCRIPTION

Coho is an Indian word for this salmon, but *Oncorhynchus kisutch* is also widely known along its range as the silver salmon from its overall silver appearance. The fish is quite similar in shape and coloration to the Chinook salmon, with a bluish-greenish back that gives way to a silvery white on the sides and belly. The fins are dusty and black spots appear over the back, head, and dorsal fins as well as the top lobe of the tail fin. Here the differences between coho and Chinook become apparent. The bottom or ventral lobe of the tail fin of a coho lacks the black spots. A second difference is in the area of the mouth. That of the Chinook is gray or black while the lips of a coho are white.

Also, coho and Chinook vary greatly in maximum size. The largest coho ever taken was a 35-pounder that found its way into a commercial net. The largest rod-and-reel fish was a 31-pounder taken in Cowichan Bay, British Columbia, in 1947. Adult coho fresh from the sea range between 8 and 12 pounds with a fair number of fish reaching the 20-pound class. As they prepare to head upstream while still in salt water they go on a feeding binge and during their last two to four months put on considerable weight.

DISTRIBUTION

Coho salmon are found in the Pacific from California to Japan but not in the Arctic. They frequent every river and bay from as far south as Monterey Bay in California north to Alaska. However, they are extremely sensitive to pollution and one vast nursery area they no longer swim in is the waters of San Francisco Bay.

Chinooks, whether at sea or on their spawning trek, are great movers covering thousands of miles in migrations. Coho, however, are homebodies in comparison. Even when they enter salt water as fish often less than a year old they don't stray too far up and down the coast or offshore.

On the average, young cohos spend little time in a nursery stream, often less than a year but up to three in some waters. The adults pick spawning sites not too far away from tidal rivers and the young fish are quick to head back to the abundant food the ocean offers. Most coho spend three years at sea before returning to fresh water to spawn. A few precocious jacks return after one year and a few older fish will hold out for four years.

Salmon begin entering the bays and sounds leading to their ancestral stream after the first of July and linger in their areas until late September, when the last of the fish begin the ascent. Actual spawning takes place anywhere from October to February but most of it is over by the first of the year. The downriver migration of the young fish begins a year later.

TACKLE AND TECHNIQUES

Once a coho salmon begins its spawning migration its digestive system atrophies and the fish ceases feeding. While in salt water, however, it strikes readily at baits in an effort to put on as much poundage as possible for the migration. Like all Pacific salmon, the coho dies after it has spawned.

Trolling the bays, sounds, and estuaries leading to the spawning rivers is the most common approach to taking coho salmon. Lures like bucktail streamers with or without a spinner are trolled at varying speeds and are very effective. Many fishermen troll as many as six rods at a time. Large fly rods and reels (mooching outfits) or spinning rods with a large line capacity are used. The flies, either single or tandem hooked, are trolled at different distances behind the boat and at different levels in the water. A kidney sinker is used on the line far enough ahead of the lure so as not to affect its action.

Fly and hook sizes vary from No. 1 to 3/0 in gaudy patterns that often have little resemblance to real bait. Patterns such as Coronation, Candlefish, Silver Killer, Gray Ghost, and even Micky Finns produce good catches. Some anglers while trolling will also cast flies at right angles to the movement of the boat and pick up an occasional fish that rolls off to the side. The best hours for coho fishing are early in the morning, while the fish are near the surface. By midmorning, they may fall deeper into the bay. The tide also has an influence on when coho feed and how their bait moves. Most baitfish become confused as the tide turns and fall easy prey to such predator fish as the coho. Thus, an hour before to an hour after either the flood or ebb are usually good times to be on the water.

Birds and their activities are another way of locating a school of salmon. Gulls and terns follow the feeding fish and have the ability to sense or somehow see their presence even when the fish and bait are not busting on top of the water. When they do, the birds set up a commotion that the fisherman should respond to.

Mooching pays off for coho as well as Chinook salmon. Hook a small herring through the lips and then slip a second hook near its tail so that it is forced to form a slight arc that will drive coho wild as an imitation of a hurt fish. Fly rods are equipped with 12- to 17-pound-test monofilament and the fish are mooched at a slow troll and drifted behind a wind. Flashes and lead keel weights are used to attract the coho and get the bait down to where the fish might be feeding if they aren't breaking on the surface.

Cohos are also suckers for trolled and cast spoons and spinners. Flashy brass, silver, or chrome spoons are easy to troll and account for a lot of fish. Brass and copper spinners work especially well when the fish are in a tidal stream in the transition between feeding and not feeding. Once the fish are in the freshwater sections to stay they will strike flies and streamers but spinners and small wobbling spoons seem to have more effect—if the fish decides to strike. The quality of fishing in the streams differs greatly from one body to the next. In some, it is near impossible to get a coho to strike once it has stopped feeding, while in others the chances are much better.

Part Two

Fishing
Techniques and
Equipment

17. Fishing from Land

Even though the usual image of a fisherman today is one of mobility in a swiftly moving boat, I don't think I would be going far out on a limb to say that the greater majority of anglers are still earthbound. That is, more fishermen still line the sandy beaches of the surf, balance on the craggy rocks along the shore, or venture out over the water on banks, piers, jetties, and docks . . . or fish off bridges.

FISHING THE SURF

Fishing from land in a salty environment finds its greatest fulfillment in the surf, that tumbling, tumultuous world of sand, sea, sky, wind, birds, and hopefully the occasional fish. There's a camaraderie found among surf anglers that isn't evident in any other kind of fishing. It may be the awesomeness of the oceans that draws men together, or it may be the prospects of making a great catch while immersed in the same environment in which the fish finds itself. There is little else akin to battling a large fish with your two feet planted firmly in the sand, water rushing everywhere about you, and your rod heavily arched as a fish tries to make its way back into the ocean.

Unfortunately, the surf is one of the least productive places to fish. It's not that fish don't inhabit the surf from time to time—they do—but it's the immobility of the fisherman. He's at the whims of the fish. Whenever a school decides to move out of range of his casts, there's nothing he can do but wait until it decides to return. But, the fish are there often enough to make him come back again and again as hope blooms eternal in his mind if not always in his fish box.

Technically, the surf is that place where ocean meets land. But this is too simple an explanation. It really extends from the upper limit along the beach where water rises to its highest tide, or is driven by a wind, out into the water to the edge of an angler's longest cast. Meeting the water is a beach, usually sandy, with a slope outside the water that often is reflective of the slope under the water. The degree of slope will determine just how fishy a place your surf can be.

In the normal type of beach, one with a slope of 10 to 30 degrees, a drop-off forms under the water. This is a sharp break in the slope caused by the undercutting action of waves returning to the ocean after they have lost their force. The greater the degree of slope the sharper will be the drop-off and the larger the area fish will find to hold and search for food caught in the turmoil of the surf. Beaches with very little slope are the least likely to hold or interest fish on the move.

As waves rush onto a beach they begin to lose their force in water that becomes progressively more shallow. This loss of force builds rows or bars of sand. The bigger the surf the larger the sandbars. These bars usually parallel the shape of the beach and can number anywhere from one or two to a dozen, depending upon the structure of the slope and the quality of the sand.

Although there may be a plethora of sandbars off a beach, only the first one or two interest the surf fisherman because the remainder

Surfcasters and their beach vehicles in a scene typical of many of the lonely stretches of beaches on the Atlantic Coast.

are out of his casting range. Bars can develop at almost any distance from the beach, from a few feet away for the first one to a hundred feet away for the second. It is between these bars that migrating and feeding fish like to swim. They are searching for crustaceans and seaworms, as well as baitfish that may be working the surf at the same time.

On a rising tide, predator fish are usually found on the inside of each bar, while on an ebbing tide they seem to prefer the outside of the bar. These bars, though they run parallel to the beach, are not continuous. At intervals, each is broken by channels, cuts, or passages. These are created by the power of spent waves on the beach as they force their watery load against the sandbar until it opens. This water cannot always go back over the tops of the bars because the incoming waves possess more force or power than the spent waves.

Fish like channel bass, striped bass, and weakfish, especially the larger members of the clan, prefer to lie in waiting in these cuts for food to come streaming to them. A wise angler, one who reads water currents on top or comes equipped with Polaroid glasses, can spot these openings. He concentrates his fishing efforts in such places.

The surf creates the beach and the sandbars, but what creates the surf? The answer is not a simple one, for surf is caused by a collection of forces that may be at work individually or all at one time. The most apparent wave builder is the wind. Wind blowing from offshore in tends to begin piling water into waves. The stronger the wind, the greater the waves. The type of surf is also a factor of the wind—more accurately, of the wind's direction. How the wind strikes the beach will determine the size and shape of the waves, and from this an angler can better determine where to fish. Waves do not always strike the beach at right angles. The wind can be coming from a quarter opposite to the direction of the beach, and this develops a wave that may run along the coast.

Swells are another factor that help shape waves and create them as well. Swells are usually the remains of a storm that has passed through an area or they can even be the long-felt effects of a storm hundreds of miles at sea. Swells come from the center of the storm and do not always have to be from the same direction as that in which the wind is currently blowing upon the water. In fact, swells may strike the beach from one angle and the wind may be coming from another, creating secondary waves over the swells. This creates a very mixed sea. Where the combined forces hit the beach is usually a good place to fish. Mixed seas tend to do a lot of digging at the sand. They will loosen worms and crustaceans buried in the sand as well as riling the water. Baitfish become confused in such a sea and predator fish sense this is a prime time to be in for the feed. Many anglers, however, become discouraged when the surf is high and the water mixed with sand, and don't fish. This is the prime time to work the surf.

In addition to wind and swells, currents and tides have their effect on the waves and on where fish in the surf will locate. Either they can have a nulling effect if they work with the main forces in operation or they can create even larger waves if they work against them. A fisherman on the dunes with glasses on the sea can quickly read what is going on. And if the breeze is onshore he'd better get into the surf.

Finding fish in the surf may look like a hopeless effort at first glance. The best indicator of where the fish are is a feeding blitz. You can't mistake it. It happens in shallow water when predator species like bluefish, yellowtail, fluke, or weakfish drive a school of baitfish into the shallows and surround them, feeding wildly, splashing about in the water. At times, bluefish are so voracious in their pursuit of food-fish like menhaden that, as previously mentioned, the small fish literally are driven out of the water to escape the machinelike jaws of these "choppers."

But a feeding blitz doesn't happen every day, and the next best way to locate fish in the surf is to enlist the aid of birds. Gulls and terns are constantly scouring the beach and water looking for schools of fish that may be feeding under the surface of the water where you cannot see them. But birds, from their advantageous position, can peer into the water and with an eyesight developed far better than that of man, they can see fish. They are after tidbits left over as a pack of predator fish moves through a school of bait. Or, the feeding fish may drive the bait to the surface where the birds can dive to the water and pick up whole baitfish for themselves. Keep your eyes on the birds if you want to find fish and when they move—follow them.

But birds, like a blitz, aren't always around when you want to catch fish. There are even times when the birds don't know that there are fish in the surf. In such instances you have to work the odds, looking for the type of environment where fish should be concentrating. The physical features of the beach, its composition, and that part under the water can help you locate fish.

We have already discussed sandbars and channels as prime areas to hunt for fish, but there are others. Points of land or even small jutting areas along a ruler-straight beach are likely to create small eddies or pockets along what might normally be a mundane beach. In such areas the moving tide and current are likely to drop food of a small nature that fish can feed upon. Always work these points.

If the beach is broken by sections of exposed rocks, or is composed of graded stones and boulders, then here is another spot you should work in earnest. Rocks and boulders not only provide a place for baitfish to feed and hide from larger fish, but they provide a place for sea grasses to anchor themselves and create an even better piece of cover.

Two of the author's sons, Michael and Steven, show off their fishing prowess after tackling the surf at Cape Hatteras, North Carolina, and produce a pair of puppy drum to prove they won.

Another likely place to fish is any area where small streams, either tidal or freshwater, break the sameness of a beach and enter the oceans. Fish will tend to congregate at the mouths of such streams, especially on a falling tide, and any place that might collect fish is a good place to begin fishing. Where larger tidal streams or rivers meet the oceans, a rip will develop between the two bodies of water. These rips are always great places to fish. Predator fish, though they will chase their food when they are driven by hunger, are basically lazy. A lazy fish will tend to hang just outside the influence of a moving body of water and wait for the food to come to it.

Where two bodies of water mix forces, smaller fish are usually at the whims of the current and cannot escape as easily when chased by larger fish. Rivers entering a bay or estuary tend also to cut holes into the bottom. These spots of deeper water are great places for large as well as small fish to wait out a tide and digest their food while waiting for something else to come along, or good pockets into which a waning current drops its load of silt, debris, and food. Fish them in earnest and they'll pay off.

It's a fact of fishing that more fish are cast over than are cast to, especially with spinning equipment that makes long casts simple and effortless. When working the surf, don't fall into the habit of making your first cast your longest, hoping to interest something between the splash of the lure and your boots. Instead, stop for a minute before you begin casting and read what is evident. Then, begin by making a series of small or short-range casts in a clockwise direction around you, working from uptide to downtide. It should take anywhere from four to six, maybe even more, casts to sweep the water immediately before you.

If that first sandbar is close to the beach, then you might take even more casts before you can feel you have correctly approached all the fish in that scope. Fish will line up along a beach facing the direction from which the current is flowing. Fish don't like to see a bait or lure come sweeping across their backs from the outside bar. Their first impression might be that it is something coming after them. Instead, they'd rather have their potential food coming from ahead of them—uptide.

On the next series of casts, extend your range by another 30 to 50 or so feet. Repeat what you have just done. Then extend your range another limit, even to its extreme, before walking into the surf. You need get into the suds only when you are sure you have combed all the in-close waters and are trying to put your lure on the outside of the second or third bar.

As long as you are now way out in the water, to the top of your chest waders, and have swept every cast in the half-circle, then begin another series of casts upcurrent and parallel to the beach. Next, turn around and continue another series casting downtide and retrieving toward you.

To all these directional variations you can add still another dimension in your fishing that can change the attitude of watching fish—the speed of your retrieve. For some fish, a steady, even retrieve provides the most interesting action for a lure or bait. Others might like an erratic retrieve, one with a lot of stop and go to it. A few fish won't hit anything unless it looks as though it were being chased by a whirlwind. Change your retrieval speed and you may encourage a lethargic striped bass or drum to take your lure.

The depth at which you fish the surf is still another variable to add to your surf lore. Some fish, like striped bass, are prone to taking lures off the surface of water, while other fish, like channel bass, never take their eyes off the bottom. To catch them your lure must be bouncing along the sand. Other fish, like seatrout or bluefish, will follow the bait at any level in the suds if it interests them.

Not all our fishing in the surf is done from a clean, sandy beach. In many sections along the Pacific side of these United States and along the Atlantic coast in New England, surfcasters are more than likely to be working from rocks and boulders. Reading and fishing the surf along such areas is an entirely different ball game. The bottom, that part of the beach under the water, can be almost any shape, though what's outside the water can give you a clue to what is under the surface.

The best way to learn the beach along a rocky coast is at low tide with an offshore wind. Study those sections of the beach you will fish more often or plan to fish for the first time. At low tide and with an offshore wind, the water is likely to be at its lowest. When the tide rises and fills the holes and surrounds the boulders, you'll know where to fish or where the fish should be hanging out.

On a rock beach, your tackle will also change. If you aren't losing gear then you aren't fishing the better spots. Longer leaders and heavier lines will be called for to resist the abrasion of rocks. You'll also have to switch to more surface lures or lures that run at midrange depths, or else you'll be planting them regularly along the bottom. Live-bait can be swum in the wash, but you'll probably opt to use lead sinkers to get them out. This calls for sinker designs that won't hang on rocks and ledges. A pyramid sinker is designed to hold in sand, and you'll never get one back if you fish it among rocks.

Safety in the surf is something that cannot be stressed too often or too loudly. A fisherman walking into a pounding surf, dressed to the arms in chest-high waders, wearing a loaded tackle pouch, and whipping a heavy rod and reel, is liable to all kinds of events if he doesn't keep his wits about him. The returning water has a tendency to eat away the sand under his boots and if it is strong enough it can topple him before he knows it. Getting to your feet with waders on can be a chore, especially if you are fishing at the ends of the season when cold water and weather slow down your every movement.

A lot of fishermen pick buoyant jackets if they don't wear a life jacket. Most wear ice creepers on their feet when clambering over the rocks, or felt-bottomed boots that do not slide on moss-covered stones. A good idea is always to fish with a buddy, so in the event that one of you finds himself in trouble the other can lend a hand. Use your ability to cast to reach that outer bar, rather than trying to walk to it. More than likely, if you are in deep water on the outer bar, there are a lot of fish behind you that you have missed. Don't risk it!

FISHING FROM BANKS

The bank as a place to fish from in a marine environment is not as frequently met with as those found in freshwater situations. Banks are formed primarily by rivers and in estuaries that are rather well protected. The open beaches seldom if ever form banks because of the action of waves on land where the two meet. Therefore, most marine bank fishing is done where streams, creeks, and rivers flow into salt water, or in protected bays and coves, usually parts of a tidal river.

Even in a large freshwater stream, the effect of the tide is felt up some portion of its length until the height of land rises above the highest rise of the tide. In reality, the tide is felt even farther up a stream than this point, because it backs up the flow of fresh water until the tide turns. What this back and forth action of the tide does to the land is to shear it, producing a near vertical surface where the water depth drops off rapidly . . . in other words, it creates a bank.

Banks are great places from which to fish because they bring the angler immediately next to deep water or bring the fish closer to his "reach." They give the angler a greater reach than when he is bound to the beach and a surf. But there are also drawbacks to the bank. One is its unstable character. The daily flow and ebb of the tides is the reason. Tides both build and destroy banks, undercutting them on one location and rebuilding them in another. Banks, especially sod banks, are very unstable places to plant your feet.

Because of this fact, a bank fisherman should get to know his fishing spot at low tide. One great way is to walk the bottom of the tidal stream—provided, of course, it is not too deep—at low tide and study the composition of the banks at this time. Most banks have a tendency to be undercut and these are great places at which to fish for weakfish, striped bass, and flounder at high tide.

The best time to fish from banks is between the extremes of the tide, because most banks of the sod type are covered with some degree of water at high tide. At low tide most of the water is gone from their bases, and you must fish the holes in the streams themselves, away from the banks.

Banks are great to fish because they are veritable feed bins for fish. All sorts of mussels and clams inhabit the sides of the banks and the roots of the grasses that grow on their sides and tops. Barnacles abound where the banks have partial outcroppings of rocks. Crabs and other crustaceans, as well as seaworms, burrow into the soft mud that forms the banks. It is then only natural that fish should come here to do their food shopping and that the angler in turn should come here looking for fish.

Because most fish in bank fishing are liable to be located along the base of the bank, anglers usually fish either up or down its side, depending upon which direction the tide is flowing. If you work artificial lures, then most of the casts are made out to midstream and swept along the bank by the current and retrieved uptide. The mobile fisherman will catch more fish than the one who decides to set up camp on the side of a bank. Some anglers prefer to do their walking in waders, but that can have its problems if you step into a hole or step off the bank when the tide is in. I'd rather walk with just hipboots, or better, during the warm months of the year, wearing shorts and sneakers tied on with extra laces.

Not all banks in an estuary are formed on its edges. In many large bays and sounds, sod banks or islands form wherever the current loses its force and drops its load of sediment. These sod banks in the middle of a bay can be extremely productive for such fish as striped bass and seatrout. The banks are usually laced by drainage canals or guzzles that remove the water from their surfaces as the tide falls. Banks are formed at these guzzles and at times a hard bottom is almost nonexistent or too far below the length of your waders to be useful. These spots are best fished by getting to them in a boat, anchoring the boat on the bank, and then getting out and walking the banks, casting as they become exposed by the falling tide.

FISHING FROM PIERS

A pier is no more than the equivalent of an extra long cast. It can also resemble a bank that is extended over the water. What a pier does best is to get you farther away from the surf or shore and into deeper water, which some species of fish prefer to the tumbling next to the beach.

Fish like striped bass, fluke, and flounders have little fear of the surf and swim readily into it searching for food. But other fish, like red and black drum, cobia, and fish that will feed off a pier's pilings, like sea bass and blackfish, prefer the deeper water just off a beach in which to search for a living.

Piers are, then, extensions of the beach into deep water that allow the angler to fish without getting his feet wet or making long casts to where the outer bars have formed. Most pier fishing is more closely akin to bank fishing than surf fishing, because it has more of an up-and-down nature to it rather than a cast-and-retrieve activity. The baits are usually fished after being cast away from the pier, better downtide than uptide, and held there by sinkers. Some casting is done with artificial lures, but not a great deal, because many piers are so high above the water they make casting lures impractical and the retrieve short and ineffective.

Fishing from a pier, while introducing you to more fish, also introduces you to more anglers. Because of the very nature of pier construction, more anglers are thrown together than might be the case if they were fishing the surf. And, manners for fishermen become extremely important. If you can't take crowds, don't take to pier fishing. But, if you can adjust to other fishermen's ways, and like to take your angling sitting down and at a modest pace, then maybe it is for you.

Most anglers who become specialists in fishing from piers develop a real body of knowledge about the art. Most also use two or more rods to increase their opportunities of catching fish. The rods are held in portable holders that can be clamped on to a railing or easily screwed on with wing nuts. Rods can also be propped against

If you are a gregarious fisherman you can get your fill by angling from a pier. Here anglers are taking advantage of weakfish that have moved close to the pier and beach to feed.

the top rail of the pier, but then the chances are good for a large fish to come along and take the entire rig.

One drawback in fishing from piers is that it is difficult to retrieve a hooked fish once it has quit the fight. In many instances the fish must be hauled up the side of the pier and this means rather stout lines, rods, and reels to accomplish the task with anything but the smallest of fish. Some piers are designed so that you can walk down a short catwalk or ladder to a lower level and there gaff or net your fish. Many piers are commercial ventures and the operators, knowing that retrieval is a difficulty of pier fishing, provide long-handled gaffs and landing nets if they don't have ladders, so that the fish can be hauled up in this way.

The only other alternative is to work your fish toward the beach and then walk off the pier to land it in the surf. This can be a tough chore because many piers have fences around their bases so that nonpaying fishermen cannot get onto the pier beyond the toll gates.

The pilings of piers do attract and concentrate fish. In a way, they act as artificial reefs or homesites for fish over what might be barren stretches of sand and surf. Pilings collect barnacles, grass, and weeds. These in turn provide protection for many small bait- and food-fish, and the big fish come in search of food. In this way, the pier is an attractor of fish as well as fishermen and supports its own purpose.

FISHING FROM JETTIES

Jetties or groins are man-made structures that extend from the beach into the ocean. Their reason for existence is to slow down the speed of tides and currents along the beach and diminish their erosive effects on the sand, stabilizing the beach. Construction materials for jetties vary widely from poured concrete to long collections of boulders or rip-rap. Those jetties that are porous, or made of oddly shaped and oddly sized units of material, are best for fishing, because they provide caves, caverns, and havens for small fish, cells almost impenetrable by larger fish. The more porous a jetty the better the fishing, usually.

A jetty-jockey, however, leads a precarious life. In most areas, a jetty is built just high enough so that it stops the current flow at an average level of high tide. This means that, for the most part, the top of the jetty is usually under some degree of water at most high tides. Walking back can be difficult at high tide because you can't see where the rocks are, and if the wind and waves are pounding you from the outside the desire to trek back is strong enough to make you walk where you cannot see. That can mean trouble.

As a result, jetty fishermen, even though they can venture farther into the water than the surfcaster, pay a price for their added mobility. But if the needed precautions are taken, it can be a rewarding way to fish. The jetty-jockey is usually fitted out with a pair of waders, hipboots, or knee-length boots. The shorter, the better, from the standpoint of safety. Over the short boots he dons a pair of rain pants to keep the waves that crash on the rocks from filling his boots. And in lapstrake fashion he dons a hooded rain jacket that he secures around the waist with an outside belt.

Felt-soled shoes or ice creepers mounted on the boots are an important part of the paraphernalia of the complete jetty fisherman. Because he is usually working over rocks that receive water at some part of the tide, they are also likely to be covered with grass or moss, which makes walking upon them an art. Add to this the buffeting effects of a strong wind or the occasional lashings of the waves, and the ice creepers become a necessity and not a luxury.

The fishing gear one uses on a jetty will be a compromise between the long wands of the surfcaster and the stubby equipment of the pier fisherman. Because his fishing already begins a cast away from shore, the jetty-jockey doesn't need the big sticks to make long casts. In reality, as mentioned earlier, a lot of his casting will be parallel to the jetty or groin upon which he is standing, because fish coming to the area are really investigating the numerous cubbies for feed.

As a result, a 7- to 8-foot rod with a spinning or level-wind reel is all that he'll need. In addition, terminal rig should be finished with a wire leader because of the chances of abrasion on rocks or materials that make up the jetty.

There is a unique way of working a jetty that expert fishermen have developed over the years. A jetty sticks into the current and because of this it has its character changed with the changes of the tide. Thus, there is a downtide side and an uptide side to the jetty with respect to the directional flow of water. The pros have found that it is best to begin working a jetty from the downstream side, at its base with the beach. The cast is made on a quartering angle with the jetty and as it approaches the angler the lure is swept near the rocks. The angler takes a position, tosses several casts, and then takes a dozen or so steps and repeats the process. When he gets to the end of the jetty he combs the water with his casts from the downtide to the uptide positions so that he won't cast over the backs of any feeding fish.

After he has swept the end of the jetty, he works his way back toward the beach, casting this time on the upstream side. Once he has used up all his new water he returns to the far end of the jetty and if he is casting alternates swipes at the upstream, then downstream side with intermittent casts off the end, toward the open water. If he is fishing live- or cut-bait, he usually casts off the end but faces downstream.

When tides and weather really boil, and storms lash the beach, the fish are still in the combers feeding. But it is nearly impossible for a surfcaster to get to them. However, the jetty is safe to a point and allows a casting platform to be maintained in the face of the weather. It is at times like this that the jetty fisherman has a real advantage and can take fish if they are there. But caution is also called for, because it is easy to be swept off the jetty by a large wave, or knocked off your feet. However, if the jetty is high enough above the water and you can find a secure spot, it's likely to provide some great fishing.

18. Fishing from Boats

Boats free the land-bound fisherman. With a boat, he need no longer sit on the beach and watch schools of fish swim beyond his casting reach. The boat allows an angler to follow. In a sense, the boat is an extension of the beach, but over the water. But it is also a lot more than that, because this mobility allows the angler to introduce a whole new set of techniques that effectively take fish.

CASTING FROM BOATS

Casting from boats is not really that much different in technique and style from casting from the surf, off a low pier, or from the edge of a bridge. The major difference is in equipment size. Because the angler can chase fish in his boat, he does not need rods and reels capable of casting a hundred yards or lines stout enough to resist the pull of a fish from the beach. Instead, he can follow.

The boat thus becomes a portable casting platform for the fisherman and allows him to use shorter rods, lighter and less line, as well as smaller reels, and still accomplish the same task—taking fish successfully. Today most casting from boats in saltwater situations is done with spinning gear. These rods range in length from 6½ to 8½ feet, depending, of course, upon the size and the species of fish you are after. The rod's action varies from medium to heavy, again depending upon the fish. Lines are basically monofilament and test anywhere from 6 to 17 or 20 pounds. The lighter the line, the longer the possible cast.

Lures also vary somewhat from those cast by the land-bound fisherman. They can be the same style of lure but because lighter lines are used the lures usually drop down in size to match the rest of the outfit. Smaller lures are often better designed and respond with more action in the water to entice fish.

The ideal casting situation is one man casting from one boat. But because a single fisherman cannot cover more than 180 degrees at any one time, toward either the bow, the stern, or one of the sides, two fishermen can usually work from a boat if they are not located back-to-back in an extremely small craft. No matter how large a boat, two casters still remain better than several. But more than two can fish and cast from a boat if they are constantly aware of the presence of the others. A plug loaded with a gang of treble hooks is always something to be reckoned with on either a fore or back cast.

Unless you are casting to a school of surfacing fish, most casting is done blind. However, even though you may not see the fish on the water, with the mobility of your boat you can go to places that provide structure, rips, or channels where fish should be. You can comb this water with the boat adrift, and each angler sweeping his side of the boat, or at anchor if the spot is an established hotspot, hole, or rip that regularly produces a lot of fish.

You don't need to make long casts from a boat. When sweeping an area, take it at your ease. Then move the boat forward and start a new set of casting sweeps.

TROLLING FROM BOATS

Trolling is little more than making a long cast last. The lures are paid into the water astern of the craft as it moves forward and then secured at the desired distance. The real merit of trolling lies in the fact that it is a great way to explore a lot of water looking for fish, in an easy and usually efficient way. Almost any number of lures, from one to four or five, can be trolled from a boat. The ideal number of lures is two, one trolled from a rod located on each corner of the boat. Additional lures can be trolled off outriggers and on really large craft a fifth rod-and-lure combination can be operated from the middle of the transom. But for most fishing situations and fishermen, two rods and lines are enough to maintain.

A trolling boat is the sedentary platform of a bank fisherman, but under way. It allows him to set his rods in holders, adjust the drags, and then move the entire operation about over the surface of the ocean, bay, or estuary. It also allows the angler specifically to locate his baits or lures at a prescribed level in the water. If you use Dacron, nylon, or monofilament lines that ride high in the water, then you'll need lead weights or diving planes to take your lures and bait to deeper levels. However, there is only so much lead you can add to a line before it becomes self-defeating, developing curves in the line that create water resistance on the material that won't allow it efficiently to sink deeper.

When you reach this point and still need more depth, then you must switch to metal lines: copper, stainless steel, or Monel. Only the latter two are employed in salt water, and they work quite effectively. Wire lines, because of their inherent weight, will take lures deeper. But because they also have a smoother surface that offers less resistance to the water than braided Dacron or nylon lines, they sink deeper.

Still another factor that affects how deep the lures will go and the amount of resistance built up on the line is the speed of your trolling craft. The rpm's (revolutions per minute) of the engine or engines determine how high or how low the lures will ride. A slower-moving craft will drop lines deeper, while a faster-moving boat keeps them closer to the surface because of water drag or resistance.

In tidal river situations, or near rips and points of land where ocean currents or tidal flow are measurable, these forces will also control or affect the depth of the lures. If you troll into a current or tide, it has the same effect as increasing your rpm's, while a reversal of directions will let the lines fall deeper. To keep them from fouling unnecessarily on the bottom you may have to maintain a higher speed or more rpm's while running downtide.

Stemming is a form of trolling, using the force of the tide or a tidal river against which to work. Stemming is usually practiced over a point of land or in a constriction between islands or parts of the mainland where the tide is forced to concentrate and run somewhat faster. Such locations are also ideal places to find predator types of gamefish. Trying to fish them by trolling in the regular manner gives the angler only a passing shot, and a short one, at any fish in these waters. Instead, he stems. The boat, under power and trailing the lines, is brought uptide to where the lures and fish should meet. Then the skipper pulls back on the throttle to a point where his effective forward speed is zero, or nearly so. The boat is just maintaining its way in the water, but in relation to the bottom it isn't moving. Then, with a slight turn of the wheel, the boat slips back and forth over the area with the lures sweeping the fishing spot. To pick "new" water, the angler simply pushes the throttle ahead slightly and the boat will creep forward in the current.

Stemming is a very effective technique that isn't difficult to master, requiring but a little experience. It is best practiced by two fishermen so that the skipper can spend his full time on the wheel and throttle while the second is tending to the lines and fish.

Trolling is basically an exploratory adventure, but this doesn't mean that it should be done haphazardly or without direction. If you troll an area where water boils over rocks and underwater reefs, off points of land, where a stream enters the salt chuck, or around islands, you are not really trolling blind. These are areas that should interest and concentrate fish. If you see breaking fish on the surface of the water, or flocks of birds wheeling and diving over an area, you should troll to them. Again, you know where you are going and what you are doing. But these are not situations you will usually encounter when you troll. Instead, you will be trolling blind, but still not haphazardly.

Experienced fishermen, even when they do know where fish may be, or at what level in the water they may be holding, develop patterns to their fishing. They methodically work the lures through a given body of water. The technique is to troll in one direction and then reverse it, going over the exact same course, but with a different presentation before moving slightly off that path to begin a parallel run.

Once you have thoroughly worked a patch of water in one back and forth direction, then attack it at right angles. Do the same as you did on the previous series of runs. If there are any fish in that body of water with a penchant for striking a lure or bait, you will have given them every opportunity.

While you are trolling on a prescribed or imaginary course, you should always be taking ranges. A range is a set of two points that will give you a line. To return to the same point on the line you need a second set of ranges at right angles to the first. The first range should be along the axis of your boat with points on the horizon. Pick a feature of the land ahead of you and one directly behind you and these two points will give you one line.

At right angles to this line, pick another set of land features, if possible on opposite sides of the boat's beam. As you move, so will the ranges on your beam, but the fore and aft points should remain the same. The value of these ranges lies in the fact that if a fish strikes you can return to the same approximate area after you have landed the fish. Because many saltwater fish move in schools, the ability to return to where you had the strike will mean more fish in the box.

You can also toss out markers that, with their lead weights attached to a string, unwrap and the float will remain on the location. These are fine when you are fishing alone in rather shallow water. But if there are other fishermen trolling around you, as is too often the case, you are likely to incur their wrath if their lines foul your marker floats. You might also foul your own lines if you are alone and hauling two or three sets of wire and lures. Better learn to take ranges automatically as you scan the horizon for signs of birds and fish or disturbances in the water's surface. It will pay off in the long run.

JIGGING FROM BOATS

In jigging, the fisherman works one of the oldest lures known to saltwater anglers, the lead-headed, bucktailed jig. This lure, in various weights from one-half to 3 and 4 ounces, effectively simulates a baitfish or squid working its way through the water. Its erratic course attracts the attention of fish and entices them to strike.

Jigging is practiced in two ways. The most common way is from a slowly trolled boat. The line is paid out to the required depth and the fisherman near the transom edge works the rod tip back and forth. He uses sharp jabs to bring the jig ahead in the current. Then he allows it to sink rapidly for a foot or two, only to be quickly jerked or jigged ahead again. The depth at which you jig and the amount of fall in the lure in between retrievals are determined by the amount of line in the water and the speed of the craft.

For jigging deep or along the bottom the best technique is to cut the engines and drift. This is best accomplished where there is a good tide running around points of land or between islands. The angler runs his boat to the head of the water he wishes to fish, cuts the engine, drops the jig to the bottom in free spool, begins to lift it off the bottom, and then lets it sink quickly. A slight variation on this theme, where the amount of rise and fall should be greater than what you can lift with a sweep of the rod tip, is to crank madly for a few turns on the reel and then slip it into free spool to let the lure fall. This is usually done in time with the raising of the rod tip, to exaggerate the action.

On days when the wind is rather fresh, you can drift over currentless areas using just the wind. In really deep water, drifting under the influence of the wind is one of the few ways you can effectively get your lure to the bottom. And the bottom is where the greatest number of fish congregate, because their source of food is usually there unless they are strictly fish-eaters.

The bucktailed jig is designed to be bounced along the bottom and not foul too frequently. The lead head is constructed with the eye or the line attachment on top to place the majority of the lure's weight on the bottom. The hook is then mounted in a turned-up position to minimize snagging of the bottom. Feathers and deer hair are added around the hook and these help to keep the hook from catching grass and weeds. The bucktailed jig is a very efficient lure.

DRIFT FISHING

Fishing from a drifting boat is little more than a very slow troll without power. The direction you drift is given by the current in which your boat sits or by the wind. Drifting can be a very effective way to fish when you want to work live-baits or rigged-baits that won't troll without twisting your line. It is also a good technique to use when you want to fish deep, or on the bottom, or when you want to fish very slowly for fish species that cannot swim rapidly to catch their food.

In a boat driven by wind, the lines should be paid off the windward direction. Otherwise, your lines will run under the boat and might become caught on its bottom. You will also lose touch with the terminal ends of the lines if they cross under the boat. Several lines can be drifted off the windward side of the craft. These should be fished at various depths unless you are after fish that feed specifically in one part or other of the ocean.

Drifting is a great way to cover a lot of bottom slowly and expose your lures and baits to a great number of potential fish. The amount of line you use will be determined by the depth of the water

Hugo Uhland of Mastic, Long Island, New York, illustrates the correct way to gaff a striped bass. Uhland, an expert drift fisherman, works the waters of Plum Gut with bucktails and porkrinds.

and the speed of your drift. If the boat is moving too fast, it can be slowed down with sea anchors or by tying off buckets and gear to offer more resistance to the water.

Getting your line to the bottom is a function of the lead weight you use. The size again is determined by the speed of your drift. It is desirable to keep as much bow or belly out of the line as possible. If you don't, you'll miss too many fish strikes. A large sinker helps reduce the amount of sag, but it also reduces your sensitivity to what is happening on the terminal end of the line.

Drifting is not as aimless as it might first appear to be, especially if you drift under the influence of the tide or of an ocean current. There are prime places to drift over, the same as those you'd pick in trolling. Larger fish tend to congregate, as we have seen, where smaller fish or bait have protection. This includes such diverse areas as submerged rock piles, sudden drops in the bottom, the edges of unexposed sandbars, places where two currents come together, the waters off points of land, and areas just outside the influence of a tide current where fish can rest or lie in wait for food to come their way.

The technique here is to run your boat to the head of the area you want to drift over, or a length or so ahead of it. Cut your power, let the boat settle into a posture, and lower your lines over the side so that once you drift over *the* spot everything will be down and ready for action. Drift past it or until you feel you are out of the productive area. Turn on your engine and take a circuitous route back for another drift. Avoid running a boat over the area you hope to drift so you don't alarm fish or chase them off. In really deep water, when you are fishing the bottom, this isn't a real factor. But in shallow water you can ruin your fishing by running the boat over the fish.

FISHING AT ANCHOR

This is one of the most contemplative ways to fish, and puts us only a notch away from the sedentary bank fisherman. What you have done is move your stationary spot out over the water. The nice thing about this type of fishing is that after you have "worn out" a hole, you can move on and fish another. Fishing at anchor has a lot of inherent advantages, the foremost of which is that you can forget about running a boat and concentrate all your efforts on the fishing at hand.

The first act is to know how to anchor. That might sound a bit silly at first, but anchoring is a part of fishing. Selecting the right type of anchor and using it under the correct conditions of wind, weather, and bottom make your fishing more efficient. The amount of rope or line you will need depends upon the depth of the water and the size of your boat. As a rule of thumb, you must pay out in rope anywhere from four to six times the depth of the water to get a Danforth-type anchor to hold well in a mud or sand bottom.

Don't drop your anchor where you expect to fish. If there is a tide force at work, figure how far above the spot you want to fish you must run and stop there. Then ease the hook over the side, pay out the estimated amount of line needed, and when it takes hold you should be over the area you wanted to fish. If you have only the wind with which to contend, then determine its direction, get upwind of the spot you want to fish, and repeat the process. Dropping the hook on the immediate area you want to fish will spook fish and when it takes hold you'll find yourself off location.

After the boat weathercocks you can drop over one, two, or three lines, more if you can handle them. The lines go off the downwind side and you'll need lead to get them to the bottom or balloons to keep them on top. If you are using live-bait, then you might not want to fish the bottom, but let the bait swim freely and at will. But if the live-bait must be on the bottom, for such fish as fluke or drum, then a sinker is used, usually off the end of a three-way swivel.

Fishing at anchor, bottomfishing or stillfishing, as it can be called, is a slow way of angling and requires a good deal of patience on the part of the angler. But at times, it is the only way to approach certain species of fish, and every angler, even the most aggressive spin-fisherman, should develop stillfishing techniques. It may be the only method he can employ to take fish.

CHUMMING FROM BOATS

Fishing at anchor is usually slow because it requires that the fish come to you rather than you seek out the fish. The action can be good if you know that fish are below, feeding on natural baits, and are called to the area by them. Otherwise, it is just the scent of your bait—and usually live- or cut-bait is the primary come-on for stillfishing—that calls the fish to your hook.

However, you can hasten the process by calling or attracting fish to where you are angling. Another word for this is chumming. Chumming, as we have seen, is no more than doling out pieces of bait—fish or fish ground into a paste and mixed into a gruel with seawater, then added to the current from time to time.

Most fish that feed on other fish are attracted by a bloody or oily chum. One of the most universal chum fish is the oily menhaden or mossbunker. The fish is plentiful, easy to obtain, and almost worthless as a tablefish. It is best used in a chum. But some fish, like flounder, can be better attracted to a spot by using crushed mussels or clams. Some anglers in the Northeast even chum flounder by using canned whole-kernel corn. There is nothing in a flounder's environment that looks like whole-kernel corn but it does attract flounder.

Striped bass are especially partial to being chummed and one great chum is sea clams and their parts. There's a coastal industry that specializes in packing sea clams and making chowders. The by-products are called clam bellies. These can be purchased packed and frozen, ready to go. The angler need only thaw them out, select a spot to chum, and begin doling them into the water.

Weakfish and seatrout are extremely fond of grass shrimp and sand shrimp, and many anglers along the Atlantic Coast chum these fish, using small shrimp. The shrimp are kept alive and cast into the water at intervals behind the boat. In every handful several are pinched so they fall to the bottom or can't swim out of the chumline.

Chumming is usually done from an anchored boat but it can also be doné off a point of land, under a bridge, or alongside a bank. But it is more easily accomplished from a boat. Though most chumming is done at anchor on the open water or in large bays, it can also be done while drifting. This is especially true when fishing for sharks or bluefish on open or large bodies of water.

Regardless of what you chum, you should always disperse the ingredient so that it maintains a continuous line. A chumline that is broken or too sparse will make it difficult for fish to find your baited hook. The opposite is also true. If you chum too heavily, especially with larger bits of fish, the prey may never reach your hook, being satiated on the way. How much to chum is best determined by experience, one's success or failure. How long to chum is another tough question to answer. In some cases, the fish immediately respond and come to the feed. In others, especially where there is little current, fish may take hours to arrive or don't come at all. A moving current is essential to successful chumming because it helps you advertise that you are handing out food. Most fish have an uncanny ability to taste or smell the water and anything that is swimming or dissolved in it. By chumming, you are taking advantage of this ability. The chumline is spread over a greater area if you drift away from it and the tide carries it away from you. You are covering more ground and the chances of interesting a fish are thus highly improved.

Chum should never be so generous that the fish are satisfied by it. Instead, the chum is just a drawing card to the real fare. If you chum with menhaden, then the bait should be a piece of cut-menhaden or similar oily fish. With bluefish, it is better if the bait is whole and small. Butterfish make good bluefish bait. For fish like sharks, it doesn't matter much. For seatrout, when chumming with shrimp, several of the shrimp should be skewered onto the hook, or invest a few cents in larger, commercially caught shrimp, those you might eat yourself. Use them for bait. When chumming for flounders with clams or corn, clams will do on the hook, but they are hard to keep there and a sandworm in the clam chum is taken just as readily.

HANDLING A FISHING BOAT

How to handle a boat while fishing is something that cannot be learned from books. It first requires that you know the characteristics of your boat, how it handles in various types of water, and just how your power plant responds. The only way to develop your boating prowess is to do a lot of boating, using the craft at every possible opportunity and under all conditions. Only then will the boat become second nature to you, a means to an end, and not the end in itself.

Operating a boat along the surf, between the waves and breakers, is one of the most productive methods one can use in salt water. But it requires that you pay keen attention to all the forces around you. One of the greatest places to cast for fish like striped bass, bluefish, and weakfish is in the tumbling surf—from the outside in. Taking a boat into the waves can be tricky but it is safe if you watch what is going on.

Waves are regular occurrences and when they do change their characteristics they do it gradually. If you want to fish a school of bass that is between the inner and outer bars, sit outside for a while and watch how the waves make up, where they break, and the frequency at which they form. With this in your gray-matter computer, you can plan your timing and move in with a wave, riding its back, have it dissipate underneath you, and fish the inside until you are ready to break back through to the outside.

At times, the waves can be too violent to ride through but you can fish up to their backs, the point in their travels where they still ride under you without crashing down upon you and your craft. The boat will let you cast in to the fish from the outside and you pull them through the rough water. Fishing in this manner does require a bit of cool. From time to time the waves might come a bit larger and unexpectedly break against the gunwale of your craft, dumping water inside. But if you can take your eyes off the fishing periodically you can spot a bad wave and quickly turn the bow into the wave and ride it out.

Fishing in this type of environment is usually done with the engine—or better, engines—in neutral and running. If a wave should turn on you, you can quickly slip the engine into gear and bring the boat about. It also requires that you have a fairly well-developed sense of balance because the level of the water on the beach rises and falls with each oncoming wave. Here is where you'll find out what you and your boat can take. Do it gradually, that is, not totally committing yourself to the melee but leaving enough margin to escape.

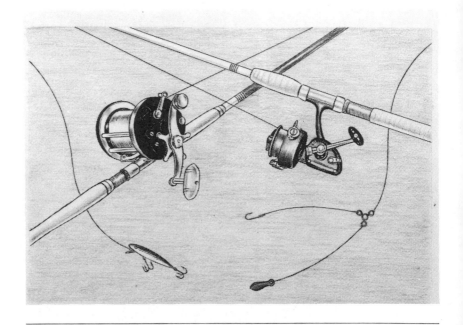

19. Fishing Tackle

There is such a vast array of tackle on the market today that it can easily be confusing to an angler, either one just beginning to fish, or even one who has been at it for a while. As is often the case, novice anglers make use of whatever tackle is on hand, for whatever species of fish they may be after. But as one's angling prowess expands there is a tendency to match the tackle to the species as well as the size of fish. A balanced outfit makes fishing that much more enjoyable. To accomplish the task one needs but a small amount of common sense and a little bit of "inside" knowledge concerning what is available.

There is no such thing as one rod, or even several rods, that can handle all the fish an angler may encounter. Rods and other pieces of equipment in the fisherman's locker have become extremely specialized so that they can perform with greater efficiency the tasks they have been asked to do.

RODS

Picking the correct rod for the right type of fish is not difficult once you learn the requirements for that type of angling.

Fishing can be divided roughly into three areas: fishing from the surf; from bank, pier, or jetty; and fishing from a boat. Within these three general areas we can use either conventional rods and reels, spinning rods, bait-casting rods, boat or popping rods, and trolling rods. All have characteristics that make each do its peculiar job that much better.

Fishing the surf requires rods that can toss a rather heavy plug or large piece of cut-bait for a considerable distance. It is a simple law of physics that the larger the rod the farther it will throw a lure. This is valid, however, only up to a point. That point is the physical capabilities of the fisherman. This places a natural limit on the size of a surf rod. Remember, too, that rather than casting everything to the last bar, 300 yards or more from the beach, there are a lot of fish within the first 100 yards of the shore and you can work lighter and smaller equipment with more dexterity under the reduced conditions.

Most surf rods are large, both in length and diameter. This is to make them capable of tossing long casts using heavy lures and bait. Most of these rods range in length between 9 and 10 feet. There is a collection of smaller rods, between 8 and 10 feet long, for lighter lures, and some really long rods, up to 12 or even 14 feet in length, are available for big baits and long casts.

At one time all rods used in the surf were conventional rods with conventional or level-wind reels attached to them. These long rods had eyes or guides that were all about the same size and shape. Line spilled off a revolving spool when cast, pulled by the weight of the lure. To make it stop before the bait landed in the water required thumb pressure applied at the right time. If this didn't happen, the spool would over-revolve and the fisherman wound up with a bird's nest to unravel for the next hour.

With the invention and development of the spinning reel and a rod adapted to handle the free-flowing line, anglers adopted them eagerly—at least those did who had never developed the educated thumb necessary to handle the conventional outfit. Anglers new to the surf found they could become halfway proficient with a spinning rod and reel in just a few casts. It often took weeks of training with the conventional outfit to cast without backlashes.

As a result, most anglers today fish the surf with spinning outfits, except for a few die-hards. True, you don't have quite the control when fighting a fish on a spinning outfit that you do with a conventional system, but this is more than compensated for by longer and easier casts, using lighter lines and lures, and by the shorter learning period.

As a result of these innovations, surf rods have steadily declined in length from 12- and 14-foot models to 9- and 10-foot versions that can do the same job with half the effort. Long rods are still needed, however, in special instances. When large bait and only large bait will do, they pay off. When the big lures must be tossed out to the first

Rods for surf fishing vary greatly according to the size of the fish an angler expects to catch and the size of the bait and lures he throws.

bar that forms 100 yards away, only a big stick can handle the requirement.

The key to a spinning rod's efficiency lies in a stationary spool that allows the line, easily and almost without friction, to spill off the reel in large rolls. Guides on a conventional rod would offer the large rolls of line resistance. Instead, on a spinning rod they have been replaced by larger eyes. Close to the reel the guides are as large as the spool's diameter. They diminish in size as they approach the tip.

All rods have an inherent action that reflects how well they will cast a lure. Heavy lures demand a rod that is fairly stiff from butt to tip. A bit of whip is desired, of course, in all rods. If the lure is too light to evoke a whip response from the tip, then the rod is too stiff or it is overpowering the lure. Rod actions are termed soft or light, medium, or heavy. Most manufacturers mark on the butt of the rod what type of action it possesses or what weight lures and line it was designed to handle.

The common sense that you must provide is a relative comparison to tackle to the size of the fish you expect to catch. It would be ridiculous for you to take a 10-foot rod into the surf loaded with 200 yards of 25-pound-test line when you are after 2- to 3-pound seatrout. Instead, drop down to a 6½- to 7- or 8-foot rod and light line to match the potential of your fish.

Surf rods, then,—both spinning and conventional types—can be divided roughly into three categories: light rods, medium rods, and big sticks for heavy-duty-type fishing. Light rods can range from 6½ or 7 feet up to 8½ feet in length. They can easily be worked with either one or two hands and are capable of tossing lures weighing 1 to 2 ounces. Lines to match them range from 4- to 17-pound strengths.

The next range, medium rods, are a little longer, generally between 8 feet, 10 inches and 9½ feet in length. They are made with a bit more power in the butt and are often stiffer toward the tip so that the power of the cast imparted by the fisherman is not dissipated in the backlash of the tip. Medium rods can handle lures weighing between 2 and 3 ounces on line of between 10- and 24-pound test.

Big sticks or heavy-action rods range between 10 and 12 feet in length, with some specialized rods even longer. All rods in this grouping can handle lines with a breaking strength between 20 and 45 pounds and lures weighing between 3 and 5 ounces. As you might guess, some of these rods are real man-killers and are used only by skilled fishermen under special conditions.

The butt sections of rods in both medium and heavy weights differ from light rods in that they are usually two-handed affairs. They are longer, between 30 and 32 inches, and designed with sections of cork or other nonslip material both before and behind the reel seat. These two, separated areas then act as fulcrum points to multiply the power of your cast and give the lure added speed as well as distance.

Nowadays, almost all surf rods are constructed of hollow fiberglass material. It is both light and strong and almost totally resistant to moisture and salt. The ideal rod is constructed in one piece and many surf rods are one-piece affairs. The reason is the superior action of a continuous fiberglass blank as opposed to one made of two or more sections. However, not all fishermen have the room or penchant to tote about 12-foot rods and as a result, multiple-section rods are popular, and practical. Older rods had joints made of aluminum or brass-nickle alloys. But the corrosive effect of salt water seemed to seal them shut after a while and made them worthless, even with a lot of care. Today, most good rods have glass-to-glass ferrules which have eliminated this problem. At the same time, they have given multiple-section rods better action while reducing their weight.

Rods designed for fishing from a bank, pier, or jetty are almost the same rods one would use in the surf. The basic difference between these rods and surf rods is length. Because the bank-, pier-, or jetty-jockey gets closer to deep water, there is not as compelling a need to make long casts. The shorter casts make shorter rods not only practical but desirable.

Typical jetty sticks range in size from 6½ to 8 feet for spinning rods and between 6 and 7½ feet for conventional rods. Butt sections are also respectively shorter in this category of rod, ranging in length between 21 and 25 inches, because of the tighter elbow room available for casting. As a rule, these rods are generally a bit stiffer than ones of the same length used in the surf, because a cast in a tighter area, or balancing on the rocks of a jetty, requires more wrist and arm action rather than shoulder and leg action, as is the case in the surf.

Conventional rods are often termed bay or popping rods, and are equipped with conventional or level-wind reels or bay reels. These latter are used primarily for fishing live- or cut-bait and are as much at home off the edge of a dock, bridge, pier, or jetty as they are over the gunwale of an anchored boat.

Fine-tuned action or response is not a built-in characteristic of most popping rods. Sturdiness and an ability to handle 5-, 7-, or 9-ounce sinkers or a big chunk of bait without folding up are what is called for in such equipment. Rods of this nature are equipped with four or five stainless steel or chrome guides. The tip guide is usually made of tough tungsten carbide to withstand the constant cutting action of rapidly drawn monofilament line.

Butt sections on these rods are divided into two parts, a fore section ahead of the reel that is usually smaller in size, and an after, butt section, longer and usually covered with cork or neoprene so it won't slide in wet hands. Less-expensive rods have butt sections of turned hickory or oak.

Boat rods are another category of specialized rods and include various spinning and conventional rods with built-in features that adapt them to the needs of a boat fisherman. In addition to spinning and conventional rods, boat fishermen make great use of trolling rods, a specialized form of the conventional rod, and popping rods designed for a lot of up-and-down fishing from drifting or anchored craft. Also, because boats are designed to meet fish at home, sometimes very large fish, you'll find the greatest development of rod sizes in boat use, including rods capable of handling 162-pound-test line, or more, and landing fish over 1,000 pounds.

Spinning rods in boats reach the height of their development and capabilities when used primarily with artificial lures. Because a boat is a mobile fishing platform, the angler is in no great need of long casts. As a result, rods can be designed to match the weight and action of the cast lures rather than the distance needed to send them to the fish. The spinning rod typically found in most boats is considerably shorter than that found in the surf or on jetties. The biggest difference is in the length of the butt. While the rods themselves are seldom over 8 or 8½ feet, the butt size drops down to from 15 to 18 inches.

A fixed reel seat adorns the butt of a rod of this type, whereas a surf rod usually has an adjustable reel seat. Most boat spinning rods are designed for two hands but can easily be handled with one hand when the need arises. Some, however, are designed primarily as one-handed rods and are used only for lightweight fish and smaller species.

Shorter rods are desired in a boat because of the limited room compared to the beach. To compensate somewhat for this shortening of the stick, the rods usually have a somewhat stiffer action. This is required to throw some of the larger surface plugs that are a favorite to work through a boiling surf from outside to inside.

Trolling rods find little use anywhere else in fishing and are designed for boat use—moving boat use. The lure cannot be cast and getting it away from the boat demands that the boat be under power. The rods are all rather stiff when compared to other types of rods. Most have a plethora of guides to help keep the line in the track and these are either simple loops or finished with small rollers to reduce the amount of friction between line and guide.

The tip almost always has a roller guide because line here leaves the rod on an angle. Friction would quickly wear out the guide if rollers were not a part of it. The butt is always divided into two sections, a fore section ahead of the fixed reel seat and an after section that terminates in a slotted butt end. This fits into a pin or groove on a gimbal attached to the fighting chair or rod holder.

Rod length varies somewhat according to the diameter of the rod and the weight class to which it belongs. Six class distinctions are defined by the International Game Fish Association (IGFA), beginning with a 20-pound class and including 30-, 50-, 80-, and 132-pound classes. Most trolling rods are between 6¼ and 6½ feet long, with a few reaching 7 feet. The butt constitutes a large part of the trolling rod's length—as much as 24 inches—and is built large for extra gripping power. The surface is covered with cork or neoprene to keep slipping to a minimum. In some inexpensive models the finish is only wood.

Not all trolling rods fall into these weight classifications. There are many custom rods that have characteristics of more than one line-test classification, and there are many special, custom-made rods above the 130-pound class. There are also numerous smaller rods, sticks under the 20-pound classification that are used to troll for small fish. Some of these rods are really bay rods or popping rods designed more for bottomfishing than trolling, but they do an adequate job at each.

The wire-line rod is a specialized trolling rod designed for use with metal lines rather than monofilament or Dacron. Ordinary metal guides, even with rollers, would soon have grooves worn in them by the abrasive lines. To compensate for this, special tungesten steel guides that will not wear have been developed for use with wire lines. Wire-line rods are also built with a somewhat stiffer action than comparable trolling rods because of the heavier line they are called upon to handle. Wire-line rods aren't made in all the same classifications as trolling rods, but are available in 20-, 30-, and 50-pound classes.

The bay rod or boat rod is still another modification of the trolling rod. It is used primarily for fishing up and down, either while drifting or at anchor. The special guides used on wire-line rods are not needed for boat rods, nor are roller guides to compensate for the mad rush of line when a large fish takes it. Instead, boat rods are simple, equipped with standard guides that can handle a fair amount of pressure. Such rods are between 4 and 7 feet long, with the average close to 5 feet. Their action varies considerably and is matched to the anticipated weight or voraciousness of the fish. Some are produced with rather light actions for small flounder and porgies, while other, rather stout rods are capable of handling 16 ounces of lead or a 50-pound cod or sea bass.

REELS

The basic purpose of a reel is to store line when it is not in the water—either pulled there by a fish or paid out by the fisherman hoping for a fish to come along. A secondary use of the reel is to help winch a fish in once it is hooked, though this is not a correct fishing technique. More important, the reel winds back lures and bait that are offered to fish and in doing so gives them a live or swimming action. Three, possibly four types of reels are of interest to sportfishermen in salt water—spinning and spin-casting reels, bait-casting or level-wind reels, and trolling reels, a modification of the level-wind reel.

Spinning reels are relatively modern fishing devices, developed just prior to World War II in Europe and introduced into the United States and Canada in the late 1940s and early 1950s. Their real value lies in their ability to let a light, or even heavy rod cast light lures

Spinning reels provide a speedy way for beginning anglers to master the art of casting. Here are four different size reels to match to the fish. *Left to right:* Quick Microlite, Daiwa 8300, Zebco-Cardinal 7, and Garcia-Mitchell 402.

long distances with light lines. The difference between a spinning reel and a conventional reel is that the spool is fixed, and doesn't revolve when the lure is cast. This immediately removes line friction that would shorten the length of travel by a lure. The bail, an outside arm, picks up the line and revolves around the spool replacing it on the arbor. When the lure is to be cast, the bail is pulled back out of the way and the line is free to roll off the spool.

As a result, light lines and small lures, baits that don't overpower a fish, can be used. This also means that lures with better, more sensitive action could be developed to interest fish. If the pull of a fish becomes too strong, the spool is allowed to slip or drag on its axle. The amount of slip or drag is controlled from the back of the spool. Smooth, efficient drags have now been developed that make playing a large fish easy and almost foolproof. It is difficult to break a good line when the drag is properly set. This gives beginners a jump on fishing ability and compensates for any mistakes they might make.

But the real value in a spinning reel is the ease and speed with which its use can be mastered. Any person with just a slight amount of physical coordination can begin casting almost immediately. It takes but a slight sense of timing to determine in a cast when to let go of the line.

A spincast or closed-face reel operates in much the same way as a spinning reel. However, the release of the line is accomplished by releasing a button. The pick-up of the line is automatic as soon as the reel handle is cranked forward. It simplifies the art of casting even further, and this type of reel is preferred by some anglers over an open-face spinning reel. One disadvantage to these reels is the limited amount of line they can handle. Another is that they are made only in sizes for light to medium rods. Some anglers also claim that they aren't quite as sensitive to the fish's action when hooked as open-face spinning reels.

Spinning reels, on the other hand, come in a great range of sizes, from ultralight models for small fish to big "coffee-grinders" capable of throwing large lures or baits for the biggest surf rod and still possessing a great amount of line for fighting a large fish. Generally, they can be grouped into about five size ranges, though these are not hard and fast. The lightest is the so-called ultralight group. These are matched to light rods, 5 to 6½ feet in length, and light lines, from 2- to 8-pound-test. Next in size is the standard reel often found in use on fresh water. This is an all-around reel for light saltwater fishing and is used more often in a boat than in land-bound situations. The reel will handle 250 yards of 8- to 10-pound-test line, or can be worked with lighter and slightly heavier lines. It is matched to rods that range from 6 to 8 feet in length.

Next in line is the standard saltwater spinning reel, slightly larger than the freshwater version and capable of holding 300 to 400 yards of light line, or less of heavier-diameter line. This size reel is also found quite often in boats and is the largest used in boat fishing. It is also a favorite with jetty and pier fishermen because it works well on rods up to 9 or even 10 feet in length.

In the next-to-the-last class we find the standard surfcasting spinning reel. It has a rather large diameter and can hold a goodly amount of line, of from 10- to 20-pound-test. The rod is usually between 9 and 11 feet in length and the reel is sized to match it. It can handle almost all the demands of the surfcasters, except when using really big baits and heavy lures. To meet this challenge, a number of really large reels are manufactured and, though cumbersome, these function as well as lighter reels. These reels and rods are not designed for a great deal of casting and retrieving and would soon wear down a fisherman. Instead, they are fished most often with live- or cut-bait. The rods, after casting, are placed in a sand spike (a rod holder driven into the sand) or one mounted on the side of the fisherman's beach vehicle.

Conventional or level-wind reels have been around for nearly a century. They were designed first for use in fresh water by bass fishermen, but were quickly adapted to salt water. The modern conventional reel is an efficient piece of fishing equipment and still finds wide use by today's anglers. At one time, it was used almost exclusively by surfcasters, but there has taken second place to the spinning reel. Some anglers, however, still prefer it today because they feel they can fight a large fish better from this type of reel than with a spinning reel.

A star-shaped wheel at the base of the handle on this reel controls the amount of drag produced on the spool of the reel. Minute adjustments are possible and this makes fighting a large fish almost a sure thing. The drag works only when the clutch is engaged and when the arbor rotates in a direction in which line is pulled out, not when it is reeled in. To eliminate the drag when casting or letting line fall to the bottom, the clutch is disengaged and the reel is in free spool. A clicker on the side is the only mechanism now slowing the revolutions of the spool, and even this can be snapped to an off position.

When casting, the spool would continue to unwind once the lure has hit the water. The only way to stop it is with pressure applied by your thumb to the line on the arbor of the reel. This requires what is often called "an educated thumb" The trick is to know just when and how much pressure to apply. Too much, too soon will shorten your casts; too little, too late will let the line over-run and form a nasty backlash tangle. That is the major drawback to this kind of reel for casting.

Trolling reels are basically the same reel a bait-caster uses for bass in fresh water. Most do not possess a device for laying the line on the spool. Instead, this is done by directing it back and forth with the aid of the thumb. The major differences between freshwater bait-casting reels and saltwater trolling reels are size and materials. The

Trolling Reels—Designed basically for boat fishing are these four reels. *Left to right:* Daiwa 40, Garcia-Mitchell 620, Garcia-Mitchell 624, and Penn No. 180.

fish encountered in salt water are larger, and larger-diameter lines are needed for them. To meet these problems, larger reels are produced. Also, salt water raises havoc with metals. Only those that are proven to resist saltwater corrosion are used in the making of trolling reels. This also is true for spinning reels used on salt water.

More than a dozen reel sizes await the fisherman in need of a trolling reel, ranging in size from a 1/0 to a 16/0. They differ only in size and in the sophistication of the drag device. Larger fish require more mechanics to control their surging runs. Reels from 1/0 to 3/0 are the lightweights, used more for stillfishing or bottomfishing and are often termed boat reels, to match boat rods. They are designed for flounders, weakfish, small redfish, or porgies. The 3/0 is capable of holding approximately 350 yards of 30-pound-test Dacron or 375 yards of 30-pound-test monofilament. The lighter the line the greater the amount that can be spooled.

Reels from 4/0 to 6/0 are near to what we might call a standard for most medium-range fish and fishing conditions. These can be used for big game but are considered light reels when used for the big fish. They work best in the hands of experienced fishermen who know their limitations. A 4/0 will load approximately 450 yards of 30-pound-test Dacron line or 800 yards of 20-pound-test monofilament. The larger 6/0 reel has a capacity of 400 yards of 50-pound-test Dacron or 1,050 yards of 20-pound-test, 650 yards of 30-pound-test, or 415 yards of 50-pound-test monofilament. The 6/0 is a great reel for fishing many species of shark under the 300-pound mark.

LINES

At one time the saltwater angler was limited in his line selection to braided linen and cotton lines. Today lines have been created to match almost every angler's need, from gossamerlike strands of monofilament to the sturdy, abrasion-resistant stainless steel lines used by deep trollers.

Monofilament lines are used today by a wider range of fishermen than any other lines. These lines are manufactured by drawing a fluid, plastic material through a series of dies. Each die grows progressively smaller and smaller until the line reaches the last die at the required dimension. This produces a fiber with a smooth, hard surface that offers little resistance to guides on a rod or when pulled through the water. It is one of the chief lines used in spinning and spin-casting and is growing in popularity even with trollers.

One reason for the latter is that it offers less resistance to the water than either nylon or Dacron lines when dragged through the water, and allows baits to sink somewhat deeper without the use of weights or diving devices.

A certain amount of stretch in a line is desirable under some fishing conditions. When monofilament was first produced a few decades ago it had too much stretch. Since then the degree of elasticity has been brought under control and now it is used to the advantage of the fisherman. When trolling for big fish, the sudden strike would yank everything loose in a boat but the stretch in a line tends to act as an absorber and softens the blow. Too much stretch, on the other hand, makes setting the hook in the mouth of a bony fish nearly impossible. It also makes it difficult to feel fish that strike softly. Good monofilament is a compromise between the two extremes.

One drawback of the mono line is that it comes equipped with a built-in memory. That is, if it is wound too tightly on a spool or used without swivels with line-twisting lures, it takes a set or curl. This can be eliminated by removing all terminal gear on the line, paying out 100 or so feet into the water and dragging it behind a moving boat. The current will take out the twist, relieve the tension on the curl, and your line again becomes easy to cast.

Strength or line tests in monofilament are produced in a great variety of ranges, thirteen classifications in all, that include: 2-, 4-, 6-, 8-, 10-, 12-, 15-, 20-, 25-, 30-, 40-, 50-, and 60-pound-test lines. Occasionally some off-strengths are introduced to the market, like 17- or 27-pound-test. These are usually lines that were designed for lower strength tests but worn dies or other variable factors in production changed the diameter specifications. Rather than discard all the line the manufacturer will label it correctly and place it on the market.

While stretch can be controlled in monofilament lines, control is better achieved in braided Dacron line. Dacron line was used almost exclusively for trolling prior to the development of monofilament. Many anglers today still use it, feeling that it is superior to plastic lines. The lesser inherent amount of stretch in Dacron makes setting the hook easier and the movements of a hooked fish near the bottom are telegraphed more accurately to the angler on the rod with Dacron than any other line.

Dacron's drawbacks include expense, it being more costly to produce, with more steps in the process. Another drawback is that because it is braided it will naturally offer more resistance to water when it is trolled and thus won't sink as deeply by itself. A third is that braided lines are more susceptible to fraying than monofilament. But when used for its intended purpose, Dacron easily fills the bill as a top trolling line.

Because so much of it is used for big-game fishing and, hopefully, record fish, it is manufactured in classes that correspond to those categories determined by IGFA rules. It comes spooled in 6-, 12-, 20-, 30-, 50-, 80-, 130-, and 162-pound-test, in quantities from 50 to 1,200 yards.

Nylon lines were the first synthetic lines to be produced and quickly replaced cotton and treated lines in saltwater fishing circles. Nylon is still manufactured today, even though it has been largely replaced by Dacron. Nylon is often referred to as squidding line because it was first used by surfcasters, whose habit it is to use squid as live-bait.

These lines are made of high-tenacity nylon that creates a smooth, flat, supple line. Stretch in the line can be easily controlled, developed to the required degree, and then fixed or set by special heating devices while the line is being wound in manufacturing. The braided line offered a lot of friction when first produced, but nowadays special silicone lubricants are added that help eliminate the internal friction that develops within the line. Also, nylon used to absorb water when wet, but new waterproofings have all but eliminated this drawback. Squidding lines come in a variety of strengths and include 12-, 18-, 27-, 36-, 54-, 63-, 72-, 90-, and 110-pound-test.

A highly specialized line that is a cross between the flat-running Dacrons and monofilaments, and the deeper-running wire lines is the lead-core line previously mentioned. When you must troll deeper and don't want to load your line with lead weights or diving planes, you can switch to a lead-core line. It is just that—a hollow braided nylon outer line wrapped around an inner core of soft lead. The supple strand in the middle gives the line its weightiness while the outer nylon gives it its strength. Such lines are easily handled on any trolling reel. Most are color-coded, that is, they change colors every 10 yards, and the angler can easily figure just how much line he has in the water by counting the number of colors that have passed through his fingers. Lead-core lines are produced in interconnected coils in 100- and 200-yard lengths and in four strength classes: 18-, 25-, 40-, and 60-pound-test lines.

Wires lines are used almost exclusively by trollers and by a few bottomfishermen who angle at great depths and who must feel exactly what is happening all the time to set the hook on lightly-striking fish. For the most part, they are used by the troller, from striped bass fisherman to shark angler, whenever he wants to get deeper into the water than other lines will allow.

Though copper lines are used in fresh water their longevity

would be short in salt water. Instead, almost all wire lines for marine use are of either stainless steel or Monel. Stainless steel wire is a bit more difficult to handle than Monel because it possesses a memory. It has a tendency to uncoil whenever the strain is taken off the end of the line and produce tangles nearly impossible to unravel. This tendency increases as the strength of the line grows. As a result, it is most often used for lighter-test lines. When heavier wire is needed, the angler usually switches to Monel, a somewhat more supple wire.

Wire lines cannot be allowed to twist or they will eventually break from fatigue. A twist is a very large knot, and knots in wire will quickly weaken and break. If uncoiled improperly, wire will kink, and the breaking strength of the line can be reduced by as much as 90 percent in the area of the kink. If a kink is unwound in the same direction as it was created it can be eliminated. This is easier done with Monel wire than stainless steel. A good way to eliminate kinks or pressure from building in a wire line is to splice swivels every 100 or so feet.

Few trolling reels are spooled completely with wire lines. Instead, a backing of either monofilament or Dacron is added to bring the line on the spool near to the top. The last filling is done with either 100 or 200 yards of wire, depending upon how much you normally use when fishing.

Wire line is produced in strengths of 20, 30, 40, and 60 pounds, with the most popular lines in the two middle class tests. Heavier-test lines will take a lure deeper than lighter-test lines even though the increased diameter offers more resistance to the water. Anglers, however, elect to use lighter-test lines when possible because wire lines in these ranges are easier to handle.

LEADERS

Leaders are special pieces of line attached to the end of the line before terminal tackle is added. Leaders are designed to take more punishment than the body of the line or to camouflage the line before it is attached to the lure or bait. Leader material can be as simple as doubling the body line for the last 10 or 15 feet of its length. This is often the practice with Dacron lines.

In many trolling situations, the line is unlikely to come in contact with rocks or the angler is after fish with few or no teeth. In this case, he need only double the end of his body material.

In some fishing situations, the main body of the line might be too visible and would spook fish that might take the bait. In this case, clear monofilament line is made into a leader for the Dacron line. In some cases where monofilament is the body line and a leader is needed, but not necessarily wire, the leader is also monofilament but of a heavier gauge or color different from the body line.

In still other cases, where the lines are likely to come in contact with rocks when trolled, or be taken there by hooked fish, or be severed by the fish's sharp teeth, wire leader is added to body lines of Dacron or monofilament.

In the case of wire lines, the body line might spook fish and a heavy-gauge monofilament, often clear, is added to act as a leader. When wire leaders are used they can be of different materials. Stiff wire leaders are desired for many mackerel species, especially when feathers are to be trolled. In some cases, where flexibility in the end of the line is a must, braided wire leaders coated with plastic are best.

TERMINAL TACKLE

This part of the fisherman's equipment is often the most important, yet has the least attention paid to it. It includes snaps, swivels, and hooks that make contact with the line and then the bait or plug. Terminal tackle should be closely matched in size and strength to the line. Many anglers have a tendency to use terminal equipment—snaps, swivels, and hooks—that is far too large. Even the smallest barrel swivel tests out at 30 pounds.

In many rigs, the lure or hook is attached directly to the line. This is fine if the lure won't twist your line or you don't expect to change it too often. But if there is a chance of twisting and many substitutions, attach a swivel with a snap on its distal end. Sometimes snaps interfere with the action of lures and the lure must be tied to the line or swivel.

Most swivels are constructed in the shape of a barrel with wire eyes on each end. One is attached to the line and the other to the snap or lure. In some cases, expecially when bottomfishing, three-way swivels do a better job of keeping lines separated and untwisted. A

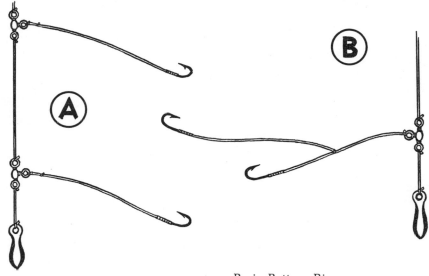

Basic Bottom Rigs

The two rigs shown here are commonly used for many bottom species. Rig (A) is the popular shore, pier, partyboat rig also called the "deep-sea rig." A variation of this rig is to use just one hook. Rig (B) is another good bottom rig for species such as flounders, blackfish, and others that feed right on the bottom.

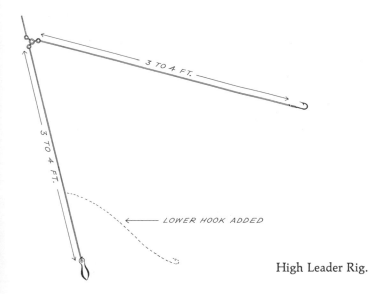

3 TO 4 FT.

3 TO 4 FT.

← LOWER HOOK ADDED

High Leader Rig.

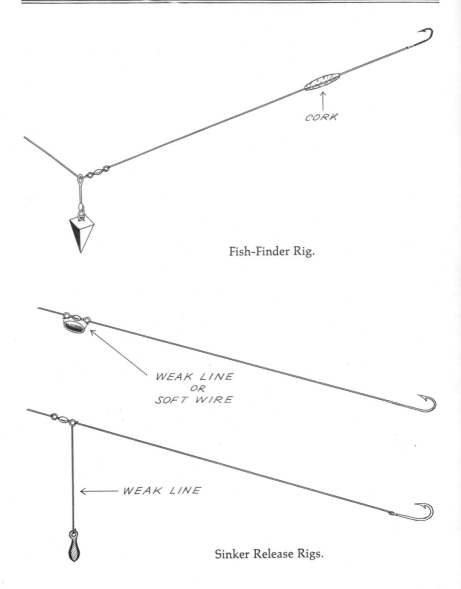

CORK

Fish-Finder Rig.

WEAK LINE
OR
SOFT WIRE

← WEAK LINE

Sinker Release Rigs.

three-way swivel is simply a center ring with three wire eyes attached to it. Each eye is free to revolve and thus keep twist off the line. One eye is attached to the line, the second to another line to which a sinker is tied, and the third to another line that eventually has the hook tied to it.

Getting a lure to stay on a certain depth, or a bait and hook to stay on the bottom, is best accomplished by lead weights. These come in various shapes to meet the conditions of being pulled through the water and in weights from fractions of an ounce to more than a pound. Some are beaded to be added into a line to bring trolled lures down to greater depth. These are called trolling drails, while a slight variation is the kidney sinker. Both are beaded so they won't twist the line.

Pyramid sinkers are so designed that the pull of the line works against the face of the lead and digs or anchors it into sand. Bank and Dipsey sinkers hold by weight alone and are designed without corners or edges so that they can be used over rock surfaces and won't catch. Still other, in-the-line sinkers are barrel sinkers, lead shaped like a barrel or torpedo with a hole through the center through which the line passes.

Hooks come in a great variety of shapes and sizes and most are specialized for a particular type of fishing. There are between thirty and forty hook sizes which range from No. 22, the smallest, to 16/0 for tuna and sharks. If you want larger hooks, they can be made on special order. Most manufacturers don't agree on hook sizes and numbers, so a No. 6 by one maker can be a No. 10 in another's catalog.

Some hooks are designed primarily to hold bait, others are part of the lure and are hidden. Their value lies in how they snag a fish's mouth. Still others are designed to impart an action to a lure or tube. If the hook is on a lure it should be made of stainless steel or treated to resist salt water. Otherwise, one dunking will quickly encourage it to rust.

Most hooks are single-shafted with one point. A few models come with two points and are used primarily when rigging bait to be trolled. Still others come as treble hooks, used primarily with artificial lures, plugs, and spoons. If you can find a need for a special hook, I'll bet you that someone has already made the hook to match it.

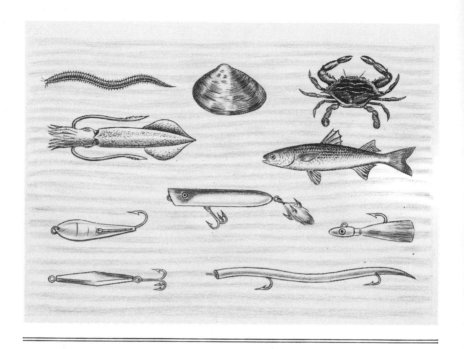

20. Baits—Natural and Artificial

Fishing is a big con game. The fisherman tries to fool the fish, offering it tempting natural baits, either alive or cut, or elaborately designed and constructed artificial baits. But they all have one catch in them . . . a hook. Hook-and-line fishing has been going on for more years than man has been able to record. In the early days, however, it was so inefficient that one could easily understand why man readily turned to nets and traps as they were invented.

Nowadays, however, hook-and-line fishing can be very productive, especially when practiced by experienced fishermen. Today's catches by sportfishermen of many species of fish annually equal or even exceed those made by commercial fishermen. One reason for this is the improved gear; another, a greater number of anglers; and last, improved artificial baits and greater knowledge of natural lures and how best to use them.

NATURAL BAITS

The saying that nothing is quite as good as the real thing has direct application in fishing when it comes to lures. The real thing, live- or cut-bait, has a quality in taste and smell that cannot be duplicated by artificial lures. This alone makes natural baits desirable. Add to this the inherent motion or activity of a live minnow or worm and you have a killing combination.

Many anglers who might call themselves purists frown on the use of live-bait. They insist that the only sporting method for taking fish is on artificial lures. I don't agree with this concept. The first premise to agree upon is whether or not you want to catch fish. If you do, then there are times in the life of a fisherman where no amount of casting, skill, or working an artificial lure will get a lethargic fish to strike. But swim a live-bait past its nose and the ball game changes.

Therefore, every complete fisherman must know how to fish natural as well as artificial baits. It extends his prowess and effectiveness as an angler. In addition, it makes fishing a lot more fun. Natural baits for most fish can be divided into four classes: worms, mollusks, crustaceans, and fish. The greater the angler's knowledge of each of these classifications of bait, the more successful will be his angling efforts.

Some fish feed on almost anything that swims in the oceans and on a lot that doesn't. Other fish, however, are extremely selective. That is, they may feed strictly on other fish, a few on only clams or mussels, while some never get their noses out of the sand and worms make up the bulk of their diet.

WORMS

There are scores of marine worms that swim in the ocean, but not all are available to the angler or make good baits for mounting on hooks. Terrestrial worms might be employed in a pinch, but because they discolor so quickly they might discourage rather than encourge a fish to strike. Three species of marine worms often are available from bait dealers or can be picked up easily by an angler who really gets into his sport. These include bloodworms, sandworms, and "tapeworms." The first two are annelids and saltwater cousins to the garden worm, whereas tapeworms, really ribbonworms but called tapeworms because they closely resemble them, are members of another phylum.

The sandworm, or clamworm, as it is also called, is the most popular marine worm in more northerly waters. It is distributed along the sands and muds from Cape Hatteras in the Atlantic north to Nova Scotia. When it is fully grown it is anywhere from 12 to 18 inches in length.

Sandworms trolled slowly behind a spinner are a very effective bait for many species of saltwater fish.

It is sometimes known as a clamworm because it frequents the same mud or clay beds enjoyed by clams and mussels. These worms burrow into the mud, usually around the low-tide mark on a beach, and spend most of the daytime inside. But come night, sandworms become real prowlers. They swim about much like an eel, aggressively seeking food and even latching onto small fish.

Sandworms make great bait and can be trolled or gently cast with a spinning or popping rod. One of the most effective striped bass baits is a sandworm or two, skewered by their heads only, onto a hook. The hook is attached to a spinner and this affair is slowly trolled around bays and inlets in shallow water. Hook size for such a rig is usually a 2/0 to 4/0 Eagle Claw or beak-type hook.

Sandworms also make good baits in the surf and when used with a fish-finder rig effectively catch almost any species of fish that might be working the suds. A fish-finder rig is composed of a large swivel in the line between the terminal swivel and the reel. The line can be pulled through the large eye on the fish-finder when a fish takes the bait. The free end of the fish-finder is tied, via a length of line, to a pyramid sinker. It is stopped from coming off by the larger swivel on the end. To this swivel a hook is attached by a varying length of monofilament and one or two sandworms adorn the hook.

In most cases, the sandworm will lie on or near the bottom, but for some traveling species of fish like stripers or bluefish, which don't always nose the mud, the sandworm should be off the bottom. This can be accomplished with the fish-finder rig and the addition of a small cork float a few inches behind the hook.

In my estimation, bloodworms are almost as good as sandworms. They are closely related and resemble one another as well. However, bloodworms are often slightly smaller and colored more of a red when compared to the rust or brown of the sandworm. When a hook pierces their skin, a goodly amount of the body fluid escapes; hence the term bloodworms. They are far more fragile than sandworms but when used properly make an effective bait.

Bloodworms range on the Atlantic Coast from the Carolinas north to Canada and on the Pacific Coast from California to Mexico. Like sandworms, bloodworms are also aggressive feeders. They possess a pharynx that can be flipped out to expose a proboscis armed with dual pincers that grab at anything moving.

Unlike the wandering nocturnal sandworms, bloodworms spend more time in and near the home burrow. Because they have softer bodies they cannot work into the hard clays and sands other worm forms choose. Instead, they stick to soft, muddy bottoms.

Wherever you use a sandworm, you can substitute a bloodworm. They are just as readily taken by feeding fish and maybe a bit more so, if they have been punctured. Because of the thinner skin and fragile body, bloodworms are best impaled on smaller or thinner hooks. Choose hooks that have small barbs on their shafts, called bait-holding hooks. These help bloodworms stay distributed along the hook rather than gathering at the curve or bend.

Ribbonworms are good bait, but because they look so much like tapeworms, many anglers avoid them. Their white, almost colorless bodies are flat and break easily when pulled from the mud or a burrow. These worms are not segmented like annelids. Unlike annelids, they grow to much longer dimensions. Seldom do you see both ends of a ribbonworm in the mud. If you did, they would be as much as five feet apart. One worm provides a lot of bait. If you get it all, it can be cut into fishable segments and dangled from a hook.

Because of these greater lengths, an angler should use tandem or multiple hooks on his terminal rig when using ribbonworms. Hook the first one near the head, then form a slight loop with the rest of the body. Leave enough trailing in the water so that it flutters and you'll have one real enticing bait.

MOLLUSKS

Unlike most animals, mollusks have their skeletons outside. These soft-bodied animals live inside their houses and are well protected from the elements and other animals. This group is made up of several classes, two of which are important fish foods and readily adaptable as bait. The first is a class composed of clams and mussels, and the other is a closely-related form, the cephalopods or squids.

A few fish can break their way into clams and mussels, while squid offer little or no problem. But most fish must be fed clams in the shucked state. Whole clams are not too difficult to string onto a hook. Make sure that after it is all piled on, the hook goes through a muscle so that it won't all slip off on the first cast.

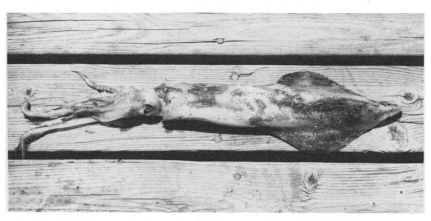

The squid, an unrecognizable mollusk. But regardless of what you call it, squid makes excellent bait either whole, in parts, or when cut into strips.

Clams and mussels are not only good for bait but also make excellent chum. The clams, shells and all, are smashed in the bottom of a bucket. The internal juices alone are enough to create a gruel and this can be doled into the water. The shells, covered with flavor, fall to the bottom first and the meaty parts drift farther away from the boat.

Skimmer or sea clams make the best clam baits because they are the largest and have ample muscle into which you can secure a hook. The beach is usually littered with them after a good onshore storm and you can walk along adding them to a bucket to be frozen and used whenever you want to fish. Otherwise, skimmers are difficult to obtain yourself because they prefer deeper, offshore water. However, draggers and commercial fishermen are often a good source if your bait shop doesn't carry them.

Hard clams, the cherrystones, Littlenecks, and quahogs of the dinner table, make excellent bait. But because man is in direct competition for them with fish the price of hard clams is so high that using them for bait is expensive. These clams can be used in much the same manner as skimmer clams. But because they are likely to be smaller, more than one are usually added to a hook. This is especially true if you are after potentially large fish like cod or striped bass. But as flounder or seatrout bait, a single shucked hardshell clam is more than enough.

Soft clams, or steamers, as they are often known because of the way they are prepared for human consumption, are an excellent bait. But here again, because they taste so good, they are sold at fish markets for a good price. However, they are so numerous and so easy to obtain that we can consider them good fish bait. The best way to collect a bucketful is to go armed with a pitchfork or basket rake at low tide and begin digging wherever the bottom is a combination of mud and sand.

Because their shells are softer, these clams can easily be smashed into a good chum. Their internal bodies are also somewhat softer than those of hard clams, and getting one to stay on the hook is a difficult but not impossible chore.

Razor clams can also be used as fish bait. Because they are not as numerous, they are not often used for the job. Their full bodies, however, make good baits and skewer nicely onto a hook. Big razor clams are fast burrowers and they can often beat you into the mud.

Mussels constitute another group of mollusks that make both good bait and chum. Most mussels grow in vast beds that are partially exposed at low tide. Collecting them is often just a matter of wading onto the flat and breaking them apart from the colony. This is especially true of the more numerous blue mussel. Its shell is rather soft and can be pounded into a pulp for chumming. For the hook, pick only the larger blue mussels, because even they are extremely soft-bodied and have little flesh that holds on a barb. As with many clams and mussels, holding them on the hook may require a little help, and wise anglers carry a bag of small rubber bands in their tackle boxes. A few turns with the rubber bands and the mussels will last through a cast or two.

Ribbed or bank mussels can be picked up at low tide by walking the streams or marsh drains in a tidal estuary. These mollusks often work their way to the edge of the high-tide mark to expand their colony and find more food. Bank mussels are not as colonial as blue mussels and you may have to walk farther to collect a creditable quantity. Like their cousins, they make good baits and stay on a hook with a little help. They also make a good chum when pulverized and ladled into the water.

It is difficult for anyone but a biologist to believe that squid and clams are close relatives. The fast, swimming squid of the inshore as well as offshore waters has a mobility clams can never emulate. The shell in a squid has been reduced to a rudimentary affair buried within the body and seldom noticed. But, like a clam that can get around by squirting, squid have developed this form of locomotion to its highest. The squid is an aggressive feeder, a highly organized animal that swims around in schools similar to fish.

Because of the squid's wide range of distribution many gamefish have become familiar with it, depending upon it for food. Large schools of squid are often pursued throughout their lives by feeding bluefish, striped bass, weakfish, and other species that like to chase their dinner.

As a bait, squid can be fished on the bottom, rigged in a somewhat free-swimming manner for the surf, or trolled. Or it can be cut into pieces or strips and used as an adjunct with other baits. In most instances the squid is used whole for large fish or cut for smaller ones, depending upon the size of the squid. In some cases, the head is pulled off and stuck onto the shank of a 3/0 claw-type hook equipped with barbs to hold it in position. This can be cast into the surf, eased into the water from an anchored boat, or drifted and fished in shallow water without lead weights. With a three-way swivel and snelled sinker it can be fished in deeper water or when the current in shoal water is too strong to let the squid fall to where fish may be cruising.

An entire squid can be rigged in numerous ways. One of the easiest is to hook three or four O'Shaughnessy hooks in tandem to each other—that is, through the eye of one and then the eye of the next to form a sort of chain. The last hook is passed up to the barb into the space between the eyes of a squid. The second goes into the bulk of the body and the third is planted not far from the tail. In larger squid, simply add more hooks. If the squid is fresh and the meat firm, it may stay on the hook without help. If you troll it in a fast current or fish it in a river with a strong tidal flow, it may need a few wrappings of line or sewing thread to keep it all together on the hook.

Squid strips make excellent trolling baits, either alone or when on the hook of a bucktailed jig or spoon. When used for this purpose, the outer covering is skinned off the squid and the firm, white meat sliced into longitudinal strips that are tapered on their distal ends.

The larger part of this wedge-shaped piece of squid should always be attached to the hook, allowing the other end to flutter in the water. If you are drifting or stillfishing squid strips, you can change their shape to add more meat to the morsel, with shorter but chunkier slices.

CRUSTACEANS

Shrimp and crabs are crustaceans familiar to us and are equally adored by fish as food. Where they are easily obtained they constitute a part of the diet of local fish and should be used for bait whenever possible. There are few fish that will pass up a wiggling crab or swimming shrimp and these can be used either as the bait or as chum to bring fish to the bait.

Three species of shrimp are used: grass shrimp, sand shrimp, and the edible shrimp *Penaeus*. Both grass and sand shrimp are small, with almost transparent bodies that help them camouflage naturally against any background. Grass shrimp frequent shallow bays, marine estuaries, and tidal creeks where beds of grass afford them protection from predator fish. The best way to catch shrimp is by sweeping a net through and along the edge of the grass during midtide.

Sand shrimp are a bit more abundant than grass shrimp and slightly larger. Instead of the backside of a bay they prefer to cope with life along the open beaches and over wide stretches of sandy bottom. Because they are so translucent, they are almost impossible to see until they move.

Weakfish and seatrout are especially fond of shrimp and can be caught using shrimp as both chum and bait. But because the shrimp are so small, it takes two or three on a 2/0 beak-type hook to make a mouthful.

There are bigger shrimp that can be bought from a fish store or a bait dealer if you don't have any friends who trawl for shrimp. The bigger, edible shrimp are native in the Atlantic from Cape Hatteras south. When using them as bait you can chum with grass or sand shrimp or crushed mussels. Depending upon their size, usually one or two are all that is needed on the hook.

Crabs, either whole, halved, or quartered, make great baits. Their attraction is natural for many fish from cobia to striped bass. They are easy to hook and hold, and the bait survives for a long time if hooked properly. The list of crabs suitable for baits includes almost every species that crawls or swims and the well-known blue crab, calico crab, green crab, fiddler crab, hermit crab, and sand bug, a specialized kind of crustacean.

Blue crabs in many states are protected by law because they are in demand for the dinner table. But when you have an old striper resident in a hole that won't be fooled by anything, drift a hooked soft-shelled crab into his lair and you can almost guarantee that he'll give it a tumble.

To add to the longevity of a blue crab, don't hook it under the carapace as is often the style, but secure it to the hook with a pair of wide rubber bands. The calico or lady crab is a bit more hardy and you can slip a hook under a part of her shell and she won't even flinch.

The distribution of the calico crab is greater than that of the blue crab and ranges from Cape Cod in the Atlantic south to the Gulf of Mexico. Rather than trapping it in crab traps like the blue, the calico can be taken by sweeping the outer beaches with a net. It can be fished whole or cut into pieces when bait is scarce.

Green crabs are one of the best baits available for blackfish. Though these crabs are found inside the estuaries, and along the creeks and guzzles where blackfish seldom venture, blackfish seem especially fond of them. Fiddler crabs, with their one large claw, are more gregarious than green crabs and set up housekeeping in colonies along the banks of salt creeks and tidal marshes. As the tide floods these areas, many species of fish come searching for food and it is the fiddler that provides them with a treat.

Hermit crabs are specialized crustaceans that have given up their tough, outer carapace covering for a life of mobility in someone else's shell. Most often, they take over the dead shells of moon snails, or the like. As they grow, they abandon the shell for the next size larger. They also make great baits without their shell; they can be hooked out or the shell crushed and the crab then placed on the hook.

Sand bugs, though not a bug in the true sense, are specialized crustaceans that make a home burrowing in the soft sand of the intertidal zone. When knocked loose by a pounding surf they make a ready meal for any fish on the spot. Seldom are they for sale in bait shops so you'll have to catch or dig them yourself from the beaches. Most specimens are small, but they do grow as large as 2½ inches and one of these monsters can make a good mouthful for a wandering channel bass or striped bass.

FISH

Most fish are piscivorous—they don't mind eating other fish. Some are even cannibalistic, making no distinction as to what fish they will eat. Then there are a few species which feed basically along the bottom and won't usually take a live fish. Still, they are scavenger enough to take dead fish or pieces of cut-fish. So almost every fish will eat other fish in one form or another.

Fish as bait can be divided into two groups. The first is composed of food- or forage-fish found on the menu of other fish. These seldom grow very large and are low on the food chain leading to bigger species. These fish usually maintain their populations by vast reproduction capabilities, and sheer quantity alone keeps them around. The other group is composed of larger fish, fish that often find themselves on one end or the other of the food chain. In immature form, these make excellent bait for larger fish.

In the first group we find small fish like spearing, sand eels, killifish, butterfish, anchovies, sardines, mullet, and menhaden, to name just a few. Bigger fish used for bait consist of such species as mackerel, whiting, blackfish, bluefish, sculpins, weakfish, and eels, any of which make good gamefish as well as bait.

Of all these fish I think the menhaden, mossbunker, or just plain bunker, is the most versatile baitfish. Bunker, when in the small stages of their lives, provide a great amount of food for other fishes. As adults of 2 to 3 pounds they are prime targets for king mackerel, striped bass, bluefish, and a host of other aggressive feeders. Bunker are so adaptable that they fill numerous niches as bait. First, they can be fished alive, hooked through the skin on the back, through the nostrils, or through one or both lips. This fish has great endurance and stays alive even when worked hard. Or, the fish can be used when dead, either whole or in part. Chunks of cut-bunker are favorites of the surfcaster and when hooked to a fish-finder rig take a lot of punishment from casting and surf.

As cut-bait the bunker's best portion is its head, sliced just behind the gills, or long slabs can be cut from each side. When used as a head bait, a 5/0 to 10/0 Siwash or O'Shaughnessy hook is buried in the flesh from the back and curved downward through the bottom jaw. The hook must be hidden at all times. As a strip-bait, it is sliced into wedge-shaped fillets and the hook pinned in the widest part of the flesh.

Eels make one of the most sought-after baits available in salt water. Most eels are trapped from creeks in wire cages or boxes, or they are readily available at any bait shop worth its salt. Eels have tremendous endurance and survive a lot of casting as well as fish strikes.

With fish like striped bass or cobia that take all their bait head first, only a single hook through the eel's jaws is needed. But with marauders like bluefish that bite off the tail and then come back for another chunk, hooks must be placed in the tail as well as the head.

When fished dead, the eel is usually hooked through the head with a specialized hook embedded in lead and shaped so that it gives the eel a swimming action when trolled. In such cases, the eel is rigged, or a wire passed through its body from the hook in the head to the eye of a second hook embedded in its tail.

ARTIFICIAL LURES AND BAITS

A vast plethora of artificial lures are available to today's sportfisherman. In fact, there are far more examples than the diversity of real baits they are supposed to imitate. Large numbers have no counterparts in real life, but they do catch fish, and that's what artificial lures are all about. Within each group there is even greater variation in sizes and colors.

Artificial lures work because their concept and construction are based on several principles that make them inviting to fish. If this were not so, fish wouldn't strike at them. Artificial lures work best on aggressive gamefish, those that feed on other fish. As a result, one group of lures is designed and colored closely to imitate real fish, usually smaller fish, those used basically as forage.

Color becomes a characteristic that can either enhance a lure or detract from it. Most lures are colored to duplicate the real thing as closely as possible. However, some lure colors have no counterpart in real life, but because of their contrast, hues, and attraction, they interest fish enough to make them strike at the lure.

Still other lures attract fish because of the way they swim, or vibrations they create in the water that a fish's sensors can tune in to. This can mean food to a fish, make it angry, excite it, or goad it into striking when it really isn't interested. Some lures have weights or rattles in them that set up a sound under water. Others have cupped faces, especially floating lures, that pop the water and chug along making a sound that gets the attention of fish.

Smell and taste, two senses difficult to separate in the water, elicit the first response from fish. Fish can taste or smell water or anything in it, at far greater distances than they can see or hear. This is one reason why live-bait is so effective in drawing fish from long

Plugs come in a variety of constructions and through design and weighting can be made to run on the surface, on the bottom, or anywhere in between. Here is a collection of various plugs. *Top to bottom:* Rebel, diving plug; Rapala Countdown, a weighted medium plug; Cordell Pencil Popper, surface plug; Old Pal 101 Hydron, surface plug; Arbogast Scudder, surface plug; Cordell Big-0, medium-running plug; and Cordell Red Fin, under-surface plug.

distances. A few lure manufacturers have added scent to their lures, and on some occasions and for some species, it seems to work. But because of the inconsistencies of fish and water, the scented lures have not proved too dependable.

At first glance there might seem to be far more lures than are needed or their variety may seem an endless hodgepodge. They can, however, be easily categorized. All lures can be grouped into a few classes that include plugs, spoons, jigs, and natural reproductions.

PLUGS

Plugs still carry the generic name of the first lure made in this style, a converted plug of wood that had hooks added to it and an eye to which the line was secured. The basic concept has changed very little since the first plug. Real innovations have been new shapes and new materials from which plugs are constructed. Only a very few plugs today are wood; plastics have invaded this area, and their superiority is difficult to match or beat.

Functionally, plugs are the devices that carry line from the rod to the fish. They can be measured in one of two ways, either by length or by weight. They can be further divided into sinking and floating plugs. The latter are often referred to as surface plugs. The diving plugs can also be subdivided into shallow-running, medium-running, or deep-diving plugs.

Top-water or surface plugs are made of buoyant materials, either wood, plastic, or hollow metals that allow them to float. Their main attraction for fish is the ruckus they can create on the surface to demand the attention of fish swimming below. Some fish swim with their eyes always on the bottom, so it would be a waste of time to try to attract them with a surface plug. But most gamefish feed from bottom to top and surface plugs are a very effective way to catch them.

Surface plugs develop their characteristics from the front face of the body. It can be cupped, as noted above, to create a chugging sound as it is pulled through the water; slanted so that it forces the water to rush over it in a wave; or shaped so that it swims madly on the surface with exaggerated movements.

Swimming plugs that work under the water's surface can be

either floaters or sinkers. Floating plugs, when pulled through the water, submerge because of their shape or design. Some are designed with shallow lips so that they do not run at great depths, but only down to three or four feet. When the retrieve is stopped, the lure rapidly floats to the surface. A plug of this nature can be worked to float-and-swim, float-and-swim, and resembles the erratic movements of an injured minnow.

A somewhat different type of plug, one whose density is slightly less, swims somewhat deeper when retrieved and with more action because it isn't trying to rise. The shape of the planing surface determines just how deep it will run. On the other end of the scale we have the deep-running or diving plugs. These plugs are almost always sinking plugs with a density greater than that of the water in which they swim. Some are even weighted to take them deeper but most have exaggerated lips or diving planes that force them to run deep when pulled through the water. The location of the eye or ring at the head of the plug also has an effect on where and how well a plug dives. In diving models it is likely to be farther from the front of the plug than in other varieties.

What plug to use will be determined first by the type of fish you are after and that part of the environment it chooses to swim in most frequently. Then comes the choice of colors . . . deciding whether you want the plug to imitate the real thing or display a color that will tempt the fish into striking for some other reason. One criterion you can follow is to attempt to match what bait or food the fish in the area are currently feeding upon. If you can duplicate it you may find success. Many fish develop a peculiar eating habit. If they are feeding on 5-inch anchovies they won't feed on any other size or kind of natural bait, even though it is available. In this case, duplicating the anchovy with a plug that closely resembles it is your best bet. If that doesn't work, then try everything you have until something scores.

SPOONS

Spoons are among the oldest artificial lures in use. The first spoon was probably just that, a spoon whose handle was cut off, a hook added to one end, and a hole for the line added to another. And like the modern plug, today's spoons vary little from this description.

Spoons are extensions of plugs and many work in the same manner, imitating fish or other natural bait. Here is a collection of just a few. *Top to bottom:* Hopkins Red & White #550; Hopkins Silver #388; Luhr Jensen's Krocadile; Tony Accetta Pet 15 (*l.*) and Spoon Squid 2 (*r.*); Hopkins NO = EQL #4 Hammered Spoon; and Abu Toby ⅝-ounce spoon.

They may have changed in hydrodynamic styling, colors, and finishes and in the metals used, but they all function pretty much in the same manner as the first one. They wobble through the water when pulled by a line. The effect is to flash light from side to side and this closely resembles the light patterns created by a swimming fish undulating through the water.

Spoons vary greatly in shape and length, from light to heavy, from fractions of an ounce to 5 and 6 ounces. Their action also varies as the weight changes. A large but thin, or light spoon has a great amount of action as it is pulled through the water, but it won't sink deeply. On the other hand, a large, heavy spoon will sink deeper, but a lot of the action is lost because it plows its way through the water rather than swimming through it. A large spoon can move better through the water, but a faster retrieve is required to make it do so. Spoon-fishing, then, is a great compromise—one reason why there are so many different and effective lures on the market today.

Oftentimes, a spoon by itself can be enough of a lure to entice a fish to strike. However, the hook can be adorned with feathers or deer hair for more emphasis, and one of the favorites is to attach a porkrind that then undulates even more than the spoon as it is dragged through the water.

Most spoons are finished in one color or material and designed to flash or reflect light. Usually they are chrome-plated. Some spoons, however, have chrome finishes on one side and brass or some other luster on the other. This produces a slightly different effect and can be

Jigs come in two varieties—bucktailed and diamond. *Top to bottom and left to right:* (1) Bridgeport Diamond Jig; (2) Small Diamond Jig with imbedded hook; (3) Abu Egon; (4) Hopkins ST Hammertail 8/0; (5) Hopkins Hammertail with Bucktails; (6) Bari Jig; (7) Smiling Bill Jig; (8) Boone Jig; (9) TriFin Jig; (10) Boone Tout; (11) Bullet-Head Jig; (12) Cordell Grub; (13) Garcia Bait-Tail.

just as good, or at times better, than a solid finish. Still other spoons are painted to resemble a mackerel or spearing and they too have their moments.

JIGS

This classification includes two contrasting lures. They are grouped together not because of their shape or construction but because both are jigged along the bottom. The first is the diamond jig, really a somewhat specialized spoon. The diamond jig, or any jig of similar construction, is made of heavy metal and is jigged off the bottom while drifting or from a slowly moving boat. This lure is often finished in a bright chrome or other reflective metal and dropped on the end of a line to the bottom. Here it is jigged up and down as the boat drifts. It relies on its reflective surface to flash light and catch the attention of fish. It is made to resemble the erratic swimming movements of a squid.

The second type, the bucktailed jig, consists of a lead head with a hook embedded in one end and an eye to which the line is attached on the other. The hook is turned up and the eye located on the top of the jig to keep the hook in an upright position. In most cases, this jig is fished with a porkrind attached to the tail to give it more action. Like the diamond jig, this one is fished along the bottom from a drifting boat or from one moving at slow speed. The lure is rapidly jerked or jigged across the bottom with upward sweeps of the rod tip.

While diamond jigs are pretty much all the same, chrome-finished, bucktailed jigs can be quite colorful. Most have heads painted white and yellow, the favorite colors with fish and fishermen. These jigs have feathers or deer hair colored the same as the head or varied. The porkrind is today an intrinsic part of the jig and can be white, red, or yellow. Many anglers mix colors, using white for the jig and yellow for the porkrind, or other combinations.

Bucktailed jigs come in assorted weights with several under an ounce and some as large as 5 to 6 ounces. Diamond jigs, however, come in an even greater range, with some used for codfish in very deep water that weigh a pound or more.

One of the most effective lures in a saltwater angler's tackle box is a bucktailed jig adorned with a porkrind on the tail.

TUBE LURES

Tube lures, constructed from plastic and rubberized surgical tubing, are a rather recent innovation. These very effective lures are made to resemble swimming eels or long strands of seaworms. They account for great numbers of striped bass and bluefish. The action of these lures is provided by a lead head so shaped that the rest of the tube wobbles or undulates in the water. A few, without the specialized head, have long-shanked hooks with a bend in them that causes the lures to spin.

For the most part, these tube lures are used singly. But more recently, numerous smaller tubes have been constructed together in a very devastating lure called the umbrella rig. This affair is designed to simulate a small school of baitfish moving through the water and can contain anywhere from four to twelve tubes. A large tube is often placed in the center of the rig and on the longest leader, so that it swims just slightly behind the rest of the "school." It is this lure that is then most often struck by a predator fish overtaking the school.

Because these lures are usually heavy and difficult to cast they are most often trolled. Single tubes usually have a weighty enough head to get them down deep, and when used with wire line they can be swept along the bottom with ease. The umbrella rigs offer quite a bit of resistance to the water, and lead is often used in their centers to drop them deeper, or occasionally a trolling drail is added just ahead of the rig for the same purpose.

NATURAL REPRODUCTIONS

The manufacture of these lures had to wait for modern synthetic materials to be developed before they could evolve. Some of the plastic lures produced today have both a lifelike texture and a coloration that rivals the real thing. The most copied bait is the eel and today dozens of different manufacturers produce eels that look almost as good as real ones and many that swim better. They come in natural black, brown umber, and even red, and all seem to catch fish.

An offshoot of this lure is the bait-tail, designed to represent a shrimp. It has a lead head for action and weightiness but a tail designed to swim in the slightest current or slowest retrieve. It can be

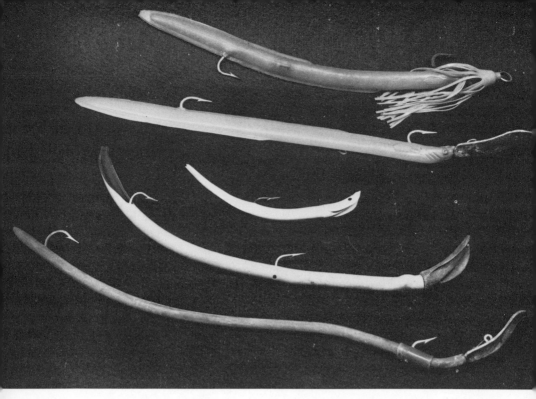

Natural reproductions today are so good that they often look better than the real thing. Here are a few. *Top to bottom:* Garcia's Wild Thing; Alou Eel; TriFin Whiptail; TriFin Tube Lure; and Garcia's Tube Alou.

jigged across the bottom with as much effectiveness as a bucktail and slid along the surface like a top-water plug.

The plastic squid is an engineering marvel. It looks and feels like the real thing, so much so that it fools a lot of fish that feed on squid. It is weighted inside with a barrel sinker and it is jigged or trolled like other lures. Most of the action, however, is imparted to the squid by the rod tip and the skill of the angler who is holding it. It takes a little effort to develop the correct jigging style but once it is mastered the imitation squid is a killer.

WORKING A LURE

The action of every lure can be as different as the man who is fishing it. Anyone can drag a lure through the water at top speed, cancelling out any effect the shape or planing surfaces might have on the way it swims. It is really up to the individual angler to get the real action out of a lure. He can vary the speed, change the address the lure makes to the water or current, or modify the hooks, plane, or eye so that the lure can do almost anything he wants it to.

Most lures will compensate for a fisherman's lack of imagination because of well-designed bodies and construction. But there are other very good lures, real fish-getters, that must be worked to make them catch fish. It is up to the angler to experiment, innovate, and reject or accept a lure. It makes fishing that much more fun.

21. Fishing Craft and Accessories

Fishing from land is fine. It is secure, pleasant, uncomplicated, and often rewarding. But if you want fishing to be rewarding more often than not, get in a boat. Fish are not bound to the beach, the bank, or the holes under a bridge or along a bulkhead. When they feel like it, they move. And if you are to continue to catch fish, you should be able to move with them. In addition, there are a lot of fish that don't come anywhere near to shore and you'll be missing a lot of action if you can't go to them.

Not only do you gain mobility by using a boat to fish but you also expand the number of methods that you can use to take fish. Fishing techniques using boats have proven so effective that today we have an armada of fishing craft dotting almost every port or point of

Typical of the boat rental fleet is this dory. You can supply your own outboard or include one in the day's fee. Oars and anchors usually come with the rental.

land on a good summer weekend. They must be doing something right or there wouldn't be so many anglers afloat.

YOUR OWN BOAT?

There are several ways to get onto the water and one of them is via your own boat. If you already have a boat there is little reason to try to sell you on the idea. But hang with us—you might find out why you bought the craft. The first step in readying yourself to buy a boat calls for a real letting-down of your hair or leveling with yourself. First, try to predict just where and how you will use your new boat. This calls for a projection into your future but you can do it, based on what you already like about fishing and doing things on your own. Just enlarge upon it, because with your own boat you'll be doing it more often and in more places.

But the catharsis isn't over yet, and here is where the real honesty will pay off. Next determine just how much money you can afford for a boat. Don't figure what you want but what you can really lay down on the desk when the marina dealer asks to be paid. Be real honest here and you won't have troubles later.

What you desire in the way of a boat will probably then be a compromise unless you are one of a small percentage of extremely affluent people around today. The compromise will be a boat you can afford, maybe not with everything on it you want. And, the payments will probably be a little higher than you can handle easily . . . but will somehow manage to meet.

Keep in mind that the first boat you get is unlikely to be your final craft. Do pick one, however, that you can improve when you get the additional monies and one that, once you decide to step up, or step down as the case might be, can be resold with a fair amount of your investment returned in the deal.

There is such a great variety of boats manufactured today that it is possible to tailor-make your choice from boats in stock. If your boat is going to be used strictly for fishing it will have one set of characteristics. If you plan to spend some time with the family in it, it will need a few additions, and if you plan to camp or just travel with it, there are other modifications that can be picked to meet your demands.

First, determine the hull you want. It can vary from a flat-bottomed boat to a modified-vee bottom, a deep-vee bottom, or a cathedral or trihedral hull. All respond differently in the water, a compromise between stability, comfortable ride, seaworthiness, and fishing functions. It is impossible to get all packed into one hull but you can try to do your best. The best approach is to visit one or two boat shows and look over all these hull configurations and talk to the dealers as well as the manufacturers. If you can wrangle a ride on the water in each type you'll have a better idea of what they can do. You don't have to be an expert to make your decision—just decide what feels best and what you like. After all, once you have bought it, you alone and not the manufacturer or dealer will have to drive it.

After you have the hull, and in the correct length to fill the requirements you have set for it, you must decide how the boat is going to be moved around. You have three options: outboards, inboard/outboards, and inboards. All three have features that make them desirable as to performance, fuel economy, initial cost, repairs, replacement, and even resale.

Regardless of which option you choose, you will have to match the power to the characteristics of your boat. It is better to have more engine pushing your craft than you normally need. One big reason is fuel economy. It takes less fuel for big engines to push a boat at a certain speed than for a smaller engine to operate at full tilt to maintain that same speed. With every boat you buy you can find a certified range for both minimal and maximum loads. Remember that your boat is likely to be loaded down with fuel, a cooler full of ice, food, and beer, probably one or two additional fishermen and all their tackle boxes and rods when you finally put out to sea. Then try to put the boat on plane. An engine should be able to jump a boat onto plane within 30 to 50 feet. If it takes longer with the engine's full thrust, you haven't got what it takes and your operating costs will be higher than they should be.

If you are going to keep your boat in the water at a mooring or in a slip you can forget about trailering and trailers. But slips cost money and aren't always available. In addition, you lose a good deal of your mobility. If you must bring it home each time you're done fishing you'll have to invest in a trailer. If your boat isn't too large or too heavy you can get away with a single axle and a hand-operated winch. But if you have weight and length you might better go to a tandem-wheeled trailer and a power winch to haul the craft aboard. The winch will help prevent hernias and the tandem wheel a bent or broken trailer suffering from overloading. Like big engines, it is also a good idea to get a trailer a little bit larger than you might need, especially if you will be trailering the boat over long distances. This is especially true of wheel sizes. The bigger and fatter the wheels, the longer they will last and the better insurance they offer for your boat's longevity ashore.

Now that you have a boat, some way to power it, and a trailer with which to haul it around, what else can there possibly be? A lot. Before you can get it into the water and go fishing you will probably have to register it with the state in which you live. You might even have to pass a boat-handling test so that you too can be licensed. Then, to meet Coast Guard requirements you'll have to find an

The size of a good headboat or partyboat is determined by the number of fishing positions along its gunwales. Here every inch is used, with favorite locations at either the bow or stern of the craft.

anchor and approved flotation devices, one for each individual aboard. The anchor is used for safety reasons when your engine fails and you don't want to drift out to sea. You'll also need some sort of whistle or horn.

The anchor is not only a safety device, but a way of keeping your fishing in one spot. There are several anchor types, so select the one large enough for your boat and the style that will hold over the bottom where you do most of your traveling and fishing. In this case, ask the boat dealer from whom you purchased your craft to help you select anchor size and style. He should know.

To make the anchor take a bite on the bottom you'll need heavy chain, from four to ten feet, depending upon the size of your boat. Attach to this enough line so that you can anchor in water at depths that don't prove impossible. As previously mentioned, the rule of thumb is that you'll need at the least three feet of line for every foot of water under you to hold the boat in a no-breeze or no-current situation. A better ratio is one to six, so if you figure that you might be trying to anchor sometime in 100 feet of water you'll have 600 feet of line in the anchor locker.

Almost every boat today comes equipped with a compass. If yours doesn't have one, get it. You can never plan on getting lost or fogged in, but it does happen, so have one installed and adjusted before you launch the boat on its maiden voyage.

In case it rains in your boat, it develops a leak, or you ship water from waves and the like, you'll need some way to get water out. A can or bucket will do but a bilge pump does it better and deeper. You can use a manual type if there is more than one of you aboard or you can take the time to stop and pump out the water, or you can have a motorized version deep in the boat's bilge that pumps out the water with a flick of the switch. One step better is an automatic bilge pump, one controlled by a mercury switch attached to a float. It takes the water out of your craft even when you aren't there and is a boat saver in a heavy rainstorm.

So far, we've hit only upon items that are considered real essentials. There are several other items that can be just as important in the right situation. One is a way to communicate with land or other boats. Today, most boaters wouldn't think of going afloat without their CB (Citizen Band) radio turned on. Though the Coast Guard does not monitor CB stations, twenty-three in all, you can always raise someone on land who can relay a message for help.

A step above CB is the VHF radio systems. These have a range greater than the dozen miles limiting the CB set and the Coast Guard monitors Channel 16 twenty-four hours a day. In addition to a place to call for help, the VHF sets keep you in constant touch with the U.S. Weather Service. It broadcasts weather conditions continually on two channels.

All boats must be equipped with lights if they are operated in the dark and today they come as an integral part of the boat. But if you plan to do a lot of night fishing you might care to install deck lights for your fishing convenience and even a spotlight for making your way around in the rocks or getting back to the dock or ramp.

If your boat doesn't have rod holders in it, and few ever come with enough, you will have to add your own. If yours is a fishing-only boat, it comes with two or four mounted in the top rail along the gunwale. You can add more to the backs of your seats or clamp-on versions that fit along the chrome rail that keeps you from falling out.

Hardly a fishing craft is afloat today without some sort of depth meter. Most are sonar-type, flashing devices that tell the angler the amount of water under his craft. They are also designed, except the digital type, to relay a message every time a fish might come between the transducers and the bottom. More sophisticated models produce a moving roll of graph paper that records depth, the presence of fish, and the texture and shape of the bottom. Each innovation, however, costs more and you must decide where to draw the line.

SOMEONE ELSE'S BOAT?

There are advantages and disadvantages to owning and operating a boat. If you don't want to incur the hassle and don't mind someone else doing all the work, you can elect to pay for these services and hire boats.

On the lowest rung of the boats-for-hire ladder we have the boat livery. There is still a lot of do-it-yourself here and you save a good bit of the costs. What you get from a boat livery is a craft that should be seaworthy, all the equipment necessary to meet Coast Guard regulations—anchor, cushions, horn—(though it's a bit cheaper if you bring all your own) and a lot of advice about where to go fishing.

From a livery you can either rent the boat alone or choose one with the motor provided, if you don't elect to bring your own. The difference is in the cost. The price can include the gas or you may be expected to provide your own. Be sure you are aware under which plan you are operating before you go around untying lines. Check also to see if there is a pair of oars stowed away somewhere—rental engines are notorious for being cranky.

The boat can be rented for the day or half-day. But half-day rentals will probably cost you as much as the full fare because the operator is unlikely to rent it for the afternoon . . . fishermen like to get away early in the day. If you lose any part of the equipment or damage the craft it will cost you. Sometimes the livery operator is covered by insurance but he'll collect from you before he tries to collect from his insurance company and have his rates increased.

Last, you'll probably be called upon to leave a sizable deposit if the owner doesn't know you. The value of boats and motors is high nowadays and some rentals have failed to return. Be a little understanding about this.

Rowboats and skiffs are suitable if you don't plan to angle far from the marina, or stay within the confines of the bay or estuary. Once you decide that you must run farther away from land you'll need a larger craft. It is possible to rent one and go yourself, but the costs are likely to be pretty stiff. In that case, you can do what most fishermen do, and find a lot cheaper—charter a sportfisherman or charterboat.

With such a charter you get the boat, all the tackle and bait you'll need, a skipper whose livelihood depends upon his fishing ability, a mate to help both you and the skipper, as well as all the costs of operating the craft for the day. At first glance, the price might make you gulp. But, if you still want to fish, you can split up the tab. Most skippers will take from four to six men and the cost can be divided up equally.

This craft is typical of those used for chartering. The fishing space is restricted to the after cockpit, and anywhere from one to three fighting chairs may occupy the space. Here the captain has left the flying bridge controls to help an angler gaff a bluefish.

There are usually two or three fighting chairs on the back of a boat and when a lot of trolling is involved, you can draw for the rotation order of who gets to fish, and when. If you are going to be fishing the bottom, then all the anglers can be leaning over the gunwale.

You are expected to bring your own food, and drinks if it is going to be that kind of trip. If you want to take some of your fish home, let the skipper know that before you begin fishing. Otherwise he is probably planning to sell most of it to offset the big increase in his fuel costs, especially if you are running offshore.

The mate on board is a lot like a waitress. He is there to help you catch fish, untangle your lines, gaff your fish, go for whatever you or the skipper needs, and clean your fish. He gets a modest salary from the skipper but, like a waitress, will expect from you some kind of tip for what he does, to make the job worthwhile. If he has been a lousy mate you don't have to feel obligated to tip him, but if he works his heart out for you and you don't reciprocate, you might not be able to charter the boat again when you want to.

There seems to be more demand nowadays for boat charters than there are boats, especially with good skippers. This means that you will have to make your reservations well in advance, sometimes a year, and probably leave a deposit. If you cannot make it, give the skipper enough warning to pick up another charter. If you do, he will probably return the deposit. But if he can't, you are likely to lose it as well as make him take a loss for the day.

For a less personalized fishing experience there is the headboat or partyboat. It's called that because you pay by the head for its use, or are a member of a larger party. There are usually no reservations required. You just show up prior to the posted sailing time, and if there is a free spot at the railing you put your money on the barrel-head and go aboard.

Partyboats are usually quite large, capable of handling anywhere from twenty to sixty or more anglers. The number of fishermen is determined by the amount of elbow room at the railing and each spot is numbered. Once you go aboard you pick a vacant spot and tie your rod to it. It is yours for the day.

Bait is almost always supplied by the skipper and figured into your costs. Rods and reels may be also, but if they are not they can be rented for a dollar or two a day. Terminal tackle is something you usually pay for. Most boats are equipped with a small food concession and you can buy lunch there, but don't always count on it.

Before you go out you'll need to know if it is a full-day or half-day trip. Some trips last for several days, or overnight, like the cod runs to the grounds off Block Island or the yellowtail runs from San Diego to the islands off Baja Mexico. These trips are special and usually require reservations and deposits.

The skipper, with all his sophisticated electronic gear, can usually put you over fish. More than likely there will be several mates on board to help you gaff fish, fix lines, clean your catch, and bag it. They too expect a tip of a dollar or two, depending upon how much use you make of their services.

Charterboats and headboats differ greatly. But the most significant difference is in the species of game they are after. The sleek sportfishermen are costly machines and are geared to angling for striped bass, bluefish, tuna, sharks, or any species of fish that must be trolled and cannot be caught easily by fishing up and down.

On the other hand, partyboats are great for this latter type of angling and a lot of fishermen can get chummy and still fish effectively. Even partyboats can work bluefish—their secret is in how they chum. Chumming is an integral part of their activity when going after many species of fish, and because of their size and bulk they can efficiently chum in a big ocean. But they must try to avoid encouraging a lot of sportfish like sharks or tuna to come around and make too many passes, or all the lines will be fouled for the remainder of the day.

22. Fish Care

Most fish can take some degree of abuse before they begin to deterio-
rate. But the longer you take to get it to the frying pan or your freezer
the greater will be its loss in flavor. The best rule is to take care of
your fish immediately after they are caught—or as soon as possible.

During the early and late months of any fishing season, outside
temperatures are often cool enough so you won't have to worry about
bacteria immediately attacking your catch. But during those months
that come between you'd better have an iced cooler waiting for your
fish or you'll lose their best flavor.

You can't always tote a cooler around with you but there are
ways to prolong the flavor of your fish, up to a point. If a cooler isn't
around, make sure you store your fish out of the direct rays of the
sun. More than likely you will be in a boat, and if so, find some shade

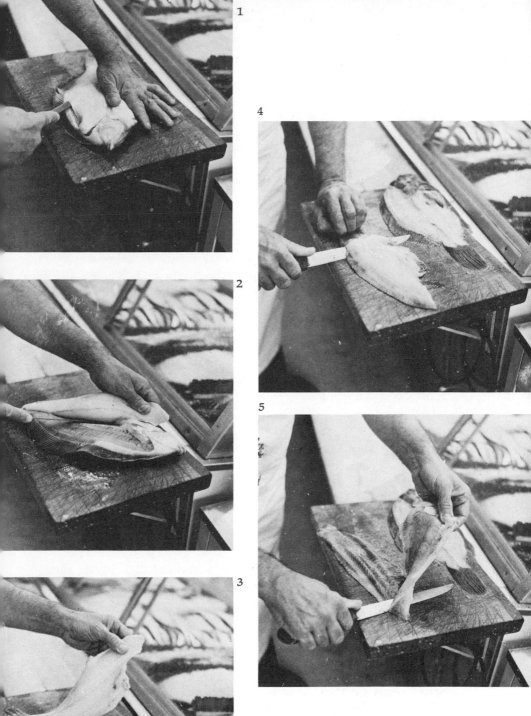

How to fillet a flounder or other flatfish.

for the catch. Then throw a towel or burlap bag over the fish and wet it down, and continue to keep it wet. If possible, place the fish in an area where the wind can ventilate them. With a wet cloth over them and a breeze, the evaporation of the water will cool the fish.

If you are on the beach and there is no shade, dig a hole until you reach wet sand. Bury the fish in it and cover them with more wet sand. Fish in the hole will keep several degrees cooler than the temperature on the top of the beach.

If you do have a cooler filled with ice with you, there are a few other steps you can also take to insure that the flavor of your fish is at its peak. Fish should never be allowed to soak in their own blood or in melted icewater. Make sure that the drain plug is open and the chest tilted slightly so the melt will drain off. Even better, construct a small grid for the inside of your cooler so the fish can't reach water. Water, warm or cold, will immediately soften the firmest fish.

I don't like to scale a fish, but there are times when the only way you can cook them is with their skin intact. In these cases, make sure that you scale the fish soon after catching. The longer you wait the more difficult it will be. If you let the fish dry out, it will be even more of a job.

If you would rather fillet your fish, and keep most of the fish, here's a simple way to go about the job. Many fishermen lose much of their catch when they clean it, throwing away meat with the bones. And to another group, catching fish is fun, but when it comes to cleaning their catch it usually winds up in the garbage can.

Cleaning fish needn't be difficult or wasteful if you follow this simple, speedy, five-step method to better fish fillets. The two techniques differ but slightly and in each almost every bit of meat is taken off and the messy job of scaling fish is avoided. Best of all, though flounder and bluefish are used as examples of the extremes that you might find in fish forms, the techniques can be applied to almost all species of fish.

FLOUNDER FILLETS

STEP 1. First cut through skin and flesh just aft of the gills and in a parallel line with them, from the spine to the back fins. Then slip the thin blade of a filleting knife between the back spines and

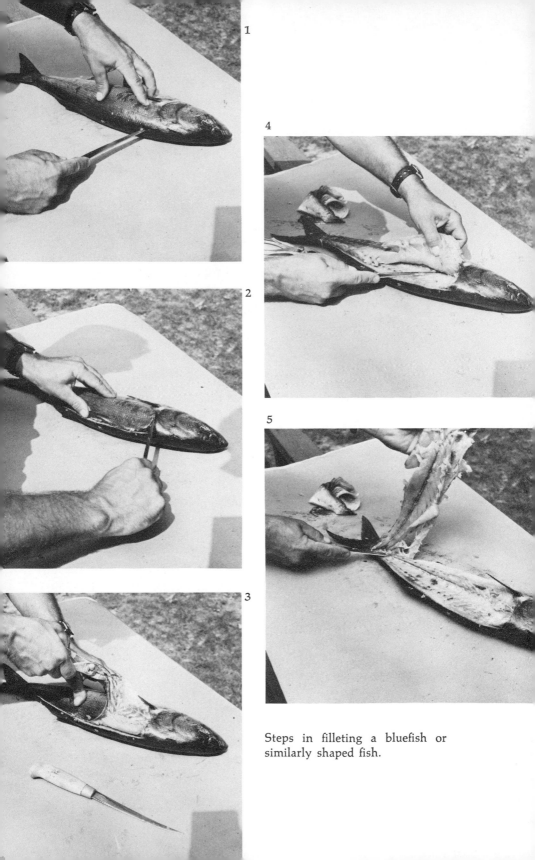

Steps in filleting a bluefish or similarly shaped fish.

the meat and cut your way back to the tail. Now you've freed the slab of meat on the top.

STEP 2. Next, follow with a second swath of the knife blade, deepening the incision to the spine, cut over the spine, and work the slab of meat free to the tail.

STEP 3. The intestines can be left unmolested if you slip the tip of the knife out of the meat just above the organs and guide it aft. Then cut the slab of meat clear of them and along the bottom of the fish's belly to the base of the tail.

STEP 4. After the entire fillet is cut off the side of the fish, flip the fillet over on its skin. Insert your knife between the skin and the flesh at the tail end. Cant the blade slightly downward, against the skin and your table.

STEP 5. With the blade canted downward, force the knife against the skin and forward. A little back and forth action will clear the fillet from the skin.

You've salvaged nearly all the meat on a flounder that it is possible to cut away, and you shouldn't have a bone in the slab. Flip the fish over and do the same on the other side.

BLUEFISH FILLETS

Because of the shape of the bluefish, a little different technique is used, though it is quite similar to the one just presented. The fish needn't be scaled if you intend to take off all the skin.

STEP 1. A cut is made along both sides of the dorsal (back) fin, just next to the fin and from the base of the head to the tail. Just break through the skin for now, not going deeper than is necessary.

STEP 2. The next cut is behind the gill covers, and in a direction parallel to them, from the cut you made on the back. Cut to the belly, using the tip only, and follow under the fish to the base of the tail. Cut only through the skin for now.

STEP 3. Pry the skin from the meat just behind the head, using the knife to cut it free. Once you have enough to take a bite with a pair of pliers, hold the flesh down with your fingers and yank the skin free all the way to the base of the tail.

STEP 4. Now you are ready to cut the fillet free from the fish. Cut along the back, next to the dorsal fin, where you made your first incision. Cut deeply, to the spine, from the head to the tail.

STEP 5. Go back to the base of the head with your knife and cut over the spine and back to the tail. Then cut another swath fore and aft, avoiding the intestines, and you've freed a boneless slab of bluefish. Because of the softer nature of bluefish meat, the job is made easier if the fish is well chilled—not frozen, but cool, so that the meat holds together during handling.

Glossary

Some of the terminology used by fishermen has developed into a special jargon that makes angling more efficient as well as more colorful. Some of it has been borrowed from the sciences, and still more from the language of the sailor. Still other terms are peculiar to fishermen, many of them having been developed in isolated parts of this country. To broaden your knowledge of these words, here is the working vocabulary of an angler.

ANADROMOUS FISHES—Fishes with special kidneys that allow them to migrate from salt water to fresh water and back again, without ill effects, for example, striped bass and salmon.

ANAL FIN—Usually a single fin on the ventral or bottom side of a fish, just forward of the tail.

ANTERIOR—Pertaining to the front.

BACKING—An amount of line on the spool of a reel used to bolster the diameter of the reel upon which the top or final line is laid.

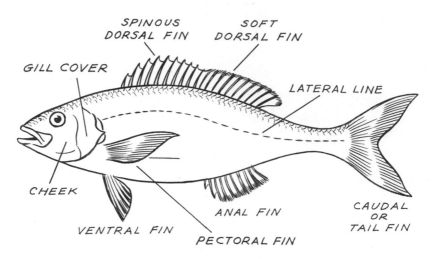

SPINOUS DORSAL FIN

SOFT DORSAL FIN

GILL COVER

LATERAL LINE

CHEEK

VENTRAL FIN

ANAL FIN

PECTORAL FIN

CAUDAL OR TAIL FIN

Parts of a fish.

BIMINI BELT—A belt with a plate in the front that holds a portable gimbal into which the butt of a fishing rod is placed to give an angler leverage when fighting a large fish.

BOW—The front of a boat.

BUCKTAIL—A lead-headed lure with upturned hook and a tail adorned with dyed deer hair.

BUNKER—A slang term for a menhaden, also known as a "pogy" in the New England states. An abbreviation of mossbunker.

BUTT—The bottom piece of a fishing rod that is grasped by the hands. It can be constructed in one or two sections. Also, the largest section of a rod when it is composed of more than one piece.

CHANNEL BASS—Another name for red drum, alias redfish.

CAUDAL—Pertaining to the end or tail of a fish.

CAUDAL FIN—Tail fin.

CAUDAL PEDUNCLE—That section of the fish's body to which the tail is attached.

CHUM—Any ground fish, crabs, shrimp, mussels, clams, or meat used to attract fish when scattered in the water and allowed to drift behind the boat.

CLAMWORM—Another name for the sandworm.

CLINCH KNOT—A knot frequently used in monofilament lines, that binds by jamming against the hook or eye of a swivel. One of the most efficient knots in fishing and the strongest that can be tied.

DISTAL—Opposite of proximal, or the end of the line farthest away from the reel.

DORSAL—The top side or back of a fish.

EBB—The part of the tide that follows after high tide is achieved. Opposite of flood.

ESTUARINE—Pertaining to that part of a river or bay where it meets the open ocean and where it loses its motion on achieving sea level.

FLOOD—That part of the tide when water is coming in or rising, and that begins at dead low tide. Opposite of ebb.

FUSIFORM—Shaped like a torpedo, cigar, or grain of rice; elongated and spindle-shaped.

GAFF—A hooked device without a barb and mounted on a handle, used to snatch a hooked fish and lift it into the boat in lieu of a net.

GAMEFISH—Usually an aggressive, sight-feeding fish that chases after its food and takes artificial as well as live bait.

GILL COVER—That posterior portion of covering on the sides of a fish that protects the gills. Another name for operculum.

GROIN—A jetty or other device placed at right angles to the beach to slow down currents and retard erosion of the beach sands.

GUNWALE—That part of the boat, usually above the deck and on the side, over which an angler leans to fish.

GUZZLE—A natural drainage creek or ditch on a tidal flat, created by ebbing water escaping to the outlet and ocean.

HYDRON—A scenting device derived from fish substances and sprayed onto lures to give them flavor as well as looks.

JIGGING—The fishing technique used with diamond jigs or bucktails to create an erratic movement of the lure through the water that resembles the swimming pattern of a squid.

LATERAL LINE—A line on each side of a fish that houses both sound and pressure receptors.

LEADER—The fore part of a fishing line, usually composed of different material, either stronger or transparent for camouflage.

LEEWARD—In the direction opposite from which the wind is coming; opposite of windward.

LIVE-LINING—Fishing with live-bait with the hook passed through a part of the fish that still allows it to swim about in a natural manner. Baitfish often used are menhaden, mackerel, or blackfish.

MENHADEN—The accepted name for bunker or pogy, a food fish widely used for bait and chum.

METABOLISM—The act of the body utilizing food, burning it up, and changing it into muscle, fat, and tissue. In fish its rate is closely controlled by water temperature, because fish have no heat-regulating mechanism. The warmer the water, the more active a fish and the higher is the rate of metabolism.

MONEL—A wire alloy used to make lines for trolling or fishing on the bottom at great depths.

"MONO"—An abbreviated term for monofilament, a plastic fishing line of exceptional strength in small diameters.

OPERCULA—Gill covers on the sides of a fish's head.

PACIFIER—A billy club or priest used to dispatch fish by tapping them on the head in the area of the brain.

PECTORAL FINS—Paired fins on the sides of a fish behind and below the gill covers.

PISCIVOROUS—Feeding almost exclusively on fish.

PLANKTON—Near-microscopic plant and animal life that floats in the oceans currents. Plankton compose the initial step in a long food chain that often ends with large fish caught by man.

PORKRIND—Strips of pigskin processed, colored, and cut to form strips or wedges that undulate easily in the water and act as an attractor to fish when added to other lures.

POSTERIOR—The back or end of an object; opposite to anterior.

PROXIMAL—That portion, as of a line, closest to the reel; opposite of distal.

PUPPY DRUM—Small channel bass or redfish, usually under 20 pounds, but in many areas under 5 pounds.

RAY—A form of flatfish. Another kind of ray supports and gives shape to softer, cartilaginous sections of fins.

REDFISH—A local name for red drum or channel bass.

RIP—A place in the water where two currents meet, usually opposing each other side by side; but often also used to denote areas where the tide runs with great strength and in a direction opposite to the prevailing winds.

RODE—Includes all the anchoring gear on a boat; the line and ground tackle, composed of anchor and chain.

SANDWORM—A marine worm that burrows into the sand and clay near clam and mussel beds and is used by anglers as bait.

SPINES—Stiff structures in fins, serving to give them support, and made of bone or cartilaginous materials.

SQUETEAGUE—Another name for weakfish, used primarily in New England waters.

STEM—To oppose the directional flow of a stream and maintain no apparent headway in the water.

STERN—The after or back section of a boat.

SURF—That part of the water on a beach from the point of highest tide to the place where breakers begin to form.

TERMINAL TACKLE—Any tackle that goes on the end of a line, for example, plugs, spoons, hooks, snaps, and swivels.

TRANSOM—The bulkhead along the stern or back of a boat.

TROLLING—Fishing from a boat while it is underway by dragging one or more lines through the water at fixed distances.

UMBRELLA RIG—A multiple fishing lure with spreader arms, similar to the skeleton of an umbrella, to which tube lures are attached. The tubes, 4 to 12 in number, with a longer tube in the center, are supposed to simulate a school of small baitfish.

VENTRAL FIN—A paired or single fin on the bottom of a fish near the vent or anal opening.

WINDWARD—In the direction from which the wind is coming. Opposite of leeward.

Index

Photo Credits

All photographs in this book were taken by the author except for the following:

Page 51, Robert Hutchinson
Page 77, Charles R. Meyer
Page 100, Larry Green
Page 106, Harlon Bartlett
Page 180, Joel Arrington

About the Author

Nicholas Karas was born in Binghamton, New York, but has spent his last 20 years living close to salt water. He was educated at Johns Hopkins and St. Lawrence universities, where he earned a degree in the biological sciences. He then attended the Syracuse University School of Journalism and was awarded a master's degree.

He is Fishing Editor of *Argosy* magazine and writes a regular fishing column in *Newsday*, the Long Island, New York, daily newspaper. He is a regular contributor to *Salt Water Sportsman, Field & Stream, Sports Afield, Outdoor Life, Fishing World* and numerous other national publications. He is also the author of a previous book on angling, *The Complete Book of the Striped Bass*, as well as three books on shooting.

Nicholas Karas has fished on all three coasts of the United States and Canada for all the species described in this book, as well as in Mexico, South and Central America, Europe, Africa and Australia. A prolific outdoors photographer as well as writer, he lives with his wife and three sons on Long Island, near some of the world's finest saltwater fishing.